After Capitalism

New Critical Theory
General Editors:
Patricia Huntington and Martin J. Beck Matuštík

The aim of *New Critical Theory* is to broaden the scope of critical theory beyond its two predominant strains, one generated by the research program of Jürgen Habermas and his students, the other by postmodern cultural studies. The series reinvigorates early critical theory—as developed by Theodor Adorno, Herbert Marcuse, Walter Benjamin, and others—but from more decisive post colonial and post patriarchal vantage points. *New Critical Theory* represents theoretical and activist concerns about class, gender, and race, seeking to learn from as well as nourish social liberation movements.

After Capitalism

David Schweickart

ROWMAN & LITTLEFIELD PUBLISHERS, INC.
Lanham • *Boulder* • *New York* • *Oxford*

ROWMAN & LITTLEFIELD PUBLISHERS, INC.

Published in the United States of America
by Rowman & Littlefield Publishers, Inc.
A wholly owned subsidiary of The Rowman & Littlefield Publishing Group, Inc.
4501 Forbes Boulevard, Suite 200, Lanham, Maryland 20706
www.rowmanlittlefield.com

PO Box 317
Oxford
OX2 9RU, UK

British Library Cataloguing in Publication Information Available

Library of Congress Cataloging-in-Publication Data

Schweickart, David.
    After capitalism / David Schweickart
        p. cm. — (New critical theory)
    Includes bibliographical references and index.
    ISBN 0-7425-1299-1 (cloth : alk. paper) — ISBN 0-7425-1300-9 (pbk. : alk. paper)
    1. Democracy. 2. Capitalism. 3. Socialism. I. Title. II. Series.

    JC423.S387 2002
    320.53'1—dc21

                                                                2002001812

Printed in the United States of America

♾™ The paper used in this publication meets the minimum requirements of
American National Standard for Information Sciences—Permanence of Paper
for Printed Library Materials, ANSI/NISO Z39.48-1992.

For
Anita and Karen
Lauryn and Carrie
the next generation
and the next

Contents

List of Figures

Preface

This book is the fourth incarnation of a set of ideas I began to develop nearly thirty years ago as a graduate student, during those heady days in the early 1970s when anything seemed possible. I was less sanguine than many of my peers about the imminent collapse of capitalism or a revolutionary upsurge here at home—"in the belly of the beast," as we called it then. Moreover, it was pretty clear to me that even if capitalism should collapse and a revolutionary government come to power, that government would not have the slightest idea as to how to restructure the economy. "Power to the people," sure, but *how* is economic power to devolve to them? What institutions would replace those of capitalism? The Soviet system had long ceased to inspire, and although great things seemed to be happening in Mao's China (not so great, we later learned), the Chinese economic model had little relevance to an advanced industrial society such as our own.

So my project became to determine how an advanced industrial economy might be structured to be economically viable, and, at the same time, embody the great ethical ideals of the democratic socialist tradition. My dissertation, "Capitalism: A Utilitarian Analysis," was its first incarnation. Although there is no mention of an economic alternative in the title, such an alternative had to be presented in the text because "utilitarianism" requires that comparisons be made. If you are going to critique capitalism from a utilitarian perspective, you have to show that some other economic system would provide a greater amount of happiness for more people.

That dissertation was later revised and published (in 1980) as *Capitalism or Worker Control? An Ethical and Economic Appraisal.* Here the alternative is named "worker-control socialism." (In the next book and in this one, I call it "Economic Democracy.") A model is presented that features worker self-managed enterprises competing with one another in a market environment, but with new investment "socially controlled." Although I've refined and adjusted the model over the years, you will see it has retained the same basic features. (Political philosopher Isaiah Berlin famously characterized thinkers as foxes or hedgehogs. "A fox," he says, "knows many things. A hedgehog knows one big thing."[1] I probably belong among the hedgehogs, for I do know one big thing: what a viable, desirable alternative to the present, pernicious economic order would look like.)

In 1993, I published *Against Capitalism*. The world had changed enormously since 1980. Most significantly, the Soviet empire had collapsed. First, its satellite states in Eastern Europe broke free of Soviet domination and repudiated their socialist heritage; then the Soviet Union itself disintegrated. These were gloomy days for those of us on the Left. Not that we were admirers of the Soviet Union; few of us were. But most of us felt, consciously or unconsciously, that the persistence of communism (indeed, its steady expansion) in the face of violent hostility on the part of the vastly richer and more powerful capitalist states, led by the United States, indicated that history was on our side. In due course, the Soviet Union and other socialist states would democratize, figure out how to run their economies efficiently, and, in the meantime, capitalism would enter into terminal crisis. So we thought.

History had other ideas. And yet I couldn't help thinking we were right. Morally, we were right—whatever history's verdict. Capitalism *is* a ruthless, predatory system, and there *is* a better way. It made me almost crazy to hear otherwise smart and decent thinkers (the philosopher Richard Rorty, for example) proclaim that we are "going to have to stop using the term 'capitalist economy' as if we knew what a functioning non-capitalist economy looked like."[2] We do know what a functioning, noncapitalist economy would look like. I wrote *Against Capitalism* to show once again—with suitable revisions to the model and additional material added—that the problem is not that we don't know what a humane economy would look like, but that forces of immense power are blocking its emergence. If intellectuals are supposed to "speak truth to power," as it was fashionable to say in those days, we ought at least say *that*.

Here I am again, writing another book on the same theme. It's at once the same book that I've written before—data updated, of course—and a rather different book. Let me highlight some of the differences. When I began writing this book, nearly four years ago, I had in mind a simple plan. I would rewrite *Against Capitalism* in a more popular key. *Against Capitalism* and its predecessors had been written for professional philosophers and economists. There were numerous footnotes and fairly esoteric discussions of technical matters, sometimes within those footnotes, sometimes in the text itself. This book was to be more "user friendly"—and I believe that it is. The footnotes remain—notes at the end of chapters, actually—but they simply source my quotes and data and occasionally suggest further reading. You can skip over them and miss nothing of substance. I've included in the text (as parenthetical remarks) side comments that I would have put in footnotes had I been writing for an academic audience. I've omitted all references to the technical debates.

I don't mean to suggest that I've "dumbed down" my presentation. Not at all. What I'm offering here is as intellectually rigorous as anything I've written. It won't be a quick and easy read. It's just that the person I have in mind as I write, with whom I am conversing, is an intelligent and concerned ordinary reader, not a scholar with philosophical or economic expertise. I want to be comprehensible to the nonexpert reader.

The original plan was simply to produce a more popular version of *Against Capitalism*, but as the writing progressed, two things changed. My first earlier works focused on capitalism as a way of organizing a national economy and providing an alternative national model. But, as everyone knows, "globalization" has become the name of the capitalist game. Therefore, this book more carefully treats capitalism as an international phenomenon (which, of course, it always has been) and more carefully specifies how a nation whose economy was structured as an Economic Democracy would interact with other nations.

A second, even more important, change occurred without my at first being aware of it. Looking back, I see that *Against Capitalism* and its predecessors were theoretical works aimed at establishing a theoretical point: those who have argued (and there are many) that a viable democratic socialist economy is impossible, given the kinds of creatures we are, are wrong. Democratic socialism, properly structured, is not contrary to human nature. It does not require extraordinary altruism on the part of its citizenry. Further, it does not run counter to deep-seated human impulses. While the present work remains theoretical, it has become theory with a more practical intent. The point here is not simply to undercut arguments advanced by various philosophers and economists against the possibility of a viable socialism, but to help ordinary people—those who will form the basis of the next great challenge to capitalism—to understand how the world works, and what can be done to make it work better.

The shift from theory with theoretical intent to theory with practical intent marked a subtle change in my thinking. I have become convinced—as I was not in 1993—that there will indeed be another sustained challenge to the capitalist world order, and that that challenge needs a clearer vision as to what is possible.

Why this shift in my thinking? Two sorts of factors were responsible. The first were of a personal nature, having to do with the reception of my work. In 1997, a Spanish translation of *Against Capitalism* appeared, published by the Jesuit-affiliated publishing house Sal Terrae of Santander, Spain, in conjunction with the social action network *Cristianisme i Justícia*. The latter arranged a book tour for me in early 1998, which took me to Barcelona, Bilbao, Tarragona, and Zaragoza. Suddenly I found myself speaking, not to exclusively academic audiences, but to ordinary people committed to social change. I also gave numerous interviews to local newspapers. Later that year, while in the Philippines, I was asked to speak to the Cooperative Foundation of the Philippines, Inc. Back home I was approached by the Eighth Day Center for Justice, a Chicago-based Catholic social action group, and asked to make a presentation. I was also invited to speak to the Midwest Center for Labor Research (now the Center for Labor and Community Research). During this same period, I began trying out chapter drafts of my new book on students, both undergraduate and graduate. As a result of these interactions, it became clear to me that there is a hunger on the part of a great many people of good will, particularly those with an activist bent, for a more concrete and comprehensive vision of present historical possibilities than is currently available. Many people are aware of injustice and want to change things but, although sensitive to many instances of social evil and working to alleviate them, they are unclear as to long-term, permanent solutions. They want to believe such solutions exist, but most have doubts. This book is intended to remove (or at least reduce) those doubts.

The other factors influencing the shift in my project toward the practical have been the changes in the world itself since 1993. A number of things have happened (or not happened) that have dampened the giddy triumphalism of capitalism's op-ed apologists so evident back then.

First, communist governments did not collapse everywhere—as was almost universally expected. All non-European communist states have remained intact. All are experimenting with market reforms—some with considerable success—but none has broken officially with its socialist past. Of course, most commentators see market reforms as leading inevitably to capitalism, but, as we shall see, that view is mistaken. There is nothing inevitable about such a transition. Markets (I argue) do not imply capitalism. Indeed, they are essential to a healthy *socialism*.

Second, what have collapsed since 1993 are not the economies claiming to be socialist, but the economies of many of the ex-socialist societies that have tried consciously to restore capitalism. Here's a recent evaluation of the Russian experience:

> The result has been an unmitigated disaster. In the first year of reform, industrial output collapsed by 26 percent. Between 1992 and 1995, Russian GDP fell 42 percent and industrial production fell 46 percent—far worse than the contraction of the U.S. economy during the Great Depression. . . . Real incomes have plummeted 40 percent since 1991. By the mid to late nineties, more than forty-

four million of Russia's 148 million people were living in poverty (defined as living on less than thirty-two dollars a month); three quarters of the population live on less than one hundred dollars a month. Suicides doubled and deaths from alcohol abuse tripled in the mid-nineties. Infant mortality reached Third World levels while the birthrate plummeted. After five years of reform, life expectancy fell by two years (to seventy-two) for woman and by four years (to fifty-eight) for men—lower than a century ago for the latter.[3]

Or consider this *cri de coeur* circulated via e-mail by a Bulgarian woman in the aftermath of NATO's war against Yugoslavia. It warns the Serbian "Democratic Opposition" about what will be in store for them. Here's an excerpt:

We, here in Bulgaria, have had U.S.-style democracy since 1989. For ten years already.

MY TEN MOST AWFUL YEARS

What happened during that most awful period of my life on Earth?

Through the ardent UDF leaders in power, the International Monetary Fund and the World Bank are successfully devouring Bulgarian industry, destroying the social fabric, and opening national boundaries. (Our national boundaries, mind you, never those of the U.S. or Germany.)

Three ways they devour Bulgarian industry:
—privatizing the Bulgarian plants and factories and liquidating them afterwards;
—directly liquidating them;
—selling them for twopenny-halfpence to powerful foreign corporations. For instance, the Copper Metallurgical plant near the town of Pirdop, producing gold and platinum as well as electrolytic copper, was sold in 1997 to Union Miniere, Belgium, for next to nothing.

Conclusion: Bulgarian industry and infrastructure (the roads for instance) have been most successfully demolished—and this WITHOUT bombing—in less than ten years. All this, just from doing what the Serbian opposition is saying the Serbs should do.

A popular joke here during the U.S. war on Yugoslavia: two Turkish pilots, flying over Bulgaria, are looking down at the Bulgarian landscape. One of them says, "I wonder? Have we dropped bombs here?" "Don't be silly," answers the other. "It is Bulgaria! It looks like that without bombing."

Side results: hordes of unemployed, as you can well imagine.

Beggars in the streets.

Children dying in the street from drugs and malnutrition.

Old people digging in the rubbish containers for some rag or moldy piece of bread.

Yesterday my brother-in-law told me he had seen the former headmistress of his son's school digging in a rubbish container.[4]

The third change that affected my thinking has been the sharp increase in global instability in recent years. In 1995, the Mexican "tequila crisis" came close to bringing down the entire global financial superstructure. According to Michel Camdessus, then head of the International Monetary Fund, who, with U.S. Treasury Secretary Robert Rubin and a handful of other powerful insiders, launched an unprecedentedly large rescue plan, they had to act, whatever the cost, or else "there would have been a real-world catastrophe."[5] Two years later, financial panic gripped Southeast Asia, bringing to its knees even the vaunted South Korean economy; the panic spread to Russia, which had to default on its internal debt, and then to Brazil. Since then, crises of varying magnitudes have broken out throughout Latin America, while Africa continues its downward spiral. Capitalism, freed from constraints, seems to have run amok, littering the globe with wreckage.

Fourth, and above all, there has been *resistance*. On January 1, 1994, the day that the famed North American Free Trade Agreement (NAFTA) went into effect, armed revolt broke out in the poor Mexican state of Chiapas, led by a movement taking its name from the legendary Mexican revolutionary of nearly a century ago, Emiliano Zapata. This unorthodox, imaginative movement, although itself renouncing violence while being subjected to harsh governmental oppression, refuses to go away. (In March 2001, members undertook a well-publicized "caravan of peace and dignity" from Chiapas to Mexico City, drawing support along the way, then staged a huge rally in Mexico City and entered the National Congress to speak to the politicians present.)

In the spring of 1995, the trade union federations of Italy called a general strike to oppose the right-wing Berlusconi government's plan to roll back pension gains. This strike shut down the country for several days, and brought 1.5 million workers, by the trainloads and busloads, to Rome. (I happened to be living in Rome at the time, teaching at Loyola University's Rome Center. Never in my life had I witnessed anything like this. My wife and I walked out of our apartment in Monte Mario, an upper-middle-class section of Rome, to find everything closed: grocery stores, fruit stands, wine shops, barber shops, newsstands, restaurants, even the gas stations. We stared in disbelief, trying to imagine something like this happening at home: the unions put out a call, and every business, everywhere—in every city,

town, and neighborhood—shuts down.) In the fall of that year, French students and workers, five million plus, also took to the streets, in a similar,
even larger action.

Protests and demonstrations began to pop up everywhere, although almost always focusing on specific issues of local or national concern. Then
came Seattle, November 1999—"Five Days That Shook the World," as writers
Alexander Cockburn and Jeffrey St. Clair termed them.[6] Thousands of pro-
testers, young and old, First World and Third World,[7] labor unions, environmentalists, anti-sweatshop activists, and many more, converged on the city
to disrupt the high-profile meeting of the World Trade Organization.

Even closer to home—here in Chicago—seven Loyola students were arrested for unfurling an anti-sweatshop banner at Niketown, a downtown
store selling swoosh products, and were scheduled to go on trial at the end
of August 2001. Nike dropped charges on the day of the trial. Everywhere
you look these days, people are resisting the ravages of our "new world order." It is impossible to predict how strong this resistance will become, or
how serious the economic crises that doubtless will continue to break out
(perhaps in unexpected places) will be, but it seems to me that whatever I
write at this point in time should contribute in some small way to that resistance. That's what this book hopes to do.

I owe thanks to many people for assisting me in refining the ideas in this
book. Two of my graduate assistants, Kory Schaff and Jason Barrett, helped
a lot in tracking down data. I've profited from student reactions—graduate
and undergraduate—to earlier drafts of this material. Particularly memo-
rable were discussions with three honor students—Dan Hoyne, Kate Hen-
derson, and Peter Gianopulos—at the Rome Center (one of whom refused
to be convinced). Appreciation should be extended to Juan Manuel Sinde,
of the Caja Laboral in Mondragon, for a useful meeting, and to Dan Swin-
ney of the Center for Labor and Community Research for extended conver-
sations as to the applicability of the model of Economic Democracy to concrete reform efforts now. I've been stimulated by ongoing debates with Al
Campbell and Bertell Ollman. Although we disagree strongly on a central
issue—the necessity of markets in a viable socialism—our discussions have
been nonrancorous and productive. I've benefitted from the commentaries
on an earlier version of this book by Patricia Mann, Frank Thompson, and
Justin Schwartz, given at the Radical Philosophy Association Conference in
the fall of 2000. I owe a lot to discussions with Michael Howard, with whom
I agree on (almost) everything. I've also benefitted from the written comments of Allen Hunter, Robert Heilbroner, Bruno Jossa, David Chandler, and
an anonymous referee. (If the referee is who I think it is, he has been
thanked by name in this paragraph.)

There are many more I should also thank. I've had the good fortune to
be able to present papers based on this book to various conferences and

meetings: in Havana, Holguin, and Camaguey, Cuba; at the Universidad de Centroamerica in El Salvador; at the University of the Philippines; at El Escorial and Gandia, Spain; at the Universitá di Bergamo in Italy; at the Université de Paris, Nanterre; and at numerous campuses in the United States. My thanks to all the organizers and inviters.

Special thanks also to my Cuban friends, Humberto Miranda, Raul Rodriguez, and Gilberto Valdez, whose courage and commitment to a humane socialism never faltered, even during the darkest days of the "Special Period," when Cuba's principal trading partner collapsed and the United States tightened its ruthless embargo. They—and so many other Cubans I've had the good fortune to meet—have been inspiring. (I've had occasion to visit Cuba six times during the past decade, almost always in conjunction with the annual Conference of North American and Cuban Philosophers and Social Scientists. I owe a debt of gratitude to Cliff DuRand of the Radical Philosophy Association, the indefatigable organizer of the North American delegation, for facilitating these visits.) Thanks also to Jean Tan for meticulous proofreading and other expert editorial assistance.

Special thanks to two other people. More than anyone else's, it was the work of Jaroslav Vanek, which I encountered while working on my dissertation, that put me on the intellectual trajectory I've since followed. I was privileged to make a presentation at a conference in his honor at Columbia University in 1999, which allowed me to express my gratitude. Let me express it again.

Finally, special thanks to Patsy—*sine qua non*.

Chicago, August 2001

Postscript

This manuscript was submitted to the publisher in August 2001, so obviously no mention was made of the September 11 terrorist attacks. However, given the significance of these events, the production schedule has been modified to allow for a postscript (and for several brief additions to the text).

"Everything has changed." This refrain was repeated constantly in the aftermath of the attacks. Is it true?

From the perspective set out in this book, the answer is "No." Not everything has changed. (As I write, widespread rioting in Argentina has brought down a neoliberal government trying to impose yet another International Monetary Fund austerity package.) The big things have not changed—although the attacks of September 11 do highlight a factor to which I paid little attention as I wrote this book.

After Capitalism documents and analyzes the destructive tendencies of capitalism, and it predicts a renewed challenge to this system. Among other things, it argues that the unrestrained capitalism that is now dominant will further widen the gap between the global haves and the global have-nots, while making life increasingly precarious for ordinary people, even in rich countries. What the book does not do—apart from an occasional aside—is consider nonprogressive reactions to economic stress and dislocation.

Yet, as the history of European fascism makes clear, modern mass movements based on ruthless, atavistic ideologies thrive under such conditions. Indeed, they are often cultivated by wealthy interests to deflect discontent and to destroy challenges from the Left. In recent times, with the socialist project in disarray, such movements have proliferated: neo-Nazi revivals in the West, the ethnic nationalisms that tore Yugoslavia to shreds and have wreaked havoc in many other poor countries, and, perhaps most significant of all, the various flavors of what I'm inclined to call "theocratic fascism"—faith-based fundamentalist movements that seek political power and do not shy away from terror.[8] Christian fundamentalists blow up abortion clinics. Jewish fundamentalists dream of a "final solution"—the ethnic cleansing in Greater Israel of "Palestinian lice" (as they were called by the recently assassinated leader of Israel's ultraright National Union Party).[9] Islamic fundamentalists set off bombs in shopping malls and commandeer aircraft full of people, which they then fly into buildings full of people.

We need to be clear about several matters.

- The cause of extremist activities is not religion per se. The vast majority of Christians, Jews, and Moslems of the world are anything but fundamentalists and are sickened by the slaughter of innocents. It is not even fair to brand all fundamentalists as theocratic fascists, although the intense *ressentiment* characteristic of most contemporary forms of religious fundamentalism point them in that direction.
- Nor is the cause poverty per se. Poverty inevitably breeds resistance, but that resistance can take various forms. Recall that not once during the Cold War era did indigenous Marxist forces fighting directly against the United States (as in Korea and Vietnam) or against U.S.-backed dictatorial regimes ever engage in terror against U.S. civilians. These forces were overwhelmingly poor workers and peasants struggling for a better life, who could see clearly that the United States opposed their efforts. But Marxism as an ideology has always distinguished between the government of a country, seen to be acting on behalf of that country's ruling class, and the ordinary citizens of the country, who also stood to gain (so the ideology proclaimed) from the movement's success. Fascist ideologies make no such distinction.
- We should also be clear that terror is not confined to fascist movements. By any objective measure, the nation now leading the charge in the "war against terror" has committed more acts of violence against

innocent people—either directly or via its support for murderous client regimes—than has any other nation of the post–World War II era. As I argue in chapter 4, had the United States been concerned to promote democracy in the world rather than capitalism, the body count of the postwar period would be many millions lower.[10] (As I also argue, there has been very little public support for the policies that have had such horrendous consequences. Successive administrations have had to expend considerable effort keeping the American people in the dark as to the exact nature of the endeavors.)

- Finally, we should remember that although wealthy interests often bankroll fascist movements, using them for their own ends, these efforts often have disastrous consequences. Wealthy landowners and industrialists backed Mussolini and Hitler to counter the Left. Saudi Arabia has funded fundamentalist movements throughout the Islamic world to legitimize its own corrupt regime. The United States gave enthusiastic (if covert) support to mujahideen fighters eager to overthrow the secular Marxist government of Afghanistan—and to drive out the Russians when they later invaded. That fascist movements often bite the hands that have fed them should come as no surprise. These movements are as cynical about their financial backers as the backers are of them. (Consider the recently published comments of President Carter's National Security Advisor, Zbigniew Brzezinski, interviewed before September 11, about the United States having given arms and advice to future terrorists: "What is more important to the history of the world? The Taliban or the collapse of the Soviet empire? Some stirred up Moslems or the liberation of Central Europe and the end of the Cold War?"[11]

What follows? The brutal events of September 11 call sharp attention to the virulence of movements that embrace terror as a "weapon of the weak" and to the threat they pose not only to innocent civilians everywhere but to domestic civil rights and liberties. Conservative forces can be counted on to exploit these events to further their own agenda. Indeed, they already have.

At a deeper level, the events of September 11 demonstrate how desperately the world needs a *progressive* alternative to the ideology of global capitalism. Capitalist globalization breeds resistance, which, when progressive responses are cut off, turns murderously ugly. Without a progressive vision—and a global movement animated by that vision—we are left with only capitalism and terror—McWorld versus jihad.[12] This book hopes to demonstrate that these alternatives, which are in fact two faces of the same coin, do not constitute our only possible future.

—Chicago, February 2002

NOTES

1. Isaiah Berlin, *Russian Thinkers* (New York: Penguin, 1978), 22. Berlin attributes the epigram to the Greek poet Archilochus, which he (Berlin) interprets as defining two kinds of thinkers.

2. Richard Rorty, "For a More Banal Politics," *Harper's* (May 1992): 16.

3. The term "Third World" gained wide currency in 1955 at the first conference of nonaligned nations held at Bandung, Indonesia, and was applied by the delegates to their countries, to distinguish them from the "First" capitalist world, and the "Second" communist world. "Third World" hints of the legacy of colonialism and emphasizes—especially now, in the absence of a Second World—the enormous gap between the two worlds that remain.

4. Nancy Holmstrom and Richard Smith, "The Necessity of Gangster Capitalism: Primitive Accumulation in Russia and China," *Monthly Review* (February 2000): 5. (I'm in basic agreement with Holmstrom and Smith regarding Russia, but not regarding China.)

5. E-mail received September 10, 1999, entitled, "With Her Eyes Opened—A Letter from Bulgaria," by Doncheva.

6. Quoted by Hans-Peter Martin and Harald Schumann, *The Global Trap: Globalization and the Assault on Democracy and Prosperity,* trans. Patrick Camiller (New York: Zed Books, 1997), 45. See pp. 40–46 for a gripping account of this near disaster.

7. Alexander Cockburn and Jeffrey St. Claire, *Five Days That Shook the World: Seattle and Beyond* (London: Verso, 2000).

8. Michael Mann labeled this latter phenomenon "combat fundamentalism." For an extended analysis, see his "Globalization and September 11," *New Left Review* (November/December 2001): 51–72.

9. See Robert Friedman, "And Darkness Covered the Land: A Report from Israel and Palestine," *The Nation* (24 December 2001): 13.

10. Noam Chomsky offers some estimates: 4 million dead in Indochina; 500,000 to 1 million dead in Indonesia; 200,000 dead in Central America (since 1978); and 200,000 dead in East Timor (since 1975). From *On Power and Ideology: The Managua Lectures* (Boston: South End Press, 1987), 24. This is only a sampling.

11. *Le Nouvel Observateur* (France) (15–21 January 1998): 76.

12. See Benjamin Barber, "Beyond Jihad vs. McWorld," *The Nation* (21 January 2002): 11–18.

1

Counterproject, Successor-System, Revolution

"A specter is haunting Europe—the specter of Communism."

So wrote Marx and Engels in 1848. They were right. Over the course of the next century and a half, this specter would indeed haunt Europe. Not only Europe. It would stalk the entire planet. Millions of people—workers, peasants, intellectuals, and assorted "class traitors"—began to dream of a new economic order and commit themselves to action. The world polarized into two great camps. Atrocities mounted on both sides. Vast quantities of nuclear weapons were readied for use. Humanity found itself staring into the abyss of MADness—"mutually assured destruction."

Now, at least for the time being, the ghost of communism has been exorcized. Capitalism has emerged victorious. It is *this* spirit, arrogant and triumphant, that now stalks the earth. It appears to us in various forms.

It appears as "consumer society"—vaguely disquieting but infinitely alluring. More astonishing than grace, invisible waves project the sounds and images of commodity happiness to all but the remotest regions of the globe. Great temples to this spirit—shopping malls that dwarf in size (and attendance) the cathedrals and mosques of earlier epochs—have spread from capitalism's heartland to almost every country of the world. Smaller shrines—from fast-food franchises to dot.com Web sites—have sprung up everywhere. Not everyone has access to these holy places, but few remain who have not felt the power of their attraction. In poor countries, armed guards screen those pushing to enter the local McDonald's and Pizza Huts.

The specter of capitalism appears to us in another form, this one more distant, more shrouded in mystery, less benevolent, but even more powerful. Global financial markets pass judgments, create and destroy fortunes, make or break countries. A hierarchy of priests—financial advisors, brokers, bankers, traders, journalists, and economists—serves the subdeities of currencies, commodities, stocks, and bonds. These clergy grasp the mysteries of finance better than the laity, but they remain servants of the specter. The markets themselves decide who will succeed and who will fail. (The most exalted of priests are sometimes humbled. Readers may recall the saga of Myron Scholes and Robert Merton, Nobel laureates in economics, who teamed up with some other financial wizards to form the hedge fund, Long-Term Capital Management—which was saved from complete collapse in 1998 only because the Federal Reserve decided it was too important to go under.)[1]

Capitalism appears to us not only as an alluring consumer society and as mysterious financial markets. Its cruelest manifestation is its savage inequality. We have all heard the statistics, although they are too numbing to remember for long. The top 225 individuals now possess wealth equal to the combined incomes of the bottom 47 percent of the world's population.[2] (Roughly, the average wealth of each *one* of these individuals is equal to the combined incomes of *ten million* people earning the average income of the bottom half of humanity.) Nations are also divided as to rich and poor, those at the bottom having per capita incomes one-twentieth or even one-fiftieth of those at the top. Life expectancy in rich countries now exceeds eighty; in poor countries, it is often under fifty-five. Infant mortality, malnutrition, and literacy rates are comparably disparate. Even within rich countries, the inequalities are staggering. In the United States, the upper 1 percent of the population owns more wealth than the bottom 95 percent. More than six million families have annual incomes of less than $7,500, whereas investment bankers and top corporate executives often make $10,000,000 per year, and the 250 or so billionaires in the country make even more. (A modest 5 percent return on a billion-dollar portfolio generates an annual income of $50 million.)

It was once believed by most respectable (comfortable) academics and policymakers that capitalism would even out these inequalities over time, bring up the bottom faster than the top, reduce the income disparities among nations, until, sooner or later, everyone consumed like a middle-class American. Nobody believes that any more. (MIT economist Lester Thurow thinks it cute to say, "If God gave Africa to you and made you its economic dictator, the only smart move would be to give it back to him.")[3] Now we simply build more prisons and more gated communities. If we happen to be in the upper-middle ranks of a rich country, we give thanks for our good fortune, and maybe buy a newspaper from a homeless person or write a small check to a favorite charity. If we are rich in a poor country, we might have to write a larger check to a favorite death squad should the peasants or workers get unruly.

The fourth manifestation of our specter is less often remarked, but no less evident: the deep irrationality of its overall functioning. How can it be that the amazing technologies we keep developing tend to intensify, not lessen, our pace of work, and make our jobs and lives less, not more, secure? How can it be that in a world of material deprivation, we must worry about industrial overcapacity and crises of overproduction? (How can there be too much stuff, when so many have so little?) Conversely, how can it be that the health of the global economy requires what ecological common sense knows is impossible—ever increasing consumption? (Economist Kenneth Boulding has remarked, "Only a madman or an economist could believe that exponential growth can go on forever in a finite world.")[4] To invoke Marx's term, how can we be so "alienated" from our products? How can it be that our own creations turn against us?

The specter of globalized capitalism: infinitely alluring, mysteriously powerful, savagely unequal, and profoundly irrational—has this spirit triumphed definitively? Have we indeed reached "the end of history," as Francis Fukuyama has proclaimed? Even on the Left, many seem to think so. Jeffrey Isaac, writing in *The New Left Review*, endorses Anthony Giddens's claim that "no one has any alternatives to capitalism":

> Now we might not like this, but Giddens is alas correct. To say this is not to regard contemporary capitalism as a "trans-historical feature of human existence" or "second nature." It is simply to remark that given the history we have inherited and the world that human beings have created, there exists no credible wholesale alternative to capitalism. The same could be said of water purification, modern medicine, electronic communication, industrial technology with all its wastes and hazards, and also civil liberties and representative government of some sort. These are all historical achievements we cannot imagine transcending.[5]

1.1 THE COUNTERPROJECT

These are strong claims: Capitalism as the end of history; capitalism as a historical achievement we cannot imagine transcending. Are they true?

This book will demonstrate that the latter claim is false. We can well imagine transcending capitalism. As to the former—let me make a different prediction. I propose that humanity's project for the twenty-first century will be to exorcize the ghost that now haunts us. If the contradictions of capitalism are as serious as I argue they are, and if they become more, not less, acute, as almost surely they will, then we will witness another sustained challenge to this most peculiar economic order. The challenge may not succeed. The forces arrayed against it are immense. But since it is becoming ever clearer that getting beyond capitalism is the best hope for our species, the attempt will be made.

In fact, a new challenge to global capitalism has already begun. One morning last July, while taking a break from revising the manuscript that became the book you are now reading, I glanced at the newspaper. The headline of the *Chicago Tribune* blared: "Riots turn Genoa into a war zone." The subhead added, "One killed, hundreds injured." While George Bush and other leaders of the G-8 (the seven leading industrial nations plus Russia—the latter added, presumably, out of respect for its nuclear missiles, not for its wrecked economy) met behind huge barricades and mouthed platitudes, at least 100,000 demonstrators, invited mainly via the Internet by an Italian network, the Genoa Social Forum, converged on the city. I checked my e-mail. Waiting for me was a first-person account, part of which reads as follows:

I think I am calm, that I am not in shock, but my fingers are trembling as I write this. We were just up at the school that serves as a center for media, medical and trainings. We had just finished our meeting and we were talking, making phone calls, when we heard shouts and sirens and the roar of people yelling, objects breaking. The cops had come, and they were raiding the center. . . . We watched for a long time out the windows. They began carrying people out on stretchers. One, two, a dozen or more. A crowd was gathering and were shouting, "Assassini! Assassini!" They brought out the walking wounded, arrested them and took them away. We believe they brought someone out in a body bag. . . . Finally the cops went away. We went down the first floor, outside, heard the story. They had come into the room where everybody was sleeping. Everyone had raised up their hands, calling out, "Pacifisti! Pacifisti!" And they beat the shit out of every person there. There's no pretty way to say it. We went into the other building. There was blood at every sleeping spot, pools of it in some places, stuff thrown around, computers and equipment trashed. We all wandered around in shock, not wanting to think about what is happening to those arrested, to those they took to the hospital. We know that they've taken people to jail and tortured them. One young Frenchman from our training, Vincent, had his head badly beaten on Friday in the street. In jail they took him into a room, twisted his arms behind his back and banged his head on the table. Another man was taken into a room covered with pictures of Mussolini and pornography, and was alternately slapped around and stroked with affection in a weird psychological torture. Others were forced to shout, "Viva Il Duce!"

Just in case it isn't clear, this is fascism, Italian variety, but it is coming your way. It is the lengths they will go to defend their power. It is a lie that globalization means democracy. I can tell you, right now, tonight, this is not what democracy looks like. . . .

Please, do something![6]

This renewed challenge to capitalism—let us call it the *counterproject*, since it opposes the project of globalizing capital—has been brewing for several years. It burst into full public view in November 1999, where, in

Seattle, union members, environmentalists, Third World activists, students, and thousands of other people fed up with watching the globalization juggernaut rampage unimpeded, decided to protest. They did so with considerable effect. In the face of massive and violent police retaliation, they shut down the World Trade Organization's (WTO) opening ceremony, prevented President Clinton from addressing the WTO delegates, and compelled the WTO to cancel its closing ceremonies and adjourn in disorder and confusion.[7] Since then, protests, self-consciously linked to the Seattle upheaval and to each other, have erupted in Quito, Ecuador (January 2000), Washington, D.C. (April 2000), Bangkok (May 2000), South Africa (May 2000), Buenos Aires (May 2000), Windsor/Detroit and Calgary (June 2000), Millau, France (June 2000), Okinawa (July 2000), Colombia (August 2000), Melbourne (September 2000), Prague (September 2000), Seoul (October 2000), Davos, Switzerland (January 2001), Quebec City (April 2001), and most recently (as of this writing—there will have been others by the time you read this), Genoa (July 2001). [Post September 11 update: A sizable contingent of protestors trekked to far-off Qatar in November 2001, where nervous WTO ministers decided to hold their post-Seattle meeting, while tens of thousands more rallied in their own countries—some thirty countries in all—to analyze and criticize the WTO agenda. In New York City in February 2002, some fifteen thousand rallied against the World Economic Forum being held there, while thousands more went to Porto Alegre, Brazil, for a "World Social Forum," which billed itself as a counter-WEF. Despite media pronouncements to the contrary, and despite the fact that governments are using the "threat of terrorism" to make protest more difficult, the events of September 11 have not derailed this "movement for global justice." (Note: Participants prefer this appellation to "antiglobalization movement," since they are by no means chauvinist or isolationist.)]

The counterproject, as a self-conscious entity, is still very much in its infancy, although its roots extend deep into the past. If it is to succeed, it will of necessity become a vaster and more complicated affair than it is today, ultimately involving millions of people who, in the process of struggle, develop a more-or-less common consciousness concerning structures of oppression and nonoppressive alternatives. It will do much more than disrupt high-profile gatherings of the world's elite. It will involve itself in the patient, difficult labor of contesting structural evil locally as well as globally, and of building counterinstitutions. If it is to succeed, the counterproject will have to avoid the major errors of past anticapitalist movements, and will have to respond creatively to capitalism's attempts, sure to come, to neutralize and destroy it.

Let me be more specific as to the general contours of this new movement. The counterproject will see itself as a dialectical synthesis of the great anticapitalist movements of the nineteenth and twentieth centuries *and* the other emancipatory movements of these centuries, especially the ongoing gender revolution, the struggle for racial equality, the fight against homophobia, the mobilizations against nuclear madness, and the efforts to halt ecological devastation. All of these struggles will be seen as part of a larger project, the counterproject, the huge, global effort to put an end to structural oppression and to ensure each and every human being a fair chance at self-realization and happiness.

In many (perhaps most) quarters, this counterproject will be called "socialist" or "communist," because, if it is anticapitalist—which it must be if it is to address the deep structures of economic injustice that pervade the world—it will be so labeled by its well-financed opponents. Of this we can be certain. As Marx and Engels noted long ago, "Where is the party in opposition that has not been decried as communistic by its opponents in power? Where the opposition that has not hurled back the branding reproach of Communism against the more advanced opposition parties?"[8]

It is pointless to contest these labels, which can in fact be worn with dignity. The counterproject will draw on the rich theoretical legacy of the socialist-communist tradition, and it will take sustenance from the many heroic struggles waged by committed individuals identifying themselves with this tradition. (These struggles have been pretty much effaced from current memory; the counterproject will have to recover its past.) It will do so without denying the shortcomings and failures—sometimes horrific—of individuals, parties, and governments that have called themselves socialist or communist. (The parallel with Christianity is exact. Progressive Christians draw strength and inspiration from the Christian tradition without denying the bigotry, corruption, and abuse that are also a part of Christianity's history.)

The counterproject will have as its goal a dialectical socialism, not a nihilistic socialism.[9] Its aim is not to *negate* the existing order, wipe everything out and start over, but to create a new order that preserves what is good in the present while mitigating the irrationality and evil. The counterproject will not be what Marx denounced as "crude communism," a communism animated by envy, which wants to level down and destroy whatever cannot be enjoyed by all.[10] It will be a project that builds on the material and cultural accomplishments of past centuries. It will embrace the political ideals of liberty, democracy, and the rule of law. It will endorse and promote such values as generosity, solidarity, and human creativity, and also self-discipline, personal responsibility, and hard work. It will not sneer at these latter values as "bourgeois." They will be regarded as indispensable to the construction of a new world.

Although it may eventually call itself socialist or communist, the counterproject will extend well beyond the confines of that tradition. It will not make the mistake of assuming that the struggle against capitalism is more urgent than other emancipatory movements, or that these other struggles are somehow reducible to the struggle against capital. Theoreticians of the counterproject will be clear on this point. It will not be claimed (because it is not true) that the struggle against the power of capital is more fundamental than, for example, the struggle against patriarchy or against the deep and bloody oppressions sanctioned by racism. It will not be maintained (because it is not true) that the dispositions and structures that sustain sexism, racism, and homophobia are less deeply rooted than those that sustain capitalism or less in need of being rooted out.

Counterproject theory will make it clear that all people everywhere who are working to overcome structural oppression are participating in a *common* project. Counterproject theory will allow individuals who have committed themselves to contesting some specific evil to identify with the hopes, fears, accomplishments, and failures of other individuals struggling against other evils. To invoke another Marxian term, it will allow us a sense of our *species–being*—the connection each of us has to all others.

1.2 SUCCESSOR-SYSTEM THEORY

In addition to illuminating the relationships among past and present emancipatory movements and among individuals committed to different aspects of what can be considered a common project, counterproject theory must also enable us to envisage—with some degree of precision—an economic order beyond capitalism. It must theorize a *successor-system* to capitalism.[11]

The concept of a successor-system is utterly lacking among the "practical Left" today—people engaged in concrete struggles against specific forms of structural oppression. Virtually all the progressive struggles being waged at present (and there are many) are taking place within the imaginative and conceptual horizon of capital.

In the advanced industrial parts of the world, progressive struggles are mostly aimed at preserving and extending earlier gains; for example, strengthening antidiscrimination and environmental legislation, increasing the minimum wage, shortening hours of work. On economic issues, the struggles are largely defensive. Capital cites "global competition" as the rationale for dismantling the welfare provisions of social democracy. Workers go on strike, and sometimes with students take to the streets to block government rollbacks of hard-won gains. In poorer countries, individuals and organizations fight to achieve what has already been achieved elsewhere with respect to human rights, democracy, labor rights, minority rights, gender equality, and environmental protection. The importance of these struggles should not be minimized, but it is hard not to notice that in none of these cases do we find articulated a specific conception of a qualitatively new way of organizing an economy—a new "mode of production." Even when activists from rich and poor countries converge to protest the policies of the WTO, International Monetary Fund (IMF), World Bank, or G-8, their concrete demands are for debt relief, tougher environmental laws, an end to "structural adjustment policies" that bleed poor countries, stricter labor law to block the race to the bottom, and so forth—worthy demands, to be sure, and well worth pressing, but demands that don't contest capitalism at its root. Even among those protestors who denounce capitalism by name—still a distinct minority, although a rapidly growing one—the lack of a concrete economic alternative is palpable.

Since the collapse of the Soviet Union, this theoretical lack has been acutely, if unconsciously, felt almost everywhere on the Left. How else explain the fact that this collapse has been so demoralizing even to those many leftists (the vast majority) who did not view the Soviet Union as the embodiment of socialist ideals? Whatever its failings, the Soviet Union represented an alternative to capitalism. It was, if far from perfect, a successor-system, and still in the process of evolution. Capitalism was not, as it now seems to be, the only game in town. (I later argue that appearances are misleading here. In fact, capitalism is not the only game in town. But without successor-system theory, we see the world through the lens of the dominant ideology.)

The counterproject needs successor-system theory. To change the world, we need to act concretely, but we also need, both as a guide and inspiration to action, theoretical illumination as to what is possible. So long as capitalism remains the horizon, all emancipatory efforts remain unduly circumscribed. Fortunately, we now have sufficient theoretical and empirical resources to construct such a theory. We are vastly better situated than was Marx or even Lenin in this respect, for we have accessible to us not only a century of unprecedented socioeconomic experimentation but also data and conceptual tools that were unavailable to the founding theoreticians of socialism. We can now say with far more warranted confidence than they ever could what will work and what will not. There is a certain irony here. At precisely the moment when capitalism appears strongest and most hegemonic, we can assert with more evidence-backed conviction than ever before that an efficient, dynamic, democratic alternative to capitalism is possible.

This book will offer a nontechnical sketch of such an alternative. As such, it is a contribution to successor-system theory, and hence a contribution to the counterproject. The model I present should not be thought of as a rigid blueprint, but as a rough guide to thinking about the future. It is meant to be an antidote of sorts to the paralyzing "bankers' fatalism" (French sociologist Pierre Bourdieu's apt term)[12] that has such a hold on the contemporary imagination. The fashionable mantra, TINA, TINA, TINA (There Is No Alternative) is not a reasoned statement. It is a poison designed to kill off a certain kind of hope. This is an exercise in poison control.

1.3 HISTORICAL MATERIALISM

Successor-system theory can be viewed as a supplement to Marx's famous *historical materialism*. In its general form, historical materialism remains the most plausible theory of history that we have. It is embraced by countless non-Marxists and even anti-Marxists—usually unwittingly, often simplistically. It has no serious rival as a theory of history. (The most powerful charge that can be leveled against it is simply that history by its very nature cannot be theorized. If it can be, then something like historical materialism must surely be true.)

In broad formulation, historical materialism asserts that the human species is a pragmatic, creative species that refuses to submit passively to the perceived difficulties of material and social life. Through a process of technological and social innovation, often proceeding by means of trial and error, we reshape the world over time to make it more rational, more productive, and more congenial to our capacity for species solidarity. The process is not smooth. Change involves losers as well as winners, so there is often class struggle. There are setbacks as well as advances, but human history, the theory asserts, exhibits a directional intelligibility that may be reasonably called "progress." We, as a species, are gaining ever more conscious control over our world and over ourselves.

When applied to the modern world, historical materialism claims that capitalism, the dominant economic system of Marx's day and our own, will be superseded by a more rational order. This successor-system has been traditionally called "socialism," and has been viewed as itself a stage on the way to a higher "communism."

As anyone who has studied Marx knows, there is a blank page at precisely this point in the theory. Marx says almost nothing as to what this "socialism" would look like. Virtually no attention is given to the institutional structures that are to replace those of capitalism and thus define an economic order genuinely superior to capitalism—that is, better able to take advantages of the technical and social possibilities opened up by capitalism but incapable of realization under that system.

When socialism descended from theory to practice, it had to confront this lacuna. Lenin, writing on the eve of the Russian Revolution, thought it would be a simple matter to replace capitalism with something better[13]—but he soon learned otherwise. Since there was nothing in the Marxian corpus to provide much guidance, the Bolsheviks had to improvise. They tried a very radical War Communism, abolishing private property, wage labor, even money—which got them through the Civil War but then broke down. They backtracked to Lenin's New Economic Policy (NEP), which reinstituted money, reintroduced the market, and even allowed for some private ownership of means of production. The NEP was successful but not wildly so. Following Lenin's death, Stalin opted for something more drastic. Agriculture was collectivized (at terrible human cost), all enterprises were nationalized, market relations were abolished, and an immense central planning apparatus was put in place to coordinate the economy. What we now think of as "the Soviet economic model" came into being.

For a rather long while, well over half a century, it looked as if this radically new way of organizing an economy was the wave of the future. The Soviet Union industrialized while the West collapsed into the Depression—as Marx had predicted it would. The Soviet Union survived a German invasion, broke the back of the Nazi military machine, and then, without any Western help, rebuilt its war-ravaged economy. Next came Sputnik, and a deep concern in Western circles that this new economic order might indeed "bury us," as Soviet Premier Nikita Khrushchev proclaimed it would. Numerous Western economists looked at relative growth rates and nervously plotted the point at which the Soviet economy would surpass that of the United States.

Leaders of the capitalist West scrambled to contain this dynamic giant, whose example was proving contagious. In 1949, the world's most populous nation declared itself a "People's Republic." A few years later the communist forces of Vietnam drove out their French colonial masters. In 1959, Fidel Castro, at the head of a guerilla army, forced the Batista dictatorship from power, and shortly thereafter proclaimed *"Socialismo o Muerte."* By 1975, the Vietnamese had defeated the vastly more powerful Americans (who had replaced the French), and began reconstructing their economy along noncapitalist lines. In 1979, a guerilla movement toppled the U.S.-backed Somoza dictatorship in Nicaragua, and although declining to call themselves communists, looked to Cuba and the Soviet Union for aid and inspiration. The course of history seemed clearly marked.

But, as we all know, a funny thing happened on the way to the future. In the 1980s, Soviet economic growth ground to a halt. The economy didn't collapse—that would come only with the attempted capitalist restoration—but the Soviet model hit its limits. It proved unable to generate new technologies or even exploit effectively those developed in capitalist countries. People became increasingly discontent. Thus, as a historical materialist would predict, with existing relations of production inadequate to new forces of production, there occurred a decisive shift in class power. To use Marx's words, "the whole vast superstructure was more or less rapidly transformed."[14] (The West did not sit by idly during this historical upheaval, but intervened with considerable success to ensure that the class it favored—the one committed to restoring capitalism—came out on top.)[15]

Does the collapse of the Soviet model, not only in Russia but also throughout Eastern Europe, mean that Marx has been proved wrong? Elementary logic says no, unless it is assumed that every attempt at constructing a successor-system must necessarily succeed. But such an assumption doesn't fit with historical materialism's basic premises. As we have noted, historical materialism regards the human species as a practical species groping to solve the problems that confront it. There is no reason to expect success right away. It is more probable to see only partial successes at first or outright failures with subsequent attempts learning from these experiences—until finally a transformation takes hold that is superior enough to the old order to be irreversible.

Neither I nor anyone else can prove that historical materialism is the correct theory of history. It is a hopeful, optimistic theory. It aims to be "scientific" but it clearly embodies elements that do not lend themselves to scientific validation. Still, it is a plausible theory, made even more plausible when supplemented by an adequate successor-system theory. This, at any rate, is what I hope to show.

1.4 CRITERIA

Let me specify more precisely what I take to be the essential criteria for an adequate successor-system theory.

- The theory should specify an economic model that can be cogently defended to professional economists and ordinary citizens alike as being both economically viable and ethically superior to capitalism. Although necessarily abstract, the model should be concrete enough for us to foresee how it would likely function in practice, when animated by the finite, imperfect human beings that we are.
- This model should enable us to make sense of the major economic experiments of this century, which have been numerous and diverse. If the human species is indeed groping toward a postcapitalist economic order, successor-system theory should illuminate that process.
- The model should clarify our understanding of the various economic reforms for which progressive parties and movements are currently struggling, and it should be suggestive of additional reform possibilities. It is a tenet of historical materialism that the institutions of new societies often develop within the interstices of the old. Successor-system theory should help us locate the seeds and sprouts of what could become a new economic order, so that they might be protected and nourished.
- Successor-system theory should enable us to envisage a transition from capitalism to the model successor-system. It should specify a set of structural modifications that might become feasible under certain plausible historical conditions, which would transform (a possibly much-reformed) capitalism into genuine socialism.

Having said what successor-system theory is supposed to be, let me underscore what it is *not*. Successor-system theory is not the whole of counterproject theory. It is not even the whole of the economic component of this theory. Successor-system theory is centered on a rather abstract economic model. It does not concern itself with the actual history of capitalism and its development from feudalism, its relationship to slavery and colonialism, its curious mix of progressive ideals and brutal practices. It does not address, except indirectly, such Marxian concepts as alienated labor, fetishism of commodities, the labor theory of value, or the falling rate of profit. It does not concern itself with the ways in which the economic "base" of society manifests itself in other areas of society.

Nor does successor-system theory address in a sustained or systematic fashion the issues of racism, sexism, homophobia, and other forms of structural oppression. These issues are important to the counterproject, exceedingly so, but they lie outside the purview of successor-system theory, at least as it will be sketched in these pages.

Successor-system theory is further restricted in that it is not a theory about Marx's "higher stage of communism," or the ultimate fate of humanity. It is concerned with what is both necessary and possible now—the immediate next stage beyond capitalism, a stage that will be marked by its origins within capitalism. One can speculate as to the evolution of a postcapitalist society such as the one I will describe, but such speculations extend beyond the range of the theory itself.

1.5 REVOLUTION

As indicated above, successor-system theory must address the transition question. Successor-system theory is meant to be theory with practical intent. If it cannot offer a plausible projection as to how we might get from here to there, successor-system theory remains an intellectual exercise in model building—interesting in its own right perhaps, and capable of providing a theoretical rejoinder to the smug apologists for capital, but useless to people trying to change the world.

The successor-system theory marked out in these pages will not offer a full-blown "theory of revolution." I am not sure that the time is ripe for such a theory. At any rate, I don't have one. Nonetheless, I do think it is possible to sketch some plausible transition scenarios, which will be done in chapter 6. I also think it possible to discern the general direction a new theory of revolution should take.

- A new theory of revolution will recognize that the old models of social revolution, drawing their inspiration from the French, Russian, Chinese, and Cuban Revolutions, are largely inappropriate to the world today, certainly to advanced industrial societies, perhaps even to poor countries. The question of armed insurrection will have to be carefully reexamined. The masses are never going to storm the White House, nor is a people's army ever going to swoop down from the Appalachian Mountains and march up Pennsylvania Avenue.

• The new theory will recognize the need for a more concrete vision of structural alternatives than has been customary in the past. (Hence the importance of the first component of successor-system theory.) It is not enough to say, "Seize state power and establish socialism." Blind faith in the laws of history or in an omniscient party has been justly discredited. The intelligence of ordinary people must be acknowledged and respected. Most workers, certainly those in rich countries, have far more to lose now than just their chains.

• The theory will emphasize the need for reform struggles now, before the conditions are right for a truly fundamental socioeconomic transformation. What we get, if and when space opens up for revolutionary structural change, will depend crucially on what we have already gotten— and on who, during the course of many struggles, we have become. As we shall see, radical structural transformation will involve a substantial deepening of democracy. But democracy, while a necessary ingredient of the kind of world we want, is not sufficient in and of itself. The output of a democratic procedure depends on the quality of the input. Hence the importance now of struggles against racism, sexism, and homophobia, against senseless violence, rampant consumerism, and environmental destruction. Hence the importance now of trying to figure out better ways of living with one another and with nature.

• The new theory will also emphasize the need for diverse strategies and diverse aims. How we get to where we want to go will depend crucially on where we happen to be. The transition to a genuinely democratic socialism will likely vary, depending on whether the country is rich or poor, on whether the country has undergone a socialist revolution in the past, and on various other historical and cultural contingencies. Although there will be commonalities of vision, there will be differences as well—of tactics, transitional strategies, and ultimate goals. Unlike the program of global capitalism, one size does not fit all. The counterproject does not envisage all nations aiming for the same patterns of development, or adopting the same technologies, values, and consumption habits. The counterproject calls for a halt to the McDonaldization of the world.

• Finally, an adequate theory of the transition from global capitalism to democratic, sustainable socialism will stress the need for an *international* social movement, not in the sense of a unified, centrally directed party, but in the sense of a common consciousness that recognizes a kind of unity in diversity and allows for cross-national cooperation and inspiration. The counterproject is nothing less than the project of our species.

1.6 A NOTE ON GENDER

The most significant revolution of the twentieth century was not the Russian Revolution or the Chinese Revolution (although the impact of each has been immense) but the irreversible transformations, still underway, in the ways men and women live with one another. We are currently living through one of the most significant moments in the history of homo sapiens. We are in the midst of a revolution that should be called by its proper name, the feminist revolution. (An ideological counteroffensive is currently underway, trying to discredit the term "feminism," its leading theorists, women's studies programs, and anyone who dares self-identify as a feminist, but the fact of the matter is, feminism has changed the world irrevocably.)

The feminist revolution, where it is most advanced, has touched virtually every facet of human life—family structure, child rearing, sexuality, work, play, love, war, our grand ambitions, and our innermost identities. It is, moreover, a worldwide revolution, far from finished but hardly confined to the relatively affluent portions of the globe. It is more advanced in some places than others, but there is no country on Earth where women are not coming together to think collectively about their common problems and about strategies for emancipation. In some countries, such strategizing is extremely dangerous, but in every such place, there are women braving the danger. In most countries, thinking is accompanied by action—from the microlevel of individual relationships to the macrolevel of national policy.

It would seem, then, given the importance and pervasiveness of the as yet unfinished feminist revolution, that successor-system theory should address the issue of gender explicitly and systematically. However, as indicated in the disclaimer offered above, I will not do so in this book. Certainly, gender concerns and feminist theorizing are germane to many of the issues to be discussed here, but in a short book such as this, these cannot be treated adequately. Still, it is worth pointing out a number of areas where gender concerns and feminist theorizing would have to be addressed to do full justice to the concerns of successor-system theory.

- *Poverty.* I consider the question of poverty, both in affluent societies and poor countries. I propose a full-employment policy as the basic solution to poverty in both rich and poor countries—a policy (as we shall see) that cannot be enacted under capitalism. I couple this with "fair trade" so that poor countries do not have to devote a disproportionate amount of their resources to catering to rich-country consumers. I recommend that poor countries engage in broad-based, labor-intensive public programs of health and education.

- Well and good—but clearly, any realistic attempt to eradicate poverty must take into account the gender dimension of the problem. How do we ensure that women as well as men have the requisite opportunities and skills for meaningful work? Should all women be encouraged to seek paid employment? What about those with young children? What about those caring for aging parents? These latter questions lead to deeper questions: Should women continue to do most of the care work in society? How should we, collectively, care for our children, for those among us with disabilities, and for our elderly?

- *Leisure.* I argue that under capitalism, there is a structural tendency toward overwork. But as everyone knows (or should know), women in paid employment are far more overworked than men, since in most cases they must bear the brunt of "the second shift"—the unpaid labor of daily domestic life. In the successor-system, we will have far more choices concerning consumption-leisure tradeoffs at work. What sorts of changes in domestic relationships are in order to insure that this leisure is fairly apportioned? I argue that ecological sustainability requires we opt increasingly for leisure over consumption. What sort of family restructuring will be needed for people to view leisure as unambiguously attractive? (As has been recently observed, many men and women prefer the structure and clear lines of responsibility they experience at work to the chaos and unpleasantness they encounter at home.[16] There is a large gender dimension to this issue that should be explored.)

- *Community.* It is possible under the successor-system to redesign local communities to make them more "user-friendly"? Each year funds are available for public capital expenditures, so that new public amenities may be instituted. Would the priorities advanced by women be the same as those advanced by men?

- *Democracy.* The successor-system to be proposed entails a large advance in democracy. Citizens will have far more opportunity than they do now to discuss, debate, and decide issues of common concern. Feminist theory has been much involved with the question of preconditions for real democratic dialogue. What is the role of argument in democratic decision making? How do we do justice to the "difference" of those with whom we engage when we talk across the borders of race, gender, class, and sexual orientation? How do we develop the ability to listen to the other? These and related questions are of profound importance to a movement that raises high the banner of democracy.

- *Revolution.* The relationship between feminism and anticapitalist revolution is complex and offers much ground for further research. Several issues stand out.
  - The feminist revolution does not fit the model of revolution that spontaneously comes to mind when we think of moving beyond capitalism. The feminist revolution has been, above all, a nonviolent revolution. Moreover, it has not been marked by decisive, watershed events that clearly mark a "before" and "after" the revolution. A new theory of revolution must pay careful attention to what has been learned from the (quite literally) millions of small and large battles fought, lost, and won as women have moved to redefine the world and their place in it.
  - The worst excesses of political revolutions have often been marked by masculinity. Angry young men have contributed courageously to revolutionary struggle, but they have also been involved in nonproductive and sometimes gratuitous violence. Those of us who lived through the sixties can recall the macho posturing that sometimes pushed us in directions we shouldn't have gone. Nor has masculine excess been confined to Western societies. The Chinese Great Leap Forward and Cultural Revolution were marked by similar excesses, as were many other radical upheavals and movements. There is a gender component to revolutionary struggle that bears analysis.
  - Women have played a huge role in virtually all the progressive struggles of the past several decades. Women have often constituted the majority of the participants, not only in struggles related to gender but those concerning human rights, nuclear disarmament, ecology, solidarity with the people of El Salvador or Nicaragua, sweatshops, and so forth. If the counterproject comes to have revolutionary potential, it will almost certainly count as many women as men among its activists, and so will have a different character and ethos from classical revolutionary movements. How different? What are the implications for organizational theory and practice?

The above listing is not exhaustive. As with race, which I address in chapter 5, theoretical and practical issues regarding gender inevitably impinge on theoretical and practical issues regarding economic structures. I regret not being able to do justice to these various intersections in this work.

1.7 AN OUTLINE OF THE ARGUMENT

Successor-system theory claims that capitalism is no longer justifiable as an economic order because there now exists a better alternative. Since this claim is comparative, the argument for it must spell out this "better alternative" in some detail, so that the two systems can be evaluated side by side. However, before considering this alternative, which will be called *Economic Democracy*, we must be clear about the nature of capitalism itself. A serious critique of capitalism cannot be content with merely noting the negative features of the contemporary world. It must show a causal connection between these features and the structures that characterize capitalism.

Chapter 2 specifies precisely the defining characteristics of capitalism and clarifies such key concepts as *capital, capitalist, entrepreneur, investment,* and *saving*. As it turns out, these terms are closely connected to certain "noncomparative" justifications for capitalism (arguments that make no reference to alternatives), which are worth considering in their own right and for the light they shed on the inner workings of the system. Chapter 2 proceeds to deconstruct these justifications. In the process, certain conclusions, quite at odds with prevailing common sense, come to light:

- Capitalists *qua* capitalists make no contribution to production.
- The stock market and other "investment games" are unfair.
- Private saving is not only *not* necessary for economic growth, but is often positively harmful—hence interest income is undeserved.

It doesn't follow that capitalism as such cannot be justified. It may be that capitalism, however unfair, is the best that we poor, finite human beings can do. To refute this claim, an alternative must be specified. Chapter 3 does this. First, the institutions of the "basic model" of Economic Democracy are set out; then evidence is marshaled in support of the claim that Economic Democracy is an economically viable system. Among the important pieces of evidence is the remarkable success of a most unusual economic experiment centered in the town of Mondragon in the Basque region of Spain.

The basic institutions that characterize Economic Democracy are defined within the context of a nation-state. However, given the economic interdependency of nations in an ever more globalized economy, principles of interaction must be specified. Chapter 3 does this also. Economic Democracy will insist that "fair trade," not "free trade," should be the governing principle, and hence will adopt a policy of "socialist protectionism."

Chapter 3 concludes with a presentation of an "expanded model" of Economic Democracy, one less pure than the basic model, but consistent with its spirit. The expanded model permits savers to earn interest on their savings, and even allows entrepreneurial individuals to become true capitalists. These allowances can be made, as we shall see, without jeopardizing the radically different principles according to which the economy as a whole functions.

Chapters 4 and 5 constitute the heart of the argument—the head-to-head confrontation of capitalism and Economic Democracy. Chapter 4 analyzes six fundamental defects of capitalism:

- Massive inequality
- Demoralizing unemployment
- Unnecessary overwork
- Excruciating poverty, nationally and globally
- Lack of real democracy
- Systematic and sustained environmental degradation

Chapter 4 shows how these phenomena are connected to the institutions that define capitalism. Chapter 5 examines the same phenomena from the perspective of Economic Democracy. In every case we will see that Economic Democracy comes off better.

Chapters 3 through 5 are concerned with satisfying the first criterion of an adequate successor-system theory, namely the presentation and defense of an alternative model. Chapter 6 addresses the remaining three criteria. We see that Economic Democracy as a model allows us to form a coherent account of the major economic experiments of the twentieth century. We see that the model is suggestive of a reform agenda that can and should be worked for now, before capitalism enters a major crisis. Concerning revolution, two scenarios are offered for a final transition out of capitalism and into a full Economic Democracy.

By way of conclusion, *After Capitalism* returns to the *Communist Manifesto* (a quote from which opened this chapter). It is proposed that something like a "New Communism," taking its cue at least in part from the original manifesto, would be highly desirable.

NOTES

1. See Roger Lowenstein, *When Genius Failed: The Rise and Fall of Long-Term Capital Management* (New York: Random House, 2000) for the less-than-edifying details.

2. United Nations Development Programme, *Human Development Report, 1998* (Oxford: Oxford University Press, 1998), 30.

3. Lester Thurow, *Head to Head: The Coming Economic Battle among Japan, Europe, and America* (New York: William Morrow, 1992), 216.

4. Cited in Mancur Olsen and Hans Landsberg, *The No-Growth Society* (New York: Norton, 1974), 97.

5. Jeffrey Isaac, "Marxism and Intellectuals," *New Left Review* 2 (March–April 2000): 114. Francis Fukuyama famously proclaimed liberal capitalism as the end of history in his *The End of History and the Last Man* (New York: Free Press, 1992).

6. Sent by Starhawk, from Genoa, July 21, 2001. Starhawk is an American author and activist who has taken part in numerous antiglobalization protests in recent years. See her Web site at <http://www.starhawk.org>.

7. For an on-the-spot account of the Seattle events, and of the demonstrations at the spring meetings of the International Monetary Fund and World Bank in Washington, D.C., the following April and at the Democratic National Convention in Los Angeles in August, see Alexander Cockburn and Jeffrey St. Clair, *Five Days That Shook the World* (London: Verso, 2000). For an invaluable source of information about past and future antiglobalization protests worldwide, see www.indymedia.org.

8. Karl Marx and Frederick Engels, *The Communist Manifesto* (London: Verso, 1998), 33.

9. For an elaboration of this distinction, see James Lawler, "Marx's Theory of Socialisms: Nihilistic and Dialectical," in *Debating Marx*, ed. Louis Pastouras (Lewiston, N.Y.: Edward Mellen Press, 1994).

10. See Karl Marx, "Private Property and Communism," in his *Economic and Philosophical Manuscripts of 1844*, reprinted in, for example, Erich Fromm, *Marx's Concept of Man* (New York: Frederick Ungar: 1966), 123–140.

11. My thanks to Patsy Schweickart for suggesting this term to me and for helping me see how fruitful this concept could be in giving practical content to what might otherwise appear to be abstract-utopian model building.

12. Pierre Bourdieu, "A Reasoned Utopia and Economic Fatalism," *New Left Review* 227 (January–February 1998): 126.

13. See V. I. Lenin, *State and Revolution* (New York: International Publishers, 1932).

14. Karl Marx, "Preface to a Contribution to the Critique of Political Economy," in Fromm, *Marx's Concept of Man*, 217.

15. For an account of the G-7 strategy to thwart Mikhail Gorbachev's dream of rebuilding the Soviet economy along noncapitalist lines, see Peter Gowan, "Western Economic Diplomacy and the New Eastern Europe," *New Left Review* (July–August 1990): 63–84.

16. Arlie Hochschild, *Time Bind: When Work Becomes Home and Home Becomes Work* (New York: Metropolitan, 1997).

2

Justifying Capitalism

If we ask how capitalism has been, and continues to be, justified by its legions of supporters, the justification that most immediately comes to mind is what I call the "comparative justification": capitalism works—not perfectly by any means, but better than any other system we humans can devise. So popular is this argument that it has been given a name: TINA—There Is No Alternative—at least, no alternative that can give us both freedom and prosperity. TINA, of course, cannot be refuted without specifying an alternative system to which capitalism can be compared.

There are other justifications for capitalism—"noncomparative" justifications—that are also significant. They constitute an important part of the intellectual armor of capitalism, protection against a question that cannot fail to occur to any decent, thoughtful person who looks at the world with open eyes: How can it be right that under capitalism some people have so much while others have so little? In particular, what do *capitalists* do to merit their stupendous wealth?

This chapter, after defining the key terms, will consider four such answers:

- The capitalist contributes his capital.
- The capitalist contributes his entrepreneurial creativity.
- The capitalist risks his capital.
- The capitalist defers consumption.

These justifications are noncomparative, in that they do not refer to alternatives to capitalism. They appeal implicitly to a commonly accepted ethical standard: it is right that people be rewarded for their contributions to the common good. They implicitly assert that the rewards accruing to capitalists

21

are more or less proportional to their contributions. As we shall see, none of these answers can withstand critical scrutiny. In seeing why not, we will come to a better understanding as to how this system we live under—more mysterious than it at first appears—actually works. We will then be in better position to address TINA—capitalism's most formidable defense.

2.1 WHAT IS "CAPITALISM"? WHAT IS A "CAPITALIST"?

In any economic system human beings interact with nonhuman nature to produce the goods and services that human beings desire. Human labor utilizes nonhuman means of production to generate products. The laws and customs that govern the relationships among these three entities (human labor, means of production, and products) constitute the economic structure of a given society. The structure of a capitalist society consists of three basic components:

- *The bulk of the means of production are privately owned, either directly or by corporations that are themselves owned by private individuals.*

Marx and the socialist movements of his day called this feature "private property," an unfortunate choice of terminology, since calling for the abolition of private property, which Marx does, conjures up images of communal food, clothing, shelter, and (who knows what those communists will do?), maybe even toothbrushes. In fact, these things are not at issue. Items purchased for one's own use are, for Marx, "personal property," not private property. Your toothbrush, your clothes, your car, and your home remain yours under socialism.

- *Products are exchanged in a "market"—that is to say, goods and services are bought and sold at prices determined for the most part by competition and not by some governmental pricing authority. Individual enterprises compete with one another in providing goods and services to consumers, each enterprise trying to make a profit. This competition is the primary determinant of prices.*

The term "free market" is often used as a defining characteristic of capitalism, but this is misleading, since some degree of price regulation—via differential product taxes, subsidies, tariffs, or outright price controls—is present in most capitalist societies. A capitalist economy must be a market economy, but the market need not be wholly free of governmental regulation nor, for that matter, wholly free of private-sector price fixing either.

- *Most of the people who work for pay in this society work for other people who own the means of production. Most working people are "wage laborers."*

Whether the income is called a wage or a salary is immaterial. In order to gain access to means of production (without which no one can work), most people must contract with people who own (or represent the owners of) such means. In exchange for a wage or a salary, they agree to supply the owners with a certain quantity and quality of labor. *It is a crucial characteristic of the institution of wage labor that the goods or services produced do not belong to the workers who produce them but to those who supply the workers with the means of production.*

There are several things to note about this definition. First of all, it defines capitalism as an economic system, not a political system. Whether or not· a society has a free press or allows its citizens to vote in competitive elections is irrelevant as to whether it is a capitalist society. Fascist Italy, Nazi Germany, white supremacist South Africa, and most of the almost-too-many-to-count military dictatorships of this century were capitalist societies.

The name or nature of the government that comes to power is also irrelevant. All postwar Western European countries have remained capitalist, even when parties calling themselves socialist have been elected, even when these parties have nationalized certain industries and/or instituted various public welfare programs. So long as most productive assets are privately owned, most economic exchanges take place through the market, and most people work for wages or a salary, a society is capitalist.

Moreover, all three structures must be present for a society to be capitalist. A society of small farmers and artisans, for example, is not a capitalist society, since wage labor is largely absent. A society in which most of means of production are owned by the central government or by local communities—contemporary China, for example—is not a capitalist society, since private ownership of the means of production is not dominant. (We will consider more carefully the controversial case of contemporary China in subsequent chapters.)

It must be emphasized that using the market to allocate goods and services does not make a society capitalist. Almost everywhere today the term "market economy" is employed as a synonym for (and usually instead of) "capitalism." This is a serious conceptual mistake. As we shall see, it is perfectly possible—and indeed desirable—to have a market economy that is socialist. Competition is not the antithesis of socialism. "Market socialism" is not an oxymoron. A viable successor-system will not be as ruthlessly competitive as contemporary capitalism, but it will by no means abandon market competition altogether.

To use "market economy" as a synonym (indeed, euphemism) for "capitalism" is not merely an analytical mistake; it is a deep ideological distortion. The term "market economy" highlights the least objectionable defining feature of capitalism while directing attention away from the really problematical institutions, namely, private ownership of means of production and wage labor. For example, the "privatization" reforms so insistently prescribed for Russia and the countries of Eastern Europe are not "market reforms." They have nothing to do with the market. They are attempts to establish private ownership of the means of production and to solidify wage labor.

If capitalism as an economic system is defined by the three institutions listed above, what is a "capitalist"? Oddly enough, in our capitalist society there is no commonly agreed-upon definition of this key term. In fact, the term is rarely used in the mass media or even in scholarly circles. We hear of industrialists, businessmen/women, entrepreneurs, and stockholders—but almost never of "capitalists"—doubtless because the word still has unsavory connotations (robber barons calling on the Pinkertons to break strikes and beat up protesting workers). Capitalists don't like to be called capitalists, at least not in public; they prefer to remain invisible—or at least be called by some other name. Still, if we are to understand capitalism, we need some sort of definition that picks out the class of people who constitute the system's driving force.

For our purposes, a reasonable definition of "capitalist" is someone who owns enough productive assets that he can, if he so chooses, live comfortably on the income generated by these assets. A capitalist is not simply someone who believes in capitalism. Nor are you a capitalist just because you happen to own a few stocks or bonds. To be a capitalist you must own enough income-generating assets that you can live comfortably without working. You may work—you probably do—but you don't have to. (As we shall see in chapter 4, the capitalist class in the United States comprises roughly 1 percent of the population.)

The capitalist class derives its wealth from its ownership of productive wealth, that is, from "capital." A capitalist receives income because he "contributes" his capital to production. But what exactly is the nature of this "contribution"? Indeed, what exactly is "capital"? These questions are more difficult to answer than one might think. Answering them carefully will allow us to see through a number of spurious justifications for capitalism itself.

2.2 NEOCLASSICAL SHENANIGANS:
MARGINAL PRODUCT AS CONTRIBUTION

To the question "what is capital?" Marx offered a straightforward answer: capital is "embodied labor"—the material result of past labor. The machine the worker is using, which so greatly enhances her productivity, is the product of other people's labor. The food the worker eats, purchased with her wages, is the product of other people's labor. When you think about it, says Marx, every conceivable good we consume comes from human beings working with and on nonhuman nature. These are the *only* factors of production—human labor (mental as well as physical) and nonhuman nature.

This is a dangerous thought. If the factors of production are only labor and nature, where does "the capitalist" enter the picture? It is clear that labor should be rewarded for its contribution to production. It is equally clear that nonhuman nature need not be. (It must be replenished or conserved, but that's a separate matter.) The capitalist also demands a reward, a "fair return on his investment"—but on what basis?

The standard answer, taught in every introductory economics course, is that goods are the product of *three* factors of production—land, labor, and capital—and that the owners of these factors are rewarded on the basis of their contributions. Well, land is clear enough—that's shorthand for natural resources (i.e., nature)—and labor is labor. But what then is *capital*? Tools? Technology? Money? Congealed time? Embodied labor? What?

Marx devoted the bulk of his greatest work (called, appropriately, *Capital*) to pursuing the implications of *his* answer. His conclusions were utterly unacceptable to the capitalist class, but not so easy to refute. Marx constructed his argument using "classical" value theory, the standard theory of his day, which had developed from Adam Smith through David Ricardo—the "labor theory" of value. It became necessary to reconstruct economic theory on a new foundation to avoid the uncomfortable implications of that particular theory. A new economics, a "neoclassical" economics, thus came into being, which zeroed in on this labor theory of value, criticized it, and offered an alternative theory, a "marginalist theory" of value. This new theory quickly replaced the treasonous old theory in all respectable quarters, and has remained to this day the dominant paradigm in the economics profession.

We needn't pursue the value controversy here, which is normally (if wrongly) presented as a controversy as to how best to understand prices. (Is the price of a commodity determined by the amount of labor it took to produce it or by the "marginal utility" of the commodity to the consumer, that is, the satisfaction that one more unit of that commodity would give?) This celebrated controversy is a smoke screen. The real heart of the "neoclassical revolution" is its theory of distribution.

The fundamental problem confronting post-Marxian economic theory is the problem of explaining (and justifying) the profits of the capitalist. If a commodity, say corn, is the product of three factors, land, labor, and capital (as the neoclassical account has it), how can we determine how much of the final product should be distributed to each of the claimants, landowners, laborers, and capitalists? To be sure, a free market will set a rental rate, wage rate, and interest rate, and so bring about a distribution—but what grounds do we have for saying that this is a *just* distribution? (Lurking in the background here is the Marxian question: If labor is the source of all value, why should the landowners or capitalists get *anything?*)

Let's forget about the capitalist for the moment and concentrate on the remaining two factors. Clearly, it takes both land and labor to produce corn. How should the product be divided between landlords and laborers? The neoclassical economist answers: it should be divided according to *contribution*. Each factor should get what it contributes.

Fine. That seems fair—but how do we know how much each factor contributes? At the end of the harvest, we have Z bushels of corn. How can we say that the workers contributed X bushels and the land contributed Y bushels? You can't just say that the competitive market will take care of the distribution. Why should we think this "invisible hand" distribution has anything to do with respective contributions? Why not just say that the workers did all the work, the landowner is a parasite, and be done with it?

John Bates Clark, one of the pioneers of neoclassical economics, acknowledged the seriousness of this question.

> The welfare of the laboring class depends on whether they get much or little; but their attitude toward other classes—and therefore the stability of society—depends chiefly on the question of whether the amount they get, be it large or small, is what they produce. If they create a small amount of wealth and get the whole of it, they may not seek to revolutionize society; but if it were to appear that they produce an ample amount and get only a part of it, many of them would become revolutionists and all would have the right to do so.[1]

Surprisingly enough, Clark and his neoclassical colleagues were able to answer the question in a noncircular manner. This is no mean feat. Here we have sacks of corn, the result of the harvest. Without making any question-begging references to competitive markets, you cannot say, can you, how much of that corn is due to labor and how much due to land? The neoclassical economist smiles and replies, "But I can. Not only that, I can prove to you that in a competitive capitalist economy, the market will set the wage rate at exactly the contribution of the laborer and the rent at exactly the contribution of the land. I can also show that if we allow monopoly—either of laborers or landowners—the market will *not* distribute in accordance with contribution but will return to the monopolists more than they contribute."

The argument is technical, but worth understanding, for it has had enormous ideological impact, and has done much to give neoclassical economics an aura of scientific respectability. Let me explain it by way of an example. Suppose we have five acres of land and ten workers. We will assume that the land is of uniform quality and that the workers are equally skilled. At the end of harvest, we have one hundred bushels of corn. How many were contributed by the land, and how many by labor? (The restless reader will want to say, "This is silly. Obviously each and every bushel required both land and labor." But wait . . .)

Let us calculate the "marginal product" of labor. Suppose one worker were to work the five acres and suppose the yield is twelve bushels. Now let two workers work the land. Because there is plenty of land, and because they can cooperate and take advantage of economies of scale, they will likely produce more than twenty-four bushels. Let us suppose they produce twenty-six. In this case, we will say that the "marginal product" of the second worker is fourteen—the gain in total production brought about by adding that second worker to the workforce. (In reality, no one is going to conduct this experiment. The point is simply that these marginal products have scientific validity because they could, in principle, be calculated experimentally.)

Now use three workers. If there are still economies of scale to be had, this third worker's marginal product might be even higher, perhaps fifteen bushels. Sooner or later, however, economies of scale give way to "diminishing returns," that basic, beloved law of neoclassical economics. After a while, the laborers begin to crowd one another. Adding a new laborer will increase production, since the land can be cultivated more intensively, but the extra output you get by adding another laborer, his marginal product, is less than what you got from the last one. If we graph the marginal product of each laborer, we have a step curve that rises for a while, but then steadily declines (figure 2.1).

Suppose we define the "contribution" of each worker to the total output of ten workers working five acres (in our example, one hundred bushels) to be the marginal product of the *last* laborer. Suppose this is six bushels. In that case, the total contribution of labor is sixty bushels, ten times the marginal product of that last laborer. Graphically, this is the shaded portion of the area under the step curve in the top graph.

This might seem to be a wholly arbitrary definition. Why should the contribution of *each* worker be defined as the marginal contribution of the *last* worker? To be sure, we have assumed them all to be equally skilled, and it is true that if we pulled any one of them from production, the total product would decline by exactly the marginal product of the last worker, but so what? If we removed two workers, the total product would decline by *more* than their combined "contribution." If we removed them all, there would be no product at all. What is so special about the marginal of the *last* worker?

Well, consider the following. Suppose we reverse our procedure and calculate the marginal product of the land. Suppose we hold our labor force constant, and have them work first one acre, then two acres, then three, four, and five, each time calculating the marginal product of the land. We'd likely

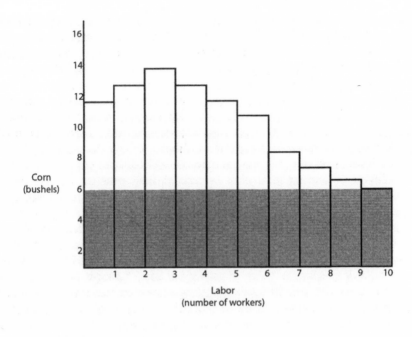

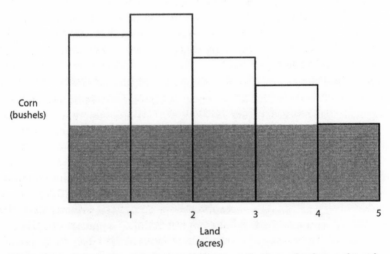

Figure 2.1   Marginalist Calculation of the Contributions of Labor and Land

see a similar phenomenon to what we observed with labor. At first, there would be increasing returns to scale, so the marginal product of land would go up, but then, after a while, diminishing returns would set in. Adding an additional acre would always increase total production, but adding that fifth acre wouldn't increase the output by as much as adding the fourth because the workers would have to spread themselves ever more thinly. Suppose we define the "contribution" of each acre of land to be the marginal product of the last acre—just as we defined the contribution of each worker to be the marginal product of the last worker. Thus, the total contribution of the land is the shaded area of the lower graph.

Notice, we have derived both the contribution of labor and the contribution of land from purely technical considerations. We have made no assumptions about ownership, competition, or any other social or political relationship. No covert assumptions about capitalism have been smuggled into the analysis. Notice too, we have a technical *problem* on our hands. We have determined, by means of a rather esoteric definition, both the contribution of labor and the contribution of land—but what makes us think these contributions are going to add up to the total product? What grounds do we have for thinking that the shaded area of the top graph will equal the white area of the bottom graph and vice versa? If they don't, then we cannot claim to have separated our hundred bushels of corn into the respective *contributions* of labor and land.

But they do add up. That's the mathematical result that gave neoclassical economics its intellectual respectability. In fact, the portions don't *always* add up. In an example such as I've given, they probably wouldn't. But if the numbers are large—of workers and acres—and if you make enough assumptions about homogeneous fertility and skills, substitutability of land and labor, and diminishing returns, then Euler's Theorem can be invoked—a purely mathematical result having nothing to do with economics per se (first proven by the great eighteenth-century mathematician Leonard Euler)—to demonstrate that the total product will in fact be equal to the contribution of labor (defined as the marginal product of the last laborer multiplied by the number of laborers) plus the contribution of land (defined as the marginal product of the last acre multiplied by the number of acres).

A remarkable result that, moreover, can be extended to include capital. If we allow capital into our story (say, money to purchase seed and tools), it can be shown that our corn harvest subdivides neatly into the contribution of land, labor, and capital. Moreover—as mentioned above—it can be further demonstrated (again with appropriate simplifying assumptions) that a free competitive market will set the land rent at the marginal product of land, the wage rate at the marginal product of labor, and the interest rate at the marginal product of capital. (Actually, the argument concerning capital is a whole lot murkier and more controversial than the argument for land and labor, but we needn't go into that.)

A remarkable technical accomplishment, separating out quantities associated with each separate factor in such a way that they all add up to the total output—*but utterly bogus as an ethical argument.* Our original objection was correct: there is something arbitrary in defining the "contribution" of each laborer to be the marginal product of the last laborer. Actually, not "arbitrary." "Deceptive" is a better word. To call the marginal product of the last laborer the "contribution" of each laborer is to invoke an *ethical* category suggesting entitlement. Since each worker "contributed" that amount, each is entitled to that amount, right? And, lo and behold, that's exactly what the free market gives the worker. In a competitive free market economy, wages are what they should be, rent is what it should be, interest is what it should be. Monopolies generate injustice, but pure competitive capitalism is fair capitalism. Workers get precisely what they contribute—and hence have no right to "become revolutionists."

But this conclusion, so much more comforting to landlords and capitalists than Marx's conclusion, in no way follows from the technical premises of the argument. Suppose our ten workers had cultivated the five acres *as a worker collective*. In this case, they would receive the entire product, all one hundred bushels, instead of sixty. Is this unfair? To whom should the other forty bushels go? To the land, for its "contribution"? Should the collective perhaps burn forty bushels as an offering to the Land-God? (Is the Land-Lord the representative on Earth of this Land-God?)

We can see that a moral sleight-of-hand has been performed. A technical demonstration has passed itself off as a moral argument by its choice of terminology, namely, by calling a marginal product a "contribution." The "contribution = ethical entitlement" of the landowner has been identified with the "contribution = marginal product" of the land. Had we not called that marginal product "contribution," it would have been impossible to conclude that our original question had been answered. We wanted to know why we should think that what the market gives the landlord has anything to do with his actual contribution. To say that the market gives him sacks of corn equal to the marginal product of his last acre multiplied by the number of acres he owns in no way answers the question. Why should that amount count as his *contribution*?

At issue here is something more than just a quantitative problem, our inability to specify the *magnitude* of the landowner's contribution. We have a quantitative problem because we have a qualitative problem. What is the exact nature of the landowner's "contribution" here? We can say that the landlord *contributed the land* to the workers, but notice the qualitative difference between his "contribution" and the contribution of his workforce. He "contributes" his land—but the land remains intact and remains his at the end of the harvest, whereas the labor contributed by each laborer is gone. If the laborers do not expend *more* labor during the next harvest, they will get nothing more, whereas the landowner can continue to "contribute" year after year (lifting not a finger), and be rewarded year after year for doing so. Labor and land (and capital) are not so symmetrical as the neoclassical tale makes them appear to be. Our "factors of production" do not meet as equals on a level playing field. The owners of one of the factors must expend their physical and mental energy year after year to continue their "contribution," whereas the owners of the other two factors need do nothing at all.

I am not saying that *in actuality* landlords and capitalists do nothing. Sometimes, they too expend physical and mental energy during the process of production (although often they do not). What is interesting, indeed paradoxical, about the neoclassical argument is that in making enough simplifying assumptions to be able to so elegantly invoke a mathematical theorem, it assumes away everything the landlord or capitalist might actually be doing to justify his reward. In the neoclassical story landlords and capitalists are wholly passive. They don't supervise workers; they don't invent anything; they don't make any decisions as to what to produce or what technologies to employ. They are wholly absent from the production process, merely *granting permission* for their land and capital to be used—in exchange for a healthy cut of the proceeds. But since "granting permission" is not a productive activity, Marx's question retains its bite. To produce material goods, we need human labor and we need nonhuman raw materials—but why do we need landlords or capitalists?

2.3 CAPITALISM'S WHITE KNIGHT: THE ENTREPRENEUR

It is precisely to distract attention from its theoretically inert landlords and capitalists that neoclassical economics complicates its initial story and introduces another character into the drama: the entrepreneur. Here is an economic actor par excellence. The entrepreneur sees an opportunity, rushes to take advantage of it, thereby benefitting not only himself but society at large. The entrepreneur develops a new product, invents a new technology, comes up with a new and more efficient way of producing or marketing. Or, more modestly, he replicates in a new location what others have done elsewhere—develops another strip mall, opens another coffee shop or dollar store or fast food restaurant. The entrepreneur is the creative principle of capitalism, celebrated, emulated, envied. Surely no one will deny that the entrepreneur makes a productive contribution to society—and hence is deserving of his reward.

No one can doubt that the entrepreneur makes a productive contribution. One can question the long-range value of specific contributions but any society, if it is to be at all dynamic, needs people who are economically creative and willing to initiate new projects. Entrepreneurial activity is vital—for capitalism and for successor-system socialism. Socialism will need entrepreneurs (though not capitalists).

The entrepreneur under capitalism makes a productive contribution, but there is a problem with appealing to the entrepreneur in order to justify capitalist income. *Most capitalist income has little to do with entrepreneurial agency.* Once again, a sleight of hand is performed in order to justify a return to capital. The entrepreneurial function has been identified with the capitalist function. To be sure, some capitalists act as entrepreneurs, and some entrepreneurs become capitalists. Nonetheless, theoretically and in practice, the two categories, capitalist and entrepreneur, are distinct. Neoclassical economic theory acknowledges this distinction. It defines the entrepreneur to be the agent who brings together land, labor, and capital, paying to the owners of each the market rate of rent, wage, and interest respectively. If the entrepreneur's project is successful, she reaps a profit.

We observe that the entrepreneur's profit is quite distinct from the return on capital. The entrepreneur is rewarded for her activity; the capitalist is rewarded for "providing capital." The real issue in justifying capitalism is not justifying profit per se. (Profit will, in fact, remain an important category in the socialist successor-system.) The real issue is justifying the income that flows to the capitalist simply by virtue of his ownership of real or financial assets.

We can see the problem most clearly when we consider income from investments that are virtually risk-free. This is what economic theory denotes as *interest*. Consider a standard textbook definition:

> The market rate of interest is that percentage of return per year which has to be paid on any safe loan of money, which has to be yielded on any safe bond or other security, and which has to be earned on the value of any capital asset (such as a machine, a hotel building, a patent right) in any competitive market where there are no risks or where all the risk factors have already been taken care of by special premium payments to protect against any risks.[2]

We observe that the theoretical definition of interest excludes income due to entrepreneurial ingenuity as well as income somehow connected to risk. (We will explore the risk connection in the next section of this chapter.) In practice, of course, financial investments are not wholly risk free, so the return on an investment usually contains a risk premium, but there are baseline, utterly safe, investments you can make. The only "risk" involved in buying an inflation-indexed U.S. government or blue-chip corporate bond is that you might make less money than if you invested in some other, riskier financial market. Barring a revolution (and maybe even then, as we shall see), those contractual interest payments will always be made.

In a capitalist society, enormous sums are paid to people who do not engage in any entrepreneurial activity or take on any significant risk with their capital. The precise amount is impossible to calculate, since "interest" as it appears in income accounts is not quite the same as the risk-free "interest" of economic theory, but it is worth noting that in 1998, personal interest income totaled $765 billion. Another $263 billion flowed as dividend income to stockholders for their (wholly passive) "contributions" to production.[3] (This is a mind-boggling total. If payments were distributed equally, which of course they are not, every household in the United States would have received more than $10,000 from these sources that year.)

To recapitulate the argument of this section: The specific function of the capitalist qua capitalist is to "provide capital"—a function unrelated to entrepreneurial activity. The capitalist qua capitalist remains the passive figure of the preceding section, who engages in nothing that can be reasonably regarded as "productive activity." Workers produce and distribute goods and services. Salaried managers coordinate production. Entrepreneurs and other creative personnel develop new products and techniques of production. The capitalist qua capitalist does none of these things. As an individual, he might also be an entrepreneur or a manager, but these productive functions are quite distinct from "providing capital"—the function that, in a capitalist economy, legally entitles him to his (often huge) slice of the economic pie. In short, not all entrepreneurs are capitalists; not all capitalists are entrepreneurs. You can't justify the income of one by appealing to the function of the other. The entrepreneurial justification for *capitalist* income is a wash.

2.4 RISK AND REWARD: PLAYING REVERSE-LOTTO

It will be objected that we have failed to take seriously the most important justification for capitalist income: except in rare cases, the capitalist—indeed any investor—*risks* his property. It is this risk that entitles the investor to a reward.

This is also a bad argument, as we shall see, but it is not without a reasonable core. It is reasonable to ask, what's wrong with rewarding people who take risks, if such risk taking is socially beneficial? If a wealthy person, instead of simply spending his money on personal consumption, chooses to back a project that ultimately enhances consumer satisfaction, society benefits, does it not? And since the investment could have failed, do we not owe this person something for the risk he ran on our behalf?

A response to this line of argument can begin by noting that we cannot propose, even tentatively, that capitalism rewards in proportion to risk. We cannot say that riskier investments earn a higher return. We can only say that riskier investments, *if they succeed,* tend to do so. If they don't succeed—and the riskier they are, the more likely it is that they won't—the investments may earn nothing at all. We can't say that because he took the risk, an investor *deserves* a return on his investment. If such risk taking conferred entitlement, then an investor whose investment failed would have grounds for demanding compensation, which clearly he does not. A bankrupt investor cannot say, "I took a risk, so I deserve a reward."

A more appropriate ethical standard for judging the rewards to risk is that of "pure procedural justice," a technical concept deriving from the concept of a "fair game." The principle is straightforward: if everyone plays by the rules, and if the rules are fair, then the results are just, no matter what they are.

With pure procedural justice, there is no independent standard of justice regarding outcome. The fairness of the procedure is determined by direct examination. If the procedure is fair, then the outcome is just, whatever it may be. Tossing a coin to decide which football team should kick off is an example of pure procedural justice, as is a poker game among (noncheating) friends. A trial by jury is not, since, even when the rules are followed scrupulously, innocent people are sometimes found guilty and guilty people innocent. (A "fair trial" is an example of "imperfect" procedural justice, since there is an independent standard by which to judge the outcome—the accused either did or did not commit the crime.) With pure procedural justice, no independent standard for evaluating the outcome exists, even theoretically. So long as no one cheated, what I win or lose at poker, no matter how much or how little, is just.

A pure procedural defense of capitalism asks us to think of capitalist investment as a game. The ethical question then becomes: are the rules fair? An objection comes at once to mind. Not everyone can play. You can play the investment game only if you have money to invest. That's one of the *rules.*

A defender of capitalism will protest that no one is legally excluded from the game, but two points must be borne in mind. First of all, the obvious point: whatever the law may say, large numbers of people simply do not have any discretionary funds to invest. They can't play at all. Secondly, among those who can play, some are better situated than others. Wealth gives access to information, expert advice, and opportunities for diversification that the small investor often lacks.

Since the rules of the capitalist investment game not only exclude many potential players but also favor some players over others, we would seem to have good grounds for questioning the justice of even "clean" capitalism, that is, capitalism without insider trading and so forth.

A defender of capitalism is sure to protest: Small investors can invest in mutual funds, and so take advantage of diversification and expert judgment. This may not have been so easy to do in the past, but it is not difficult now. Moreover—and more importantly—these investors have *freely chosen* to enter the game. They don't have to play. Surely we don't want to *prohibit* people from putting their money at risk if they so desire.

These points are well taken. Small investors (who are, after all, well enough off to have something to invest) would hardly seem to be in need of paternalistic protection. Moreover, the capitalist investment game is a *positive-sum* game. The small investor, although perhaps disadvantaged vis-à-vis the large investor, is still likely to make money on his investment, particularly if he is not too greedy. Certainly there are schemes and scams aplenty to detach the unwary small investor from his savings, but there are also lots of "legitimate" opportunities. The stock market, for example, may not be a magic carpet ride (however much it sometimes seems to be), but neither is it a fraud. Many investors, small as well as large, have made money on the stock market—a lot more than have made money playing poker.

The game-theory concept just introduced is a useful concept for understanding certain key features of capitalism. A game is *positive sum* if the total expected gain from playing, computed according to probability theory, is positive. More simply put: a positive-sum game is one in which more money is won than is lost. A *zero-sum* game is one in which gains and losses match. In such a case, being excluded does not disadvantage you, since the expected gain from playing is zero. On balance, you are no better off playing than not playing. A game is *negative sum* (for example, any gambling game where the house gets a cut) when your expected gain is negative. If monetary gain is your only reason for playing, you are better off sitting it out.

I have claimed that capitalist investment is a positive-sum game. Let me call the capitalist investment game "Reverse-Lotto," since, unlike Lotto itself, this game pays out far more than it takes in. (Lotto and other state lotteries are among the *worst* of the negative-sum gambling games, paying out barely half of what they take in. Not surprisingly, lottery outlets are far more prevalent in poor communities than in those where there are other, more favorable, games to play.)[4]

If the capitalist investment game is positive sum, then people who are excluded are disadvantaged. As we have already noted, many people are indeed excluded—anyone who lacks sufficient discretionary income to play. If capitalist investment were a zero-sum game, such people would have no grounds for complaint (no economic grounds, at any rate). If the investment game were negative sum (like a state lottery), such people could count themselves lucky at being kept out.

Is the capitalist investment game really a positive-sum game? One proxy for investment income is what shows up in the national accounts as "property income." This figure is usually about one-quarter of the national income. It is never negative. The fact of the matter is, those who play the investment game usually gain by doing so, for they are playing a game where the net gain (interest, dividends, capital gains) is massively positive. To be sure, there are losers, but overall far more money is won than lost.

But how is this possible? How is it *possible* for the investment game to be positive sum? How can more money be won at Reverse-Lotto than lost? Where does that extra money come from?

This question takes us to the heart of capitalism. Let us address it by first detouring through another question. What is the point of the capitalist investment game? That is to say, what is the purpose of stock markets, bond markets, currency markets, investment banks, and other institutions that allow those with surplus money to risk it in hopes of seeing it grow? What is the point for society? It is no mystery why *individuals* would want to play a positive-sum game, but what's in it for society at large?

Clearly, the point is not to reward risk per se. People take countless risks that go unrewarded, even when successful. Every time I cross a city street or fail to buckle my seat belt, I take a risk. There are no social institutions in place to reward me monetarily for my successful survival, nor would anyone want to propose any. The risks we want to reward are those which, when run successfully, are beneficial to society.

If we think about it, we realize that the point of the investment game is to encourage socially beneficial behavior of two distinct sorts. The *primary* goal is to foster entrepreneurial activity: actions by talented people that lead to new products, new techniques of production, and so on. Any society that wishes to be reasonably dynamic must find ways of encouraging such activity.

But in order to actualize a new idea, an entrepreneur needs *the labor of other people*. Notice, I did not say "money." It is important to realize that money is not an *essential* condition. What an entrepreneur needs is labor—the past labor of other people (in the form of buildings, equipment, and raw materials) and present labor (her own and that of her employees). At bottom, what an entrepreneur needs is *authority*, the authority to command the labor of others.

How does one acquire such authority? In a capitalist society, by having the money with which to purchase it. (It is here that money enters the picture.) Where does the entrepreneur lay hold of such money? In a capitalist society, partly from her own savings, but mostly from individuals who have money to spare. Thus we have the *secondary* goal of the capitalist investment game: to encourage those with money to spare to make it available to those who can use it effectively to mobilize the labor of others.

We can now understand how it is that the investment game is positive sum, and why it is the case that the immediate gain is (largely) at the expense of the nonplayers. One gets something for nothing because someone else gets nothing for something. Investment income, the reward to those who have "risked" their money by channeling it into financial institutions—banks, stock markets, real estate trusts, venture capital consortia, and the like—is possible only because *those who produce the goods and services of society are paid less than their productive contribution*. If capitalist distribution were really in accord with the principle of contribution (as is often claimed), the investor would get nothing. The *entrepreneur* (the person with the innovative idea) would still be rewarded, as would workers and managers, but there would be nothing left over for the person who merely "provided the capital."

What I am saying here is rather hard to swallow, particularly if you have made a little money with your investments. Let me illustrate more concretely. Let's take the case of the stock market. How do you make money in the stock market? Basically, there are two sources of income. When you buy a share of stock in Company X, you are entitled to a portion of Company X's profits. That's your dividend income. You can also make money from capital gains. If, over time, the value of your share appreciates, you can sell it and pocket the difference.

In the first case, the analysis is straightforward. Dividend payments come from net profit, and net profit derives from surplus value—the difference between the monetary value added to the raw materials by the workers (including management) and what they are paid. As any economist will confirm (since it is an analytical truth), unless labor costs are less than the value added by labor, there will be no profit. (Please note: even if profits of a particular company in which you hold stock were due entirely to some new innovation, it wasn't *your* innovation. You just own a share of the company's stock.)

What about capital gains? Here the situation is less transparent. Some part of your capital gain may be due simply to speculation. If enough investors think that a stock will rise in value, their buying it will cause it to rise, thus fulfilling their expectations. If you happen to have purchased a share of that stock prior to the speculative surge, and you sell it while the price is high, you realize a "magic" profit.

But the real basis for stock appreciation lies not in investor psychology but elsewhere. Part of a company's net profit is paid out to the stockholders in the form of dividends, but the remainder is reinvested in the company. These "retained earnings" increase the real value of the company, and hence the value of the stock itself. So the capital gains portion of stock income also derives from profit, hence from surplus value—hence from what Marx called the "exploitation" of labor.

"But wait!" you will surely say. "In buying stock I supplied the company with investment capital. Without me, the company would have made fewer profits."

In most cases, this assertion is flat out false. In the vast majority of cases, when you buy stock, you give your money not to the company, but to another private individual. You buy your share of stock from someone who is cashing in his share. Not a nickel of your money goes to the company itself. The company's profits would have been exactly the same, with or without your stock purchase.

It is true that once in a while a company will offer a *new issue* of stock, to be sold to the public for cash. This dilutes the value of the existing stock, so stockholders aren't enthusiastic about new issues, but sometimes new funds are acquired this way. But even here, there's a problem. The stock purchaser keeps getting "repaid" long after the value of his contribution has been reimbursed. Dividend checks keep coming for as long as the company endures; the reinvested profits of the company—no longer connected in any way to the original investment—keep adding to the stock's value forever. John Kenneth Galbraith—sympathetic to capitalism, but clear-eyed as to how it works—puts the matter this way:

> No grant of feudal privilege has ever equaled, for effortless return, that of the grandparent who bought and endowed his descendants with a thousand shares of General Motors or General Electric. The beneficiaries of this foresight have become and remain rich by no exercise of intelligence beyond the decision to do nothing, embracing as it did the decision not to sell.[5]

Let me be clear as to what has been shown thus far. I have explained how it is possible that the capitalist investment game (as a whole and usually in its various parts) is positive sum. In most years more money is made in the financial markets than is lost. How is this possible? It is possible only because those who engage in real productive activity receive less than that to which they would be entitled were they fully compensated for what they produce. The reward, allegedly for risk, derives from this discrepancy.

It does not follow that rewarding risk in this manner is immoral or even socially harmful. The entrepreneur engages in productive activity of an important nature. An entrepreneur must have access to funds to enact her vision. In a capitalist society, these funds come from private investors. But the entrepreneur's gamble poses a risk to an investor. Since an investor can lose, he must be enticed to take the risk. This, remember, is the secondary function of the capitalist investment game. I have shown that this part of the game is unfair because it is a positive-sum game from which many are excluded. Still, it could be argued (and often is) that unless the secondary goal of the investment game is satisfied, the primary goal, the encouraging of entrepreneurial activity, cannot be satisfied either. The game might not be fair, but it serves so important a function that, all things considered, it is justified.

Consider an analogy. A peasant community is in thrall to a theocracy. Every year the peasants turn over a portion of their harvest to the priests, who pray to the Land-God for a good harvest next year. The priests also exhort their flock to work hard, informing them that they will offend the Land-God if they do not. Thus motivated, the peasants do work hard, and do in fact produce more than they did in pretheocratic days.

Ideologically, the system is based on a lie. The productivity of the land is not due to the prayers of the priests but to the hard work of the peasants themselves. But perhaps this is a Noble Lie—justified by its consequences.[6] Without it, the people would in fact be worse off.

Perhaps people need Noble Lies—that the Land-God must be appeased, that providing capital is a productive activity, that capitalists are mostly creative entrepreneurs, that financial markets are fair.

Or perhaps we've outgrown the need for Noble Lies. What if there is an alternative—a better mechanism for providing authority to entrepreneurs, which does not involve people with wealth compounding their wealth without engaging in any sort of productive activity?

Notice, this question moves us from the noncomparative justification to the comparative one. We see that it is not risk per se that justifies a capitalist's income, but the assumption that there is no better mechanism for generating sufficient entrepreneurial energy than capitalist positive-sum Reverse-Lotto. The comparative case for Economic Democracy will challenge this assumption.

To avoid a possible misunderstanding: I have *not* argued that investing in the stock market is immoral. Financial markets under capitalism fulfill a vital function. They are also unfair. However, replacement institutions do not yet exist. To what extent should a person who can play an unfair positive-sum game sacrifice her own interests by refusing to do so? It is true that the game is unfair, but it is unclear that anyone would benefit from the refusal. These are the terms of the problem. Let your conscience be your guide.

2.5 THE UTILITY (AND DISUTILITY) OF DEFERRED CONSUMPTION

Before taking up the comparative argument, let us consider one final noncomparative justification. To understand more fully how capitalism actually works, we need to consider a concept that has been absent from the discussion so far, the concept of "saving."

Like capital, this concept might seem to be so commonplace that no analysis is necessary. To save is to defer consumption. I put away a part of my income now so that I might spend it later—on that proverbial "rainy day." Nothing mysterious here.

There is something a little *peculiar* about these savings, however. In a capitalist economy, there are places for me to deposit my savings that will pay me for doing so. This is odd, isn't it? The bank is protecting my savings: it is performing a service for me. Shouldn't I be paying the bank for this service? (When I store my luggage in an airport locker, I pay for the service.) But no, that's not how it works. In fact, the bank pays me.

Let us ask the ethical question. Why should I receive interest on my savings? I put money in a bank. There is no question of *risk* here. My savings account is fully insured by the federal government. There is no question of *entrepreneurial activity* on my part. I have not the slightest idea what the bank does with my money. All I know is, so long as I leave my money in the bank, it will "grow."

Interest may seem to be a simple thing, but interest, particularly when compounded, is remarkable. John Maynard Keynes, somewhat whimsically, calculated that the entire foreign investment of Britain, some £4 billion in 1928, could be derived from that portion of the treasure Sir Francis Drake stole from the Spanish which Queen Elizabeth invested in the Levant Company—some £40,000, compounding at a very modest 3.25 percent each year. "Thus every £1 which Drake brought home in 1580 has now become £100,000. Such is the power of compound interest."[7]

One pound grows to be a hundred thousand. Again we must ask, how is this possible? Population growth is easy enough to understand. If every couple has four children who live to adulthood, the population will double every generation. That's easy to understand. Parents were fruitful and they multiplied. If I invest $1,000 at 6 percent, my investment will double every twelve years. How did *that* proclamation take place? From whom did the $1,000 come?

Superficially, the answer is simple enough. It is possible for a bank to pay its savers interest because it charges interest to its borrowers—a higher rate, in fact, so that it can make a profit. If we ignore this profit (which is not particularly significant), and if we imagine the loan to be a consumer loan, then clearly nothing more is going on than a redistribution of income. Lenders gain at the expense of borrowers. In order to consume now, before you have saved up the full price of the item you wish to purchase, you agree to pay me for the privilege of doing so. I lend you $1,000; you repay me $1,060 a year from now. That year I can spend $60 more than I could have if I hadn't waited, whereas you can spend $60 less. This is a nice arrangement for me, to be sure, but you have no grounds for complaint, do you? You also gained something, namely, the ability to enjoy a product before you had saved enough to purchase it.

Of course, background assumptions are important here, since this process is not always benign. It is not a particularly startling fact that those who lend money typically have more of it than those who borrow. In a class-polarized society, institutions that facilitate the transfer of funds from rich to poor, to be repaid with interest, will likely make matters worse. Ancient and medieval philosophers had a point when they condemned the charging of interest, "that most hateful sort of wealth getting, which makes a gain out of money itself."[8]

Nevertheless, in a modern society, so long as the practice does not get out of hand, consumer loans seem harmless enough. Paying for the privilege of consuming before saving need not be prohibited. Indeed, a network of savings and loan associations to facilitate home buying and other consumer purchases can be part of a well-organized *socialist* society—as we shall see in the next chapter.

However, this sort of saving and lending is *not* the sort of saving and lending that forms the cornerstone of capitalism. This sort of saving and lending redistributes income, but it has no direct effect on production. I can consume $60 more a year from now than I otherwise could, but you can consume $60 less. Ancient and medieval philosophers may have found the transfer of wealth from poor to rich repugnant. We may appreciate the convenience of being able to buy on credit. Neither of these judgments has anything to do with the economic function of saving *under capitalism*. Neither draws any connection between savings and *economic growth*.

We smile now at the railings of Aristotle or Thomas Aquinas against "taking payment for the use of money lent."[9] They failed to realize, we tell ourselves, how interest can function as a mechanism for enhancing production, so that in the long run, *everyone's* consumption goes up. Consumer loans are a sideshow. What are crucial under capitalism are business loans—savings loaned out, not for consumer gratification, but for the purpose of productive investment.

We all know the story that Aristotle and Aquinas did not know. Frugal savers put money in the bank. The bank loans it out to entrepreneurs who use these loans, not for personal consumption, but to open new businesses or otherwise expand production. From this increase, the loans can be repaid with interest. Everybody benefits—lenders, borrowers, workers, and consumers. The economy grows. The best of all possible worlds.

This is the *standard story*, the basic story meant to explain the social utility of interest. We need savers to supply funds to entrepreneurs so that the economy can grow. The well-known schema is savings → investment → growth. (We encountered this story in the last section. There we examined the issue of compensating investors for risk; here we will be asking a deeper question: do we really need savers at all?)

John Maynard Keynes, the most influential economist of the twentieth century, stared at the wreckage of the Great Depression and realized that the standard story had it backwards. For society as a whole, the causal sequence runs investment → growth → savings. The implications of this story are dramatic and unsettling. You don't need savings for growth. So you don't need to pay people interest to encourage them to save. (Keynes himself did not draw out these implications, since he was concerned with saving capitalism from itself, not with undermining its legitimacy, but they follow readily from his analysis.)

The Keynesian counterstory is counterintuitive. Someone must save, must defer consumption, to provide funds for investment, right? "Not necessarily," says Keynes. Consider a simple variation on the standard story. Suppose we have an enterprising entrepreneur with a project in mind. Suppose, instead of waiting for a frugal saver to accumulate the funds to finance it, the government simply prints the money and lends it to her. She can now do exactly what she would have done, had there been a frugal saver willing to lend her money—hire workers, increase production, repay the loan with interest, make a profit. As in the standard story, everyone is better off—entrepreneur, workers, consumers. Moreover, since the government has been repaid the loan with interest, it can lend out even more the next time. The pump has been primed.

The crucial thing to note about this counterstory, for our purposes, is that production was increased *without anyone doing any prior saving*. No one deferred consumption. Therefore, no one has to be rewarded for doing so.

I am not suggesting here that a society should rely on governmental printing presses to generate its funds for investment. (Where these funds should come from will be discussed in the next chapter.) The fundamental point I am making is this: In an advanced industrial society, *business credit* is necessary for a healthy economy—*but personal savings are not*. A person who wants to start a new business, or a business that wants to expand production, needs to command the labor of others. Money is an effective mechanism for exercising this authority. In capitalist societies, for historical reasons, most business credit comes from financial institutions that accumulate funds from private savers. But this credit need not come from private savers. It could come from public sources. Therefore, the payment of interest to private savers is not necessary for economic growth.

The Keynesian counterstory makes it clear that private savings are not essential to a modern economy. In fact, it points to an even more shocking conclusion. In an advanced capitalist society, saving rather than consuming can be *detrimental* to the economy. This is the part of the Keynesian counterstory never mentioned in polite company.

Keynes was the first to make theoretically explicit what should now be a commonplace: the key to a healthy capitalist economy is effective demand. The deep economic crises of capitalism are almost never supply-side crises. The recurring problem is insufficient demand for all the goods the system has produced or could produce. If demand is strong, businesses make healthy profits, and hence have plenty of money to reinvest. But when demand is weak, profits decline, investment is cut back, and workers are laid off—which compounds the problem, since laid-off workers buy less, depressing demand still further, and so on.

But if effective demand is the key to a healthy capitalist economy, then to save rather than to consume is, from an economic point of view, an antisocial act. From the point of view of the economy as a whole, the personal decision to save rather than consume decreases aggregate demand, increases the likelihood of unemployment, and exacerbates the tendency toward economic stagnation. (Remember George Bush's exhortation to the country in the aftermath of September 11, in effect: "Be patriotic! Go shopping!" The president was correctly invoking Keynes, who, in a 1931 radio broadcast, had urged: "Oh patriotic housewives, sally out tomorrow early into the streets and go to the wonderful sales which are everywhere advertised. You will do yourselves good . . . and have the added joy that you are increasing employment, adding to the wealth of the country."[10])

To be sure, the decision to save does not always have negative consequences. If the money saved is loaned out to an entrepreneur who uses it to buy raw materials and hire workers, then aggregate demand is not reduced. However, as Keynes so forcefully pointed out, there is no reason to suppose that the demand for investment loans will be sufficient to absorb the supply of savings. When it is not, the whole economy suffers. We get recession, unemployment—and the eventual disappearance of those excess savings.

It should be noted that this strange irrationality—the propensity of an economy to slump because of too much saving—becomes ever more acute the richer or more inegalitarian the society becomes, since wealthy people tend to save more than poor people. It is also important to note that banks are not the only institutions that encourage people to save. So do stock markets, bond markets, real estate trusts, mutual funds, and all the other financial institutions that offer "investment" opportunities. "Investing" in these institutions is not investing at all in the Keynesian sense, but saving. (Investing in the Keynesian sense means building new facilities, purchasing new equipment, expanding production capabilities.) These institutions are part of the problem, not part of the solution.

2.6 TINA

But there is no alternative, is there? That's the mantra: TINA, TINA, TINA. Of course there are always alternatives, but are there better alternatives, more desirable alternatives?

We must now confront what is surely the strongest argument in favor of capitalism. The reader can grant all that has been so far demonstrated:

- Providing capital isn't really a productive activity.
- Most capitalists aren't entrepreneurs.
- Those with money to risk in the financial markets gain at the expense of working people.
- No one need defer consumption in order for an economy to grow.
- Saving can be harmful to the economy.

The reader can grant all this and still doubt that any other set of institutions could produce better overall results than those that define capitalism. To be sure, the history of capitalism is full of sound and fury—imperial conquest, slavery, systematic violence against working people, internecine wars of almost unimaginable destructiveness—but now that the institutions of liberal democracy seem to have taken firm root, at least in the advanced capitalist countries, and now that the Soviet and Eastern European socialist experiments have collapsed, the comparative case for capitalist supremacy is surely strong. If we want efficiency and growth, freedom and democracy, shouldn't we stick with capitalism? Wouldn't any attempt at fundamentally altering the basic institutions, as opposed to softening their rough edges, kill the goose that is laying all these golden eggs? These are the hard questions we must now address.

NOTES

1. John Bates Clark, *The Distribution of Wealth* (New York: Kelley and Millman, 1956), 4. Originally published in 1899.

2. Paul Samuelson, *Economics*, 11th ed. (New York: McGraw-Hill, 1980), 560.

3. U.S. Department of Commerce, *Statistical Abstract of the United States, 1999* (Washington, D.C.: Government Printing Office, 2000), table 727.

4. See Bill Mosely, "The Lottery Scam," *Democratic Left* (Spring 1999), 5–6, for recent figures.

5. John Kenneth Galbraith, *The New Industrial State* (Boston: Houghton Mifflin, 1967), 394.

6. The notion of a Noble Lie was famously proposed by Plato. The citizens of his ideal republic were to be told that they were born with different metals in their blood—gold for the rulers, silver for the soldiers, bronze for the artisans. Individuals would thus recognize their proper places, and not engage in the fratricidal class struggle so common in the Greek city-states. See Plato, *The Republic,* book 3, 414c–415d.

7. John Maynard Keynes, "Economic Possibilities for Our Grandchildren," in *Essays in Persuasion* (New York: Norton, 1963), 324.

8. Aristotle, *Politics*, 1258 b2-5.

9. "It is by its very nature unlawful to take payment for the use of money lent, which payment is known as usury, and just as a man is bound to restore other ill-gotten goods, so is he bound to restore the money he has taken in usury." Thomas Aquinas, *Summa Theologica*, question 78.

10. Quoted by Elizabeth Johnson, "John Maynard Keynes: Scientist or Politician?" in *After Keynes*, ed. Joan Robinson (New York: Barnes and Noble, 1973), 15.

3

Economic Democracy: What It Is

A serious critique of capitalism cannot be content with merely noting the negative features of the contemporary world. It must show a causal connection between the structures that define capitalism and these features. Otherwise, the negatives can simply be written off as either the inevitable effects of human nature (if you are a pessimist) or the consequences of some reformable aspects of capitalism (if you are an optimist). A serious critique must show that these negative features would not be present, or would at least be far less prominent, if certain structural elements of capitalism were altered *and* that such alterations would not have other worse consequences.

Hence, we must specify precisely not only the defining characteristics of capitalism, which was done in the previous chapter, but also the structural features of an alternative to capitalism. Such a specification, even in rudimentary form, is necessarily complicated, since a modern economy is a complicated affair. But if we want to do more than simply denounce the evils of capitalism, we must confront the claim that there is no alternative—by proposing one.

3.1 ECONOMIC DEMOCRACY: THE BASIC MODEL

The model to be elaborated here and defended in subsequent chapters does not originate simply from economic theory, nor is it a stylized economic structure of some particular country or region. The model is a synthesis of theory and practice. What I call "Economic Democracy" is a model whose form has been shaped by the theoretical debates that have taken place over the past thirty years concerning comparative economic systems,

45

by the empirical studies of modes of workplace organization, and by the records of various historical "experiments" of the twentieth century, notably the Soviet Union, postwar Japan, Tito's Yugoslavia, China after Mao, and (smaller in scale, but extremely important) a most unusual "cooperative corporation" in the Basque region of Spain.

The model also derives from an analysis of two sources of felt discontent with capitalism, discontent already acute in many quarters and likely to intensify. (It is precisely this discontent that gives the model a practical dimension. If people are basically content with the way things are, alternatives, even if superior, are of theoretical interest only.) Both sources of discontent may be regarded as "democratic deficits"—lack of democratic control over conditions that affect us deeply.

The first concerns workplace democracy. It is a striking anomaly of modern capitalist societies that ordinary people are deemed competent enough to select their political leaders—but not their bosses. Contemporary capitalism celebrates democracy, yet denies us our democratic rights at precisely the point where they might be utilized most immediately and concretely: at the place where we spend most of the active and alert hours of our adult lives. Of course, if it could be demonstrated that workplace democracy is too cumbersome to be efficient or workers too ignorant or shortsighted to make rational decisions, this would be a powerful counterargument to extending democracy in so logical a direction. But, as we shall see, the evidence points overwhelmingly to the opposite conclusion: *workplace democracy works*—in fact, as a general rule, workplace democracy works better than owner-authoritarianism, that is, the capitalist form of workplace organization.

The other disconcerting feature of contemporary capitalism is capital's current "hypermobility." The bulk of capital in a capitalist society belongs to private individuals. Because it is theirs, they can do with it whatever they want. They can invest it anywhere and in anything they choose, or not invest it at all if profit prospects are dim. But this freedom, when coupled with recently enhanced technical transfer capabilities, gives capital a mobility that now generates economic and political insecurity around the globe. Financial markets now rule, however "democratic" political systems purport to be, and this rule is often capricious, often destructive.

Let us consider a socialist alternative to capitalism that addresses these democratic deficits. It's socialism quite different in structure from the failed models of the past. (I use the term "socialist" to refer to any attempt to transcend capitalism by abolishing most private ownership of means of production. Although differing in other ways from earlier attempts to get beyond capitalism, Economic Democracy shares with them the conviction that private ownership of the means of production must be curtailed if the human species is to flourish.)

Economic Democracy, like capitalism, can be defined in terms of three basic features, the second of which it shares with capitalism:

- *Worker self-management*: Each productive enterprise is controlled democratically by its workers.
- *The market*: These enterprises interact with one another and with consumers in an environment largely free of governmental price controls. Raw materials, instruments of production, and consumer goods are all bought and sold at prices largely determined by the forces of supply and demand.
- *Social control of investment*: Funds for new investment are generated by a capital assets tax and are returned to the economy through a network of public investment banks.

This *basic* model, which will be elaborated more fully below, is necessarily stylized and oversimplified. In practice, Economic Democracy will be more complicated and less "pure" than the version presented here. However, to grasp the nature of the system and to understand its essential dynamic, it is important to have a clear picture of the basic structure. (The same is true of capitalism. Economists generally use simplified models to explain the basic laws of the system.)

Recall that capitalism is characterized by private ownership of means of production, the market, and wage labor. The Soviet economic model abolished private ownership of the means of production (by collectivizing all farms and factories) and the market (by instituting central planning) but retained wage labor. Economic Democracy abolishes private ownership of the means of production and wage labor, but retains the market.

3.1.1 Worker Self-Management

Each productive enterprise is controlled by those who work there. Workers are responsible for the operation of the facility: organization of the workplace, enterprise discipline, techniques of production, what and how much to produce, what to charge for what is produced, and how the net proceeds are to be distributed. Enterprises are not required to distribute the proceeds equally. In all likelihood, most firms will award larger shares to more highly skilled workers, to those with greater seniority, and to those with more managerial responsibility. Decisions concerning these matters will be made democratically. (Disgruntled members are free to quit and seek work elsewhere, so egalitarian considerations must be balanced against the need to motivate and retain good workers.)

In a firm of significant size, some delegation of authority will be necessary. The usual solution to this general problem of democracy is representation.

Most enterprises will have an elected workers' council that will appoint a general manager or chief executive officer and perhaps other members of upper management. Management is not appointed by the state or elected by the community at large or, since this is not a capitalist corporation, selected by a board of directors elected by stockholders. (There are no stockholders in Economic Democracy.)

An important practical issue emerges at this level—getting the right balance between managerial accountability and managerial autonomy. Accountability without autonomy risks timidity and paralysis; autonomy without accountability risks despotism. Managers need sufficient autonomy so that they can manage effectively, but not so much that they can exploit the workforce to their own advantage. It can be assumed that various enterprises will handle this issue differently, the more successful models being emulated. (As we shall see, highly successful models already exist.) Whatever internal structures are put in place, ultimate authority rests with the enterprise's workers, one-person, one-vote.

Although workers control the workplace, they do not "own" the means of production. These are regarded as the collective property of the society. Workers have the right to run the enterprise, to use its capital assets as they see fit, and to distribute among themselves the whole of the net profit from production. Societal "ownership" of the enterprise manifests itself in two ways.

- All firms must pay a tax on their capital assets, which goes into society's investment fund. In effect, workers rent their capital assets from society. (More on this below.)
- Firms are required to preserve the value of the capital stock entrusted to them. This means that a *depreciation fund* must be maintained. Money must be set aside to repair or replace existing capital stock. This money may be spent on whatever capital replacements or improvements the firm deems fit, but it may not be used to supplement workers' incomes.

If an enterprise finds itself in economic difficulty, workers are free to reorganize the facility or to leave and seek work elsewhere. They are not free to sell off their capital stocks and use the proceeds as income. A firm can sell off capital stocks and use the proceeds to buy additional capital goods. Or, if the firm wishes to contract its capital base so as to reduce its tax and depreciation obligations, it can sell off some of its assets; in this case, proceeds from the sale go into the national investment fund, not to the workers, since these assets belong to society as a whole. If a firm is unable to generate even the nationally specified minimum per capita income—Economic Democracy's equivalent to the minimum wage—then it must declare bankruptcy. Movable capital will be sold to pay creditors. Its workers must seek employment elsewhere.

In essence, a firm under Economic Democracy is regarded not as a *thing* to be bought or sold (as it is under capitalism) but as a *community*. When you join a firm, you receive the rights of full citizenship; you are granted an equal voice, namely, an equal vote in the community. When you leave one firm and join another, these rights transfer. With rights come responsibilities, in this case the responsibilities of paying the capital assets tax and maintaining the value of the assets you are using.

3.1.2 The Market

Economic Democracy is a market economy, at least insofar as the allocation of consumer and capital goods is concerned. Firms buy raw materials and machinery from other firms and sell their products to other enterprises or consumers. Prices are largely unregulated except by supply and demand, although in some cases price controls or price supports might be in order— as they are deemed in order in most real-world forms of capitalism.

Since enterprises in our economy buy and sell on the market, they strive to make a profit. ("Profit" is not a dirty word in this form of socialism.) However, the "profit" in a worker-run firm is not the same as capitalist profit; it is calculated differently. Market economy firms, whether capitalist or worker-self-managed, strive to maximize the difference between total sales and total costs. *However, for a capitalist firm, labor is counted as a cost; for a worker-run enterprise, it is not.* In Economic Democracy, labor is not another "factor of production" on technical par with land and capital. Instead, labor is the residual claimant. Workers get all that remains, once nonlabor costs, including depreciation set-asides and the capital assets tax, have been paid. (As we shall see, this seemingly small structural difference will have far-reaching consequences.)

"Market socialism" remains a controversial topic among socialists. I and many others have long argued that centralized planning, the most commonly advocated socialist alternative to market allocation, is inherently flawed, and that schemes for decentralized, nonmarket planning are unworkable. Central planning, as theory predicts and the historical record confirms, is both inefficient and conducive to an authoritarian concentration of power. This is one of the great lessons to be drawn from the Soviet experience. I won't pursue the argument here.[1] I will simply assert what I take to be a growing consensus even among socialists: Without a price mechanism sensitive to supply and demand, it is extremely difficult for a producer or planner to know what and how much to produce, and which production and marketing methods are the most efficient. It is also extremely difficult in the absence of a market to design a set of incentives that will motivate producers to be both efficient and innovative. Market competition resolves these problems (to a significant if incomplete degree) in a nonauthoritarian, nonbureaucratic fashion. This is an achievement indispensable to a serious socialism.

3.1.3 Social Control of Investment

This is the most technically complex feature of our model. It is vastly simpler than the institutions that comprise the investment mechanisms of capitalism (i.e., those mysterious, omnipotent "financial markets") but it is more complicated to specify than is worker self-management or the market.

In any society that wants to remain technologically and economically dynamic, a certain portion of society's labor and natural resources must be devoted each year to developing and implementing new technologies and to expanding the production of the goods and services in high demand. In a modern society, this allocation of resources is effected through monetary *investment*. From where do investment funds come? In a capitalist society, they come largely from private savings, either the direct savings of private individuals or the retained earnings of corporations, that is, the indirect savings of stockholders. These savings are then either invested directly, or deposited in banks or other financial institutions, which lend them out to businesses or entrepreneurs. (This process was analyzed in some detail in chapter 2.)

In Economic Democracy, investment funds are generated in a more direct and transparent fashion. We simply *tax the capital assets of enterprises*— land, buildings, and equipment. This tax, a flat rate tax, may be regarded as a leasing fee paid by the workers of the enterprise for use of social property that belongs to all.

Receipts from the capital assets tax constitute the national investment fund, all of which is earmarked for new investment. ("New investment" is simply investment over and above that financed by enterprises directly from their own depreciation funds.) All new investment derives from this fund. In stark contrast to capitalism, Economic Democracy does not depend on private savings for its economic development.

Since investment funds are publicly, not privately, generated, their allocation back into the economy is a public, not a private, matter. Society must decide on procedures that are both fair and efficient. Here we have options. Not surprisingly, there's no set of procedures that can guarantee perfect efficiency and perfect fairness, but there do exist various mechanisms that can be employed to produce more rational, equitable, and democratic development than can be expected under capitalism.

At one extreme, a democratically accountable planning board could allocate all the funds according to a detailed plan. This would *not* be a plan for the entire economy, à la Soviet central planning, but only for new investments (in a country like the United States, roughly 10 to 15 percent of GDP),[2] so it would not run up against the insurmountable difficulties inherent in the

Soviet model. Such planning would be more akin to that practiced by Japan and South Korea during their periods of most rapid development—"market conforming" investment planning. For a country in which developmental priorities are relatively clear and widely accepted, such planning might be appropriate.[3]

At the other extreme, these funds could simply be distributed to a network of public banks that would then lend them out using precisely the same criteria that capitalist banks would use. This would be a kind of *laissez-faire* socialism: let the market decide investment allocation. Banks would be charged a centrally determined interest rate on the funds they receive. They would be expected to make a profit, that is, to charge more than the base-rate interest, adjusted according to risk. Bank officials, who are public officials, would be paid in accordance with performance. Banks would compete, as they do now, trying to balance the riskiness of their loans against the interest rates they charge. As under capitalism, managers of successful banks (i.e., the most profitable) would be rewarded, managers whose banks performed poorly would be sacked. In all cases, bank profits are returned to the national investment fund.

In my view, the optimal mechanism, at least for a rich country, lies between these extremes. Decision-making is far more decentralized than in the first alternative; the market is more constrained than in the second. Concerns for justice and efficiency are balanced by using a mix of market and non-market criteria. The basic idea is to allocate the centrally collected funds according to a principle of fairness first, and then to bring in competition to promote efficiency. Efficiency will be understood to include not only technical efficiency, but "Keynesian efficiency" as well, that is, full employment. (In the Keynesian view, it is not *efficient* to have able-bodied people unemployed. That's a waste of a valuable resource.[4])

The principle of fairness pertains to regional and communal distribution: each region of the country and each community within each region is entitled to its *fair share* of the national investment fund. "Fair share" is understood to be, prima facie, its *per capita share*; that is to say, if Region A has X percent of the nation's population, it gets X percent of the money available for new investment. The central implication of this principle is that regions and communities do not compete for investment funds. They do not compete, as they must under capitalism, for capital. Each region and each community gets its share, each and every year, as a matter of right.

Two ethical-sociological assumptions serve to ground this "fair share" requirement:

- Societal health requires that individuals develop intergenerational commitments and a sense of place, these being facilitated by regional and community stability.

- Although individuals should be free to move to other regions or communities if they so desire, they should not be compelled to do so—not even if there is some marginal gain in overall economic efficiency if society's labor force is reallocated.

Guaranteeing each region and each community a steady supply of investment funds each year mitigates the coercion that a purely market-determined allocation of investment funds is likely to produce. Since this guarantee enhances regional and community stability without encroaching on an individual's freedom, it should be part of the investment-allocation mechanism. (If *large* efficiency gains can be had by pressuring people to relocate, then the argument for per capita allocation of investment funds is less compelling—although the case would have to be made that the efficiency gains are sufficient to offset the real costs of labor migrations. In a truly democratic society, investment allocations would be subject to democratic control. Market allocation would not be presumed "natural," nor would efficiency concerns automatically trump all others.)

Why should "fair share" be per capita share? We observe that it would not be fair simply to return to each region the investment funds collected (via the capital assets tax) from that region, since that amount merely reflects the quantity of capital assets in that region. The fact that one region has a larger capital base than another is not due to the greater effort expended by the people in that region, or to their greater intelligence or moral worth, but to the region's specific history. It would hardly be fair to base present capital allocation on past history. Doing so would give a disproportionate share to the regions that are already more capital intensive, thus exacerbating, rather than mitigating, regional inequalities.

This, of course, is precisely what happens under capitalism. (Real-world capitalism, that is, as opposed to neoclassical fiction, where capital always flows from areas of greater capital intensity to those of lesser.) New investment tends to flow to where the capital base is already large. Cities attract more capital than rural areas. Industrial centers suck investment funds from the rest of a country. Capital tends to move to where capital is already plentiful, because that is where new investment opportunities are easiest to find. Workers must then follow, migrating to where new jobs are being created. To be sure, there are countermovements. An industrial region may decline if shifting patterns of demand or new technologies adversely affect the market for the products being produced there, or if labor unions get too strong, or if social or infrastructure problems make a desirable region less desirable. But this simply means that capital will flow elsewhere, and workers must, if they can, chase after it. (What happens at the national level also happens globally. Rich countries attract more capital than poor countries. Immigration patterns follow suit. Here, we are concerned with developing principles for allocating capital within a given country. Those principles and mechanisms for dealing with inequalities among nations will be discussed later.)

It is clear that the pattern of industrialization and capital density that an Economic Democracy has inherited from its capitalist past cannot be regarded as entitling a capital-intensive region to even more capital. Moreover, if we think about how the market works, we see that capital-intensive regions are *not* being unfairly disadvantaged by a per capita allocation. The capital access tax is, in fact, a *cost of production*, and hence covered by the market price of the goods being produced. That is to say, firms in a given industry are all subject to the same tax burden, and so they can (and will) set their prices to cover these taxes. They will not be disadvantaged competitively by doing so. Unfortunately, this perfectly legitimate price setting gives rise to a market illusion. Capital-intensive regions may think they are paying more than their "fair share" of taxes, since they get back less than they pay. What they don't realize—unless this point is made explicit—is that the market allows their capital-intensive firms to charge more for their products than they would otherwise be able to, precisely to cover these taxes. Ultimately, it is the consumers of the goods, not the firms themselves or the regions in which the firms are located, who pay these taxes; the regions, therefore, have no grounds for complaint.

If one wants a positive justification for the principle of per capita capital allocation, one can appeal to Marx's insight that labor, not capital, is the source of value, and hence of the surplus value that constitutes the investment fund. If this is so, then the investment fund ought to be distributed to regions in proportion to the size of their workforces, that is, (essentially) on a per capita basis. Or, if one prefers a non-Marxian justification, allocating investment funds to regions may be regarded as providing a *public service*. Hence, the allocation of investment funds should follow the principle used in the allocation of such public services as education and health care (at least in those parts of the world where education and health care are publicly funded and rationally distributed)—namely, per capita share.[5]

These justifications do not give the per capita principle absolute force. The right of a region or community to its per capita share of the investment fund is a prima facie right only, which can be overridden by other ethical or economic considerations. The modernization of an outmoded industry in a particular region might require that it receive more than its per capita share for a period of time. It might be desirable to allocate a larger than per capita share to an underdeveloped region or community for a number of years, to aid it in catching up. These decisions will have to be made publicly, by the democratically elected national or regional legislature, with full weight being given to the fact that if some regions get more than their per capita share, others will get less.

The principle of fair share governs the allocation of the national investment fund to regions and communities. When this share reaches a community, it is then distributed to public *banks* within the communities. These banks will make the funds available to local enterprises wanting to expand production, introduce new products, enter new lines of business, upgrade technologies—anything requiring capital in excess of what has accumulated in their depreciation funds.

Banks make *grants*, not *loans*, to business enterprises. These grants, however, do not represent "free money," since an investment grant counts as an addition to the capital assets of the enterprise, upon which the capital asset tax must be paid. Thus, the capital assets tax functions as an interest rate. A bank grant is essentially a loan requiring interest payments but no repayment of principal.

Each bank receives a share of the investment fund allocated to the community, but this allocation is no longer governed by the principle of fair share. A bank's share is determined by the size and number of firms serviced by the bank, by the bank's prior success at making economically sound grants, *and* by its success in creating new employment. (The importance of this third criterion will become clear later.) The bank's own income, to be distributed among its workforce, comes from general tax revenues (since these are public employees) according to a formula linking income to the bank's success in making profit-enhancing grants and creating employment. Unlike banks under capitalism, these banks are not themselves private, profit-making institutions. They are public institutions charged with effectively allocating the funds entrusted to them in accordance with *two* criteria: profitability *and* employment creation. (A community could impose additional criteria to better control the pattern of development in the community. For the sake of simplicity, I will restrict the nonmarket criterion to the most essential, employment creation.)

If a community is unable to find sufficient investment opportunities to absorb the funds allocated to it, the excess must be returned to the center, to be reallocated to where investment funds are more in demand. This being the case, communities have a strong incentive to seek out new investment opportunities in order to keep the allocated funds at home. Banks also have a similar incentive, so it is reasonable to expect that communities and their banks will set up entrepreneurial divisions—agencies that monitor new business opportunities, and provide technical and financial expertise to existing firms seeking new opportunities and to individuals interested in starting new worker self-managed enterprises. These agencies might go so far as to recruit prospective managers and workers for new enterprises. (As we shall see, the bank at the center of the world's most successful cooperative experiment, Mondragon's Caja Laboral Popular, did exactly that—with impressive results.)

One further element of the investment mechanism needs to be considered. In a market economy, two kinds of capital investment take place: "public" investment related to the provision of free (or heavily subsidized) goods and services (e.g., roads, bridges, harbors, airports, schools, hospitals, basic research facilities, and the like) and "private" investment related to goods and services to be sold competitively on the market. Under capitalism, these funds are separately generated: public investment is financed from general tax revenues; private investment comes from private savings. (The separation is not so clean in practice. Governments turn to the private financial markets to finance budget deficits. They also use public money—often large amounts—to subsidize favored private industries.[6]) Under Economic Democracy, all capital investment comes from the same source, namely, the capital assets tax. Thus, key decisions must be made at each level of government as to how much of the investment fund should be allocated for public capital investment, for what, and how much should be left for the market sector. (Note: "capital investment" is investment in durable physical assets. Thus, funds for school construction would come from the investment fund whereas salaries of teachers and operating expenses come from general tax revenues. Similarly, in the "private" [i.e., "cooperative"] sector, funds for new plant construction would come from the investment fund whereas worker incomes and operating expenses come from profits.)

Decisions as to the allocation of investment between the public and market sectors should be made democratically by the legislative bodies at each level, national, regional, and local. Investment hearings should be held, as budget hearings are currently held; expert and popular testimony should be sought. The legislature then decides the nature and amount of capital spending on public goods appropriate to its level, sets these funds aside, then passes the remainder to the next level down.

For example, the national legislature decides, in accordance with the democratic procedures just described, on public capital spending for projects that are national in scope (e.g., an upgrading of rail transport) and then transfers funds to the appropriate governmental agency (e.g., the Department of Transportation). The remainder of the national investment fund is distributed to regions on a per capita basis. Regional legislatures now make similar decisions concerning regional capital spending, then pass the remainder of their investment funds to local communities on a per capita basis. The communities, in turn, make decisions about local public investment, then allocate the remainder to their banks, which make them available to local enterprises. (It should be noted that there is considerable countervailing power in the system to prevent "excessive" public spending—most immediately, all those workers in the enterprises that might want to apply for bank funding, and more generally, the entire citizenry of a community, since everyone knows that a thriving community requires thriving local businesses. Democratically accountable legislative bodies must weigh the benefits to their constituents of more public spending against the need for market sector development. There would seem to be no systematic bias here one way or the other.)

We now have before us the basic structure of "social control of investment." To summarize: A flat-rate tax on the capital assets of all productive enterprises is collected by the central government, then plowed back into the economy, assisting those firms needing funds for purposes of productive investment. These funds are dispersed throughout society, first to regions and communities on a per capita basis, then to public banks in accordance with past performance, then to those firms with profitable project proposals. Profitable projects that promise increased employment are favored over those that do not. At each level, national, regional, and local, legislatures decide what portion of the investment fund coming to them is to be set aside for public capital expenditures, then send down the remainder, no strings attached, to the next lower level. Associated with most banks are entrepreneurial divisions, which promote firm expansion and new firm creation. Figures 3.1, 3.2, and 3.3 offer a schematic presentation of this summary.

A final observation: The simplified schema just presented has only local banks making grants to local enterprises. Large enterprises that operate regionally or nationally might need access to additional capital, in which case it would be appropriate for the network of local investment banks to be supplemented by regional and national investment banks. These would also be public institutions that receive their funds from the national investment fund.

3.2 THE VIABILITY OF ECONOMIC DEMOCRACY

Worker self-management extends democracy to the workplace. Apart from being good in itself, this extension of democracy aims at enhancing a firm's internal efficiency. The market also aims at efficiency, and acts to counter the bureaucratic overcentralization that plagued earlier forms of socialism. Social

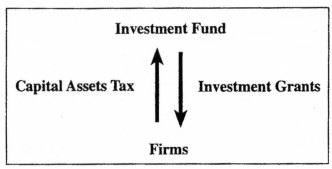

Figure 3.1   Flows to and from the Investment Fund

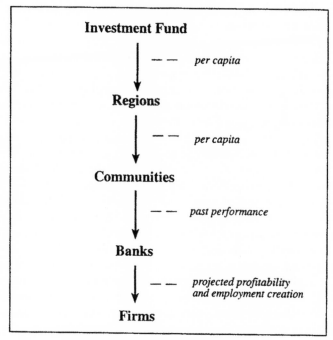

Figure 3.2   Investment Allocation Criteria

control of new investment is the counterfoil to the market, counteracting the instability and other irrational consequences of an overextended market—what Marx calls the "anarchy" of capitalist production.

"Well and good," the skeptic will say, "but will it work? Will an economy structured around workplace democracy and social control of investment be an efficient, dynamic economy, or will it soon fall apart, as did the other socialist experiments of this century—including the Yugoslav experiment in worker self-managed socialism, to which Economic Democracy bears a strong resemblance?"

This is a fair question—even if some of the background assumptions are wrong. Not all the socialist experiments of this century have collapsed. China, Cuba, and Vietnam endure—and will continue to survive (I believe), however problematic the socialist character of their economies becomes. (More on this later.) It isn't clear, either, that Soviet-model economies had to collapse. That they were in urgent need of structural reform cannot be doubted, but it is hard now not to think that reforms that moved in the direction of Economic Democracy would have been vastly preferable to the reforms actually undertaken. Even now, a decade after the collapse of communism, there are only one or two countries of the region whose income levels have reached those achieved before the collapse; even in these, the

---

The National Legislature

➤ Determines the capital assets tax rate.

➤ Decides how much of the investment fund is to be used for capital spending on public projects national in scope.
(The rest is allocated to the regions.)

Regional Legislatures

➤ Decide how much of their portion of the investment fund is to be used for capital spending on public projects regional in scope. (The rest is allocated to their communities.)

Local Legislatures

➤ Decide how much of their portion of the investment fund is to be used for capital spending on public projects in their communities. (The rest is allocated to their banks.)

Banks

➤ Decide which grant requests from local firms to honor.

➤ Set up entrepreneurial divisions to encourage the setting up of new businesses.

➤ Decide what new enterprises to fund.

Figure 3.3   Investment Fund Decisions

levels of inequality and poverty are much higher than before. In Russia itself, the human catastrophe that has followed capitalist reforms is hard to exaggerate. (Joseph Stiglitz, former chief economist of the World Bank, reports that "for eighteen of the twenty-five countries [of Eastern Europe and the former Soviet Union] poverty on average has increased from 4 percent to 45 percent of the population" and that "life expectancy in these countries on average has fallen even while world life expectancy has risen by two years."[7]

We should also be wary of a historical amnesia that blinds us to the actual accomplishments of these first experiments in socialism. Central planning—however badly done and brutally enforced—moved Russia, in less than half a century, from being the most backward country in Europe to the ranks of a global superpower. Chinese socialism, with minimal external assistance, raised more people from abject poverty to relative prosperity than any form of capitalism has ever done, and in a remarkably short period of time. (Life expectancy in China was thirty-five in 1949; it is seventy today.) The Yugoslav experiment in worker self-management sustained for three decades one of the highest rates of growth in the world, vastly improved the average standard of living, and produced a vibrant intellectual culture. Cuba, on its own today, relentlessly squeezed and blockaded by the United States, continues to record social indicators of health and education of First World order.

We must be careful in drawing facile lessons from history, negative or positive. Economic Democracy is a different form of socialism from what was initially tried. The first attempt at constructing a socialist economy abolished the market and substituted centralized planning. Economic Democracy is a market economy with workplace democracy and social control of investment. We need to ask what the historical record and empirical data tell us about the viability of *these* structures.

First, some theoretical considerations. Economic Democracy, like capitalism but unlike Soviet-model socialism, is a competitive economy. Firms compete with one another in selling their products to consumers, so the basic incentive structure is right. An enterprise has a clear incentive to find out and give consumers what they want, to avoid wasting raw materials, to employ the most cost-effective technology, to stay abreast technological change, and to be constantly on the lookout for better products, better technologies, and better ways of organizing production. Economic Democracy retains the incentive structure of a market economy, the structure that gives capitalism its efficiency strengths.

"But," it will surely be asked, "will a worker-managed firm respond to these incentives as well as a capitalist firm? Are workers competent enough to make complicated technical and financial decisions? Are they competent enough even to elect representatives who will appoint effective managers?" I can't deny that these are fair questions, but neither can I resist remarking on how curious it is that these questions are so quickly raised (as in my experience they always are) in a society that prides itself on its democratic commitment. We deem ordinary people competent enough to select mayors, governors, even presidents. We regard them as capable of selecting legislators who will decide their taxes, who will make the laws that, if violated, consign them to prison, and who can send them off, the younger ones, to kill and die in war. Should we really ask if ordinary people are competent enough to elect their bosses?

It's a question that has to be asked. The issue is too fundamental to pass over lightly. After all, workers in democratic capitalist societies do *not* elect their bosses. Perhaps they are *not* competent enough. Perhaps managers will be reluctant to impose discipline if they are subject to election, or less inclined to exert themselves fully, since they must share profits with workers. Perhaps the time and effort associated with democratic decision making will cut too deeply into productive work time. Perhaps the process will lead to worker frustration, increased alienation, and incoherent policies. Might not economic chaos result, or if not chaos, at least a precipitous decline in efficiency?

In fact, we can respond to these doubts with empirical findings that are as unambiguous as one would dare hope, given the complexity and significance of the issue. There is overwhelming evidence, based on scores of studies of thousands of examples, that both worker participation in management and profit sharing tend to enhance productivity, and that worker-run enterprises are almost never less productive than their capitalist counterparts. They are often more so.

As to the efficiency effects of greater worker participation, the HEW study of 1973 concludes, "In no instance of which we have evidence has a major effort to increase employee participation resulted in a long-term decline in productivity." Nine years later, surveying their empirical studies, Derek Jones and Jan Svejnar report, "There is apparently consistent support for the view that worker participation in management causes higher productivity. This result is supported by a variety of methodological approaches, using diverse data and for disparate time periods." In 1990, a collection of research papers edited by Princeton economist Alan Blinder extends the data set much further and reaches the same conclusion: worker participation usually enhances productivity in the short run, sometimes in the long run, and rarely has a negative effect. Moreover, participation is most conducive to enhancing productivity when combined with profit sharing, guaranteed long-range employment, relatively narrow wage differentials, and guaranteed worker rights (such as protection from dismissal except for just cause)—precisely the conditions that will prevail under Economic Democracy.[8]

As to the viability of complete workplace democracy, we note that workers in the plywood cooperatives in the Pacific Northwest have been electing their managers since the 1940s, workers in the Mondragon cooperatives in Spain since the 1950s. There are some twenty thousand producer-cooperatives in Italy, comprising one of the most vibrant sectors of the economy. The Swedish cooperative movement is also large and impressive. Needless to say, not all self-management ventures are successful, but I know of no empirical study that even purports to demonstrate that worker-elected managers are less competent than their capitalist counterparts. Most comparisons suggest the opposite; most find worker self-managed firms *more* productive than similarly situated capitalist firms. For example, Berman, on the plywood cooperatives, states:

> The major basis for co-operative success, and for survival of capitalistically unprofitable plants, has been superior labour productivity. Studies comparing

square-foot output have repeatedly shown higher physical volume of output per hour, and others . . . show higher quality of product and also economy of material use.[9]

And Thomas on Mondragon:

> Productivity and profitability are higher for cooperatives than for capitalist firms. It makes little difference whether the Mondragon group is compared with the largest 500 companies, or with small- or medium-scale industries; in both comparisons the Mondragon group is more productive and more profitable.[10]

There is also the example of Weirton Steel. In 1982, following a mediocre year and facing bleaker prospects, National Steel offered to sell its Weirton, West Virginia, plant to its 7,000 workers. The deal was completed in 1984. Weirton proceeded to post eighteen consecutive profitable quarters—at a time when many steel firms suffered steep losses, including two of Weirton's competitors, who were forced into bankruptcy.[11] United Airlines, now majority-owned by its pilots and technicians, has survived the intense competition that has brought down so many conventionally owned carriers.

The negative example of Yugoslavia? Not even Harold Lydall, perhaps the severest procapitalist critic of the pre-1989 Yugoslav economic system, argues that worker incompetence at selecting managers was the problem. Lydall acknowledges that for most of the period from 1950 to 1979, Yugoslavia not only survived but also prospered. Things changed, much for the worse, in the 1980s. How does he account for this precipitous decline?

> It is evident that the principal cause of failure was the unwillingness of the Yugoslav Party and government to implement a policy of macroscopic restriction—especially restriction of the money supply—in combination with a microeconomic policy designed to expand opportunities and incentives for enterprise and efficient work. What was needed was *more freedom for independent decision-making by genuinely self-managed enterprises* within a free market, combined with tight controls on the supply of domestic currency.[12]

The problem in Yugoslavia does *not* appear to be an excess of workplace democracy. In the judgment of one Belgrade newspaper (as summarized by Lydall), "The most convincing explanation for the present social crisis is the *reduction* of the self-management rights of workers."[13]

It is not really so surprising that worker self-managed enterprises are efficient. Because their incomes are tied directly to the financial health of the enterprise, all workers have an interest in selecting good managers. Since bad management is not hard to detect by those near at hand, who observe at close range the nature of that management and feel its effects rather quickly, incompetence is not usually long tolerated. Moreover, individuals have an interest in seeing to it that coworkers work effectively and in not appearing to be slackers themselves, so less supervision is necessary. As one expert has noted, based on his seven years of field study:

> There exist both personal and collective incentives in cooperatives that are likely to lead to higher productivity. The specific consequences of these incentives are that the workers in cooperatives will tend to work harder and in a more flexible manner than those in capitalist firms; they will have a lower turnover rate and absenteeism; and they will take better care of plant and equipment. In addition, producer cooperatives function with relatively few unskilled workers and middle managers, experience fewer bottlenecks in production and have more efficient training programs than do capitalist firms.[14]

I do not mean to suggest here that workplace democracy is the miracle cure for economic malaise. Efficiency gains are not always dramatic. Not all cooperatives succeed. Failure is often painful—as is the failure of a capitalist firm. Nevertheless, the evidence is incontrovertible that worker self-managed firms are at least as internally efficient as capitalist firms. In fact, the cited evidence establishes more than this minimal conclusion. Anyone who reviews the literature can see plainly: all else equal, worker self-managed firms tend to be *more* efficient than their capitalist counterparts.

Two key elements of Economic Democracy—worker self-management and the market—"work." The evidence leaves little room for doubt. What about social control of investment? Since no such investment mechanism as the one I have described has been put into place anywhere, it is impossible to be as certain about the efficacy of this institution. There are no economic studies to cite. Here we must proceed differently. We must ask about the specific parts of the mechanism.

Is it possible to raise investment funds by taxation rather than by private savings? Of course it is. In all advanced capitalist societies, a significant portion is already raised that way. The investments government makes in infrastructure, office buildings, schools, equipment for basic research, and so forth come from tax-generated funds. (National income-expenditure accounts hinder our seeing the obvious, since they treat all government expenditures as public *consumption.* As many economists have pointed out, this isn't right. The expenditures that finance day-to-day activities—operating expenses and the salaries of government officials—may properly be regarded as taxpayer payment for services rendered, but those expenditures for machinery, buildings, roads, bridges—things intended to enhance the productivity of the economy over time—are as much *investment* expenditures as are the expenditures of capitalist firms on machinery, buildings, and so on.)

Could the entire investment fund for a nation be generated by a capital assets tax? Of course it could. The tax is simply a flat-rate property tax applied to businesses. Uniform accounting procedures would have to be adopted, and regular audits undertaken, but these are hardly insurmountable difficulties.

Wouldn't this tax be so high that it would force many businesses into bankruptcy? No—because this is not an *additional* tax that enterprises have to pay. It is a tax that *substitutes* for existing "taxes." Under Economic Democracy, there is no need for a corporate income tax, for example. The profits that remain after costs have been met should be returned to the workers. Workers will pay an income tax, as they do now, or a consumption tax, but there is no need for double taxation. Moreover, since there are no stockholders of the firm, there is no one to whom the enterprise must pay dividends. These dividend payments, which can be thought of as an enterprise "tax" under capitalism, are eliminated under Economic Democracy, as are the interest payments that companies now pay to bondholders and private banks. In essence, that portion of a company's profit that would, under capitalism, be paid out as dividends or interest to private individuals now goes directly into the investment fund, and is then recycled back into the economy—without the mediation of capitalist middlemen. Instead of paying interest and dividends to private individuals, who (we hope) will reinvest most of them, companies make their payments directly to a public institution that injects them (all of them) back into the economy immediately.

I think it fair to conclude that there are no conceptual difficulties or serious practical obstacles that preclude generating society's investment fund by means of a capital assets tax instead of relying on private savings. To be sure, there are powerful, entrenched special interests that can be counted on to resist any move to a more rational system, but that is a separate issue, to which we will attend later. (Powerful, entrenched *feudal* interests resisted the reforms proposed by the rising *capitalist* class. Powerful, entrenched interests don't always win.)

Relying on a capital assets tax would be at least as efficient as relying on private savings to generate funds for capital investment. It would probably be more efficient. Not only would the private consumption of the capitalist middlemen be eliminated, but society would now have direct control over the quantity of funds to be invested. If funds are insufficient relative to demand, the tax can be raised. If funds are excessive, the tax can be lowered. Authorities would no longer have to cajole people into saving more, or try to manipulate their behavior by raising or lowering interest rates—indirect procedures of only moderate effectiveness, as central banks are well aware.

The second part of Economic Democracy's investment mechanism is bound to be more controversial. Economic Democracy does not rely solely on market criteria to determine capital allocation. Investment funds do not automatically flow to where financial opportunities seem to be the greatest. Instead, an ethical criterion is imposed from the start: each region of the country gets its "fair share" (per capita) of the investment fund.

Neoclassical economists will likely object: if capital flows are restricted, the outcome cannot be optimally efficient. They will draw the curves to prove it. This objection should not be taken seriously, since it is a disciplinary reflex, not a well-considered judgment. Our economists remember the beautiful theorems proving capitalist efficiency, but they tend to forget how extravagant and unrealistic the assumptions upon which the efficiency theorems are based: perfect information on the part of producers as to present and future prices and technologies, perfect information on the part of consumers as to current and future tastes and preferences, no externalities of production or consumption, and so forth. The neoclassical faith in the ultimate efficiency of free capital flows is simply that: an act of faith. It has no scientific warrant. As Keynes liked to stress, there is simply too much primary uncertainty involved in making investment decisions to expect optimal efficiency to prevail as the unplanned, uncoordinated outcome of private, self-seeking judgments. ("Enterprise only pretends to itself to be mainly actuated by the statements in its own prospectus, however candid and sincere. Only a little more than an expedition to the South Pole is it based on an exact calculation of benefits to come.")[15]

In reality, all capitalist economies interfere to some degree with the free flow of capital, some much more so than others. Japan, particularly during the postwar "miracle years," was quite heavy-handed in directing capital into certain sectors of the economy and into certain industries, while making it harder to get in others. South Korea followed a similar model with equally impressive results. It takes a mighty faith indeed to maintain that Japanese or Korean development would have been more rapid or more equitable or more efficient had market forces been given untrammeled freedom. As Nobel laureate economist Amartya Sen noted,

> It is remarkable that if we look at the sizable developing countries, the fast growing and otherwise high-performing countries have all had governments that have been directly and actively involved in the planning of economic and social performance. . . . Their respective successes are directly linked to deliberation and design, rather than being just the results of uncoordinated profit seeking or atomistic pursuit of self-interest.[16]

Even if it is conceded (as it must be) that governmental interference with the "natural" flow of capital can sometimes produce better results than the invisible hand, it doesn't follow that the specific mechanisms of Economic Democracy will have such happy consequences. To make the case that they will, we have to examine such concrete issues as unemployment, inequality, the quality and rate of economic growth, and so forth, and see which system is more likely to deal effectively with these problems. That will occupy us in chapters 4 and 5. For now, let me simply point out that there are no obvious reasons for thinking that Economic Democracy's mechanism for allocating investment funds will not work. In fact, there are at least four consequences of Economic Democracy's allocation procedure that would seem to favor it over the capitalist alternative:

- National development is likely to be more harmonious. If market criteria alone dictate the flow of capital funds, regional inequalities tend to grow rather than shrink. Capital flows to where the action is. Rich regions tend to get richer, poor regions poorer. Economic Democracy interferes with this "natural" tendency, directing capital to each region in proportion to population.
- Communities are likely to be more stable under Economic Democracy. If markets alone determine capital allocation, people will feel the pressure to move to those parts of the country where job opportunities are greater—those parts, that is, into which capital is flowing. The young, talented, and energetic will be among the first to go—not a good thing for community stability.
- One can expect community life to be richer. If communities are guaranteed an annual influx of capital, to be used for economic development, more people are likely to want to be involved in local politics, since there is more scope now for positive vision.
- Neither communities, regions, nor the nation as whole need worry about capital flight, since the investment capital of the nation, publicly generated, is mandated by law to be returned to the regions and communities that comprise the nation. Vulnerability to the sorts of macroeconomic instability brought about by the rapid flows of finance capital into or out of a region or into or out of the country itself is eliminated completely.

The drawbacks? Perhaps some allocative inefficiencies. Perhaps some bad decisions as to how a community should use the share of capital it receives. Probably some corruption—pressure put on bank officials to make inappropriate loans, perhaps some bribery. But there are plenty of allocative inefficiencies, bad investment decisions, and financial corruption under capitalism. It is hard to see why these features would be worse under Economic Democracy, let alone so much worse as to offset the clear advantages.

3.3 THE MONDRAGON "EXPERIMENT"

The case for the viability of Economic Democracy would seem to be strong. We know that workplace democracy works. The evidence is beyond dispute. We know that investment funds can be generated by taxation instead of from private savings. This cannot be doubted. And it would seem that allocating these funds in such a way that market criteria are invoked only late in the process, rather than from the beginning, promises egalitarian and stability gains. Of course there will be lingering doubts. We can't point (yet) to the great historical experiment where these institutions have been implemented on a national level. We can, however, point to a smaller scale version of something that looks very much like Economic Democracy. Although little known to the world at large, it is an experiment that, in my view, is of world-historic importance.

Here is the story in a nutshell.[17] In 1943, Don José Maria Arizmendiarrieta, a local priest who had barely escaped execution by Franco's forces during the Spanish Civil War, established a school for working class boys in a small town in the Basque region of Spain. The "red priest," as he was called in conservative circles, was a man with a large vision. Believing that God gives almost all people equal potential and dismayed that not a single working class youth from Mondragon had ever attended a university, Fr. Arizmendiarrieta structured his school to promote technical expertise as well as "social and spiritual values." Eleven members of his first class (of twenty) went on to become professional engineers. In 1956, five of these and eighteen other workers set up, at the priest's urging, a cooperative factory to make small cookers and stoves. In 1958, a second cooperative was established, to make machine tools. In 1959, again at Arizmendiarrieta's instigation, a cooperative bank was established. This proved to be a decisive innovation. The bank became the hub of the cooperative sector, providing capital and technical expertise to existing cooperatives wanting to expand and to new cooperatives willing to affiliate with it. It even developed an "entrepreneurial division" that researched new production and marketing possibilities and encouraged the setting up of new cooperatives.

The Mondragon complex spread beyond the town of Mondragon itself. It also developed a host of support structures: a technical university, research institutes, a social security organization, and a network of consumer outlets. The initial experiment, a worker-owned factory making kerosene cookers, has developed since 1956 into a system of more than a hundred enterprises, including eighty industrial cooperatives making home appliances, agricultural equipment, automobile components, machine tools, industrial robots, generators, numerical control systems, thermoplastics, medical equipment, home and office equipment, and much more. In 1991 (fifteen years after Arizmendiarrieta's death), these cooperatives, always linked via the bank, combined formally to form the Mondragon Corporación Cooperativa (MCC). MCC includes not only producer and construction cooperatives but also a bank (Caja Laboral), two research centers (Ikerlan and Ideko), the social security service (Lagun Aro), a network of retail stores (Eroski), and several educational institutions (Eskola Politeknikoa, Eteo, and others).

Today, MCC is the dominant economic power in the Basque region of Spain ("much more important to the Basque region than General Motors is to Detroit," a Basque researcher said to me). MCC's capital goods division is the market leader in metal-cutting tools in all of Spain, as is the division that makes refrigerators, washing machines, and dishwashers. MCC engineers have built "turnkey" factories in China, North Africa, the Middle East, and Latin America. The Eroski group is now the third largest retail food chain in Spain (the only one of the top four controlled by Spanish interests). Caja Laboral has been rated as being among the top 100 most efficient financial institutions *in the world* in terms of its profit/assets ratio. Ikerlan is the only Spanish research firm to have met the NASA technical specifications and hence permitted a project on the space shuttle *Columbia* in 1993. The Eskola Politeknikoa, enrolling 2,000 students, is considered by many to be the best technical institute in Spain. All in all, MCC now has a workforce of 53,000, annual sales of $6.6 billion, and assets of over $13 billion.[18]

In short, we have here a corporation comparable in size and technological sophistication to a dynamic capitalist multinational firm that has an internal structure radically different from a capitalist corporation. This worker-owned, worker-managed "cooperative corporation" is in essence a federation of cooperatives, each of which is wholly owned by its workforce. The workers of each cooperative meet at an annual general assembly to elect a board of directors, which then appoints the cooperative's management and selects delegates to the MCC Congress. These delegates, some 350 in all, then meet to pass judgment on the strategic plan for MCC, presented by a congress board, whose twenty-two members include the division heads of MCC (the member cooperatives are grouped into divisions) plus representatives of the special institutions (the bank, the research organizations, and so forth). All of the cooperatives are bound by the provisions of this plan. Individual cooperatives are free to dissolve their contract of association with MCC if they so desire, but none has ever done so. The benefits of belonging far outweigh the restrictions—wage scales, allowable income differentials, percent of profits to be reinvested in the corporation or in the community—imposed on a cooperative's autonomy.

It is beyond dispute that the Mondragon "experiment" has been economically successful, even in the face of the greatly intensified competition to which it has been subjected following Spain's admittance into the European Union. It is worth considering the values and vision that animated Arizmendiarrieta and his early disciples for insight as to why Mondragon has done so well.

The Mondragon complex did not develop as a purely pragmatic response to local conditions. Arizmendiarrieta was deeply concerned about social justice and explicitly critical of capitalism, basing his critique on progressive Catholic social doctrine, the socialist tradition, and the philosophy of "personalism" developed by Monier, Maritain, and other French Catholic philosophers. He was likewise critical of Soviet state socialism and of certain elements of the cooperative movement itself. He was particularly sensitive to the danger of a cooperative becoming simply a "collective egoist" concerned only with the well-being of its membership. From the beginning, Arizmendiarrieta insisted that a cooperative corporation must have a larger goal: "Our goal is more than simple options for individual improvement. It is more. If the cooperative enterprise does not serve for more, the world of work has the right to spit in our faces."[19]

The external goal most explicitly and operationally incorporated by the Mondragon complex has been employment creation. A capitalist firm typically aims at maximizing either profits or market share—employment creation is accidental. Indeed, when cutting labor costs becomes a central focus, job creation may conflict with profitability. (To give but one example: General Electric has tripled its revenues and profits during the past fifteen years, while shrinking its employment worldwide from 435,000 to 220,000.) In Mondragon, employment creation has always been a primary goal, with structures put in place to advance that goal. Specifically, the Caja Laboral not only provides funds for expansion and new cooperative creation but, as noted, it has also set up an "entrepreneurial division" to research market opportunities and to provide technical assistance to workers wanting to set up cooperatives. This entrepreneurial function has been supplemented by a research center (SAIOLAN) specifically devoted to developing both entrepreneurial talent and high-technology new businesses.

"Community" is also a central value. Businesses have obligations that extend beyond their membership. In Arizmendiarrieta's words,

> Cooperatives have a community dimension, which obliges them not only to give satisfaction to their own membership, but also to fulfill a social function through its structures. We must consider that the enterprise is not only our property, and therefore we have only the use of it. Calculations cannot be thought of as exclusively pleasing the membership, but rather of serving to fulfill more perfectly the mission that society has confided in us.[20]

Does MCC still abide by the ethos of its founder? So as not to paint too rosy a picture of what is, after all, a real-world experiment involving finite and fallible human beings, we should attend to the critics. One of the most prominent is Sharryn Kasmir, an American anthropologist who spent eighteen months in Mondragon. She entitled the book based on her field research *The Myth of Mondragon*.[21]

What myth does Kasmir want to debunk? First, let us be clear as to what is *not* mythical about Mondragon. Kasmir does not deny that the Mondragon cooperatives have been economically successful. Moreover, the Mondragon cooperatives have succeeded in the face of severe regional economic difficulties. Between 1976 and 1986, for example, the Basque region lost 150,000 jobs, during which time the cooperatives *increased* employment by 4,200. The early 1990s saw another deep recession, official unemployment reaching 25 percent in the region. This time, the industrial cooperatives were hit, and employment fell from 17,000 in 1991 to under 15,000 now. Still, overall employment in MCC did not decline. It remains rare for a cooperator in Mondragon to lose work altogether because cutbacks are effected through reassignment to other cooperatives and nonreplacement of retirees.

Therefore, what is mythical about Mondragon is neither its economic success nor the employment security the cooperatives provide. It is not a myth, either, that Mondragon cooperatives are more egalitarian than their capitalist counterparts, or that Mondragon workers can exert some real control over conditions that affect them. Kasmir notes that the highest-level engineers in Mondragon firms make 30 percent less than comparably skilled engineers employed by capitalist firms in the province. She observes that class differences were not nearly as extreme in the cooperative firm she selected for comparative study as in its capitalist counterpart. She points out that attempts by management to widen the allowable pay differential between the lowest and highest paid (1 to 4.5 in most enterprises) have often been defeated by workers. Workers also voted against (and hence defeated) a management proposal to cut their common four-week August vacation to two weeks with the other two weeks assigned at other times (so as to be able to keep production going fifty weeks per year).

Kasmir also acknowledges that Basque labor unions have been reluctant to criticize the cooperatives, since, in the words of one labor leader "the cooperatives [are] valuable national resources, capital that is tied to Euskadi [the Basque region of Spain]. Since the cooperators are owners, they have to vote to approve the movement of capital out of Euskadi. That would be a vote to lose their own jobs, to create unemployment. They wouldn't do it."[22]

On gender issues, there is also a difference between the cooperatives and the capitalist firms in the region. Although not many, there are more women in management positions in cooperative firms than in their capitalist counterparts. Moreover, "in my experience," Kasmir reports, "the issue of gender was debated and taken seriously in the cooperatives in a way that it was not in regular firms."[23]

If Mondragon is as good as Kasmir herself describes, what's *wrong* with it? What exactly *is* the myth? The most significant myth Kasmir wants to dispel is the image of a workplace in which everyone regards one another equals, where workers are happy with their work, and where workers actively participate in daily decision making. This image comes to mind when one reads much of the literature on Mondragon. Mondragon is often portrayed as an *alternative* to class struggle and to socialism. Kasmir rightly objects. She notes that one often hears "we're all workers here"—but only when talking to managers. In her comparative survey, in answer to the question, "do you feel you are working as if the firm is yours?" nearly 80 percent of the cooperative manual workers said "no"—a slightly *higher* percentage than those at the private firm. (Interestingly, *managers* of cooperative firms identified with their firms far more than did their private-enterprise counterparts. Fully half of the private managers did not feel a part of the firm, whereas only 18 percent of the cooperative managers felt so alienated. Mondragon's success in garnering management loyalty is no small thing; it is doubtless an important factor in explaining the success of the Mondragon cooperatives.)

As Kasmir admits, her sample size was not large, so one must be careful about drawing sweeping conclusions. One should certainly not draw the conclusion that workers are indifferent to the cooperative nature of their firm: only 10 percent of the workers surveyed by Kasmir said they would prefer to work in a privately run enterprise. These results are consistent with a conversation I had with a Mondragon worker when I visited the complex in 1995. The worker had expressed a certain cynicism about the ideals of the Mondragon experiment. "People once took them seriously, but not any more," she remarked.

"You mean it doesn't matter to you, whether you work here or at a private company?" I asked.

"Of course it matters," she replied. "Here I have job security, and here I can vote."

It must be acknowledged that Mondragon has not resolved the problem of alienated labor. I would argue that it cannot be expected to do so, so long as it remains a cooperative island in a capitalist sea—an increasingly competitive sea at that. Neither can it be expected to forego completely other mechanisms regularly used by its capitalist competitors—the use of part-time and temporary wage labor, and investing part of its profits in high-return capitalist enterprises, some of them in the Third World. Being more efficient is not always enough because capitalist firms can also avail themselves of other means for enhancing profitability, means that have to do with increasing exploitation rather than technical productivity. (Paying workers less for the same work increases profitability but not productivity.)

The presence of worker alienation and of certain practices that cut against the grain of Arizmendiarrieta's vision should not blind us to two striking lessons that can be drawn from the economic success of Mondragon. First, enterprises, even when highly sophisticated, can be structured democratically without any loss of efficiency. Even a large enterprise, comparable in size to a multinational corporation, can be given a democratic structure.

Second, an efficient and economically dynamic sector can flourish *without* capitalists. Capitalists do not manage the Mondragon cooperatives. Capitalists do not supply entrepreneurial talent. Capitalists do not supply the capital for the development of new enterprises or the expansion of existing ones. But these three functions—managing enterprises, engaging in entre-preneurial activities, and supplying capital—are the *only* functions the capi-talist class has ever performed. The Mondragon record strongly suggests that we don't need capitalists anymore—which, of course, is the central thesis of this book.

3.4 A NOTE ON THE PUBLIC SECTOR

This book concentrates on one part of the economic structure of a viable so-cialism—those institutions that allocate investment funds and those that uti-lize such funds to produce goods and services for sale in a competitive mar-ket. In chapters 4 and 5, I compare them in their consequences to capitalist institutions and defend their superiority. Very little is said during any of these discussions about those goods and services that will be provided to the citi-zenry *outside* the market, notably, child care, education, health care, and care for the disabled and the elderly. Although the socialist tradition has long insisted that such amenities be offered to all citizens on the basis of need, not ability to pay, the provision of such services, free or at nominal charge, no longer serves to distinguish socialism from capitalism, since many (although certainly not all) advanced capitalist societies do just that. (In almost all cases, such services were introduced under pressure from strong labor movements to head off their more radical demands. Social democratic re-forms are not "natural" to capitalism.)

This being the case, I do not offer a detailed specification of the public sector institutions that would be present in any real-world instantiation of Economic Democracy. We may assume that Economic Democracy will have learned from the experiences of those capitalist countries that have been most successful in providing their citizens, universally, with quality child care, education, health care, retirement benefits, and the like, and will adopt, perhaps with slight modification, their programs. (I do not mean to suggest that all hard issues in these areas have been resolved. Consider health care, for example. It is not within the means of any coun-try to give everyone the best treatment that is technically possible. Certain procedures must be rationed. How? According to ability to pay? By lottery? According to age and/or general state of health? There are no easy answers to these questions. What is certain, however, is that *basic* health care can be provided to everyone.)

Although I won't attempt here or elsewhere in this book a full-blown ex-position of the public sector under Economic Democracy, let me make a few observations about two topics that are particularly salient to the construction of a humane future—the relationship among generations and the relation-ship of income to work.

Since human solidarity is perhaps the most fundamental of socialist principles, we can expect Economic Democracy to embrace the principle of *intergenerational solidarity*. This, in my view, should be understood as follows: A citizen regards *all* the children of his or her society as being, in some sense, his or her children, and *all* the elderly as being his or her parents. (Philosophers will hear the echo of Plato's *Republic* here.) It is reasonable to think in such terms. In point of fact, each person born into a humane society is cared for and educated by many members of the older generation, not simply his or her biological parents, and each must be cared for by members of the younger generation when he or she retires from the labor force. To be sure, biological or other legally recognized parents of children have special rights and responsibilities regarding "their" children, as do children regarding their legal parents, but it remains the responsibility of each citizen to see to it that no child or older person is neglected.

Regarding children, this principle implies, minimally, that:

- Prenatal and child-rearing classes be made available, free of charge, to all parents. (Perhaps they should be required of all parents.)
- Quality day care should be available, free of charge, to all parents who require such assistance. (For parents who choose to remove themselves from the paid workforce to care for their children at home, a child care supplement might be in order. One mechanism that might be employed: all parents of preschool-aged children receive "vouchers"— government-issued certificates denominated in dollars—which can be used to pay for certified day care, or, if not used for that purpose, applied to the family's tax obligations.)
- All children should have free access to quality primary and secondary education. (Note: Socialist principles do not preclude providing parents with vouchers to be used at "private" schools. There are two basic rationales for private education. It is sometimes maintained that competition among schools enhances the quality of education. I doubt that this is true, but if a community wishes to try the experiment, it should be free to do so. Market socialism, after all, is not opposed to competition. The second rationale concerns religious education. If a society's constitution prohibits the teaching of religion in public schools, it seems not unreasonable to provide those parents who wish to send their children to religious schools with tuition vouchers. There is nothing "antisocialist" about providing free education for all our children.)

Such provisions as just listed would, of course, have to be financed from taxes—not the capital assets tax, since that tax is earmarked for capital investment only, but taxes on income or consumption. To the objection that tax rates would be too high, I would respond that it is by paying such taxes that you fulfill your basic obligation to intergenerational solidarity.

Moreover, it is very much in the interest of society to reduce the financial burden parents must assume in raising children—now more than ever, given the large demographic shift that is presently taking place. In all advanced industrial societies, birthrates are declining sharply. Among the reasons:

- With sexuality now separated from reproduction, and with opportunities for paid employment now open to women, most women are now free to choose—as they have rarely been in the past—whether to have children or not, and if so, how many.
- Children are now exceedingly costly. Whereas in the past (and still in the present, in many parts of the world), children could be regarded as an economic asset, they are now a financial liability. Children no longer contribute substantially to a family's income, nor can they be relied on to assume financial responsibility for their parents when the parents age. The economic incentives for having children have sharply reversed.
- In our increasingly meritocratic, peer-oriented world, having children is becoming ever more fraught with anxiety. Parents can no longer feel secure that their children will grow up well or will find decent jobs as adults. Advanced industrial societies are now more than ever polarized into "winners" and "losers." Parents live in terror that their beautiful offspring will turn out badly.[24]

A strong conclusion follows from these facts. If an advanced industrial society wants to maintain a stable population, it can no longer rely on "biological instinct" or even the deep gratification that having and raising children can provide. If we want to maintain a stable population, which presumably we do, we cannot stand idly by and let nature take its course. It goes without saying that we do not want to turn back the clock regarding the first factor listed above. The technological and social changes that have freed women from the burden of unwanted children are a clear advance for humanity. Therefore, we must concentrate on the other two factors. Making child care and education a public responsibility, as outlined above, addresses the second. The economic structure of Economic Democracy has implications for the third. As we will see in chapter 5, Economic Democracy greatly reduces the economic anxieties that so many people face today. The economy will be less volatile. Everyone will be guaranteed a job. In addition, communities will be more stable under Economic Democracy, thus offering a better environment for raising children. The declining birthrate problem is far more tractable under Economic Democracy than under capitalism.

Regarding care for the elderly, the principle of intergenerational solidarity points to a "pay as you go" social security system. That is to say, younger people currently working should pay, via their income or consumption taxes, what is required to maintain in dignity those who can no longer work, or who, even if able, have worked long enough and have chosen to retire. That is to say, everyone in society should come under a public pension plan that is funded by general tax revenues.

"Pay as you go" is usually contrasted with systems in which workers, during their productive years, set aside a portion of their paychecks via mandatory social security deductions and/or voluntary contributions to their pension funds so that, when they retire, they can take care of themselves. In an important sense, this distinction is illusory. If we think in terms of material resources, it is clear that *all* social security systems are "pay as you go," because, however pensions and annuities are structured, the material fact is, people who are working must produce the goods and services consumed by those who no longer work. It is more honest—and ultimately fairer—for the older generation to acknowledge frankly their dependency on the younger generation than to pretend to be independent—just as that younger generations should acknowledge the fact that their current independence (such as it is) was made possible by an older generation that cared for *them* for the first two decades or so of their lives.

The material fact that retired workers depend on those currently working—regardless of the form a pension contract takes—underlies the considerable anxiety being expressed these days about an imminent "crisis" in social security, caused by the aging of our population. As the birthrate falls and life expectancy increases, the ratio of active workers to retirees must inevitably decline. This, we all know, could spell trouble. Whatever the form of my retirement portfolio, it cannot guarantee me material security if not enough people are working.

Serious though this problem may be, it is by no means insoluble—at least if we allow ourselves to think beyond the horizon of capitalism. In material terms, the issue is whether we will have enough able-bodied workers and enough material resources to produce the goods and services needed to care for our children, those who are working, and those who have retired. Given the enormous productivity of our current technologies, the answer is surely yes, especially if:

- We begin to shift our production goals and consumption habits in the direction of minimizing waste, enhancing durability, and otherwise living in better harmony with our natural world (changes that will be required in any event, given the ecological constraints that are closing in on us).

Moreover, if we do indeed face a labor shortage:

- We can encourage older people to continue working, perhaps only part time and at less physically demanding jobs. (Given that older people are now, on average, in much better health than they used to be at comparable ages and given that many would doubtless like to continue making productive contributions to society, we can be confident that our labor force could be significantly increased if such an increase were needed.)

As we shall see, shifting our production and consumption to bring them into alignment with the requirements of ecological sustainability is far more feasible under Economic Democracy than it is under capitalism. We will also see that Economic Democracy does not require significant unemployment in the way that capitalism does, and so there will be less resistance on the part of younger people than is likely under capitalism to the prospect of older people working longer. As long as our institutions sustain, rather than contradict, the principle of intergenerational solidarity, the likelihood of a real crisis in social security is nil.

There has been significant discussion on the Left in recent years concerning the relationship between income and work, deriving from the debate concerning "basic income." Philippe Van Parijs has argued that "real freedom for all" has been, or at least should be, the ethical ideal of the Left. To best achieve this end, he says, income should be separated from work. Every citizen should be guaranteed a basic income, whether or not that person engages in paid labor. This basic income should be as high as possible. Indeed, the very criterion for determining the optimal economic structure of society should be the level of basic income it provides. Van Parijs goes on to suggest—more provocatively still, coming from a man of the Left—that some form of *capitalism* might trump all forms of socialism in this regard.[25]

This latter claim is untenable. As we shall see in chapter 4, unpleasant unemployment is crucial to the healthy functioning of a capitalist economy. However, the issue remains: should "basic income" be part of the socialist agenda? In particular, should Economic Democracy add a commitment to a maximally sustainable basic income to its institutional structure? (Michael Howard, for one, has pressed this case.)[26]

In a sense, the notion of "basic income" is noncontroversial, at least in one of its formulations, namely, the "negative income tax." (If a society has a negative income tax, you get a check from the government if you make less than a certain cut-off income, the amount being proportional to the difference between your income and the cut-off point.) Conservative economist, later Nobel laureate, Milton Friedman proposed the "negative income tax" four decades ago.[27] A version was adopted by the Nixon administration, and has been in effect in the United States ever since (where it is called the "earned income tax credit" [EITC]).

Although the EITC is currently the largest entitlement program in the federal budget, aside from health entitlement programs and social security, the amounts paid out are paltry. In 1999, the maximum benefit payable to a family with two or more children was $3,816. A childless household with no income received $347.[28] This is not the level that Left advocates of basic income have in mind. The Left's proposal is far more substantial. "Basic income" is to be set at the "highest sustainable level" so that (it is assumed) a person can live without working if she or he so chooses. This, it is argued, would give people much more "real freedom" than they currently possess. It would allow many to work only part time or to share work, and it would compel companies to provide better paid and more attractive employment, since otherwise no one would work at all.

I must confess to being skeptical on both empirical and normative grounds. It is by no means clear how high a basic income could be and still be sustainable. Basic income grants are financed from the taxes of those who *do* work. The more people take advantage of the basic income to work part time or not at all, the higher the taxes must be on those who work full time. It may well be that the basic grant would be much lower than its proponents think to be politically or economically sustainable—and hence would have fewer benefits than they suppose.

I'm also uncomfortable with the ethical principle invoked here, which allows an able-bodied person to claim a right to the fruits of other people's labor, without being obliged to contribute anything in return. Socialists have long argued that income from capital derives from the unpaid labor of those who work—and hence is exploitative. As we saw in chapter 2, this criticism is essentially correct. So long as work is not fun—which it is not for most people, nor will it magically become so under Economic Democracy—socialists should insist on a measure of reciprocity. To my way of thinking, it is far better, ethically and programmatically, to target public funds to basic health care, child care, education, and retirement, while at the same time guaranteeing decent jobs for all able-bodied citizens whose ages fall within an agreed-upon span, than to guarantee everyone an unconditional level of support, even those who can but don't want to engage in paid labor.

3.5 FAIR TRADE, NOT FREE TRADE

The structures described thus far that define Economic Democracy pertain to a national economy but, as everyone knows, we now live in a global economy. How would Economic Democracy fare in this "new world order"? Is Economic Democracy possible in one country or would it have to be implemented on a world scale to be effective? What should be the nature of the economic linkages between an Economic Democracy and other countries? These are the questions we must now consider.

From an *economic* point of view, there is no reason to think that Economic Democracy would not be viable in one country. If other countries, however internally structured, do not react with military aggression or an economic blockade, a country structured along the lines of Economic Democracy should thrive. Of course, if the country were poor, it would be difficult to bring the foreign multinationals situated in that country under democratic control—but even in such a case, some sort of peaceful accord *might* be possible. (Much would depend on the state of the counterproject internationally.) It might also be difficult to attract foreign investment, since investment would confer no control over an enterprise. (A worker-controlled enterprise would not be precluded from accepting capital from abroad in exchange for a contractually stipulated share of the profits, but investors do not get to vote.) As we shall see in the next two chapters, lesser reliance on private foreign capital may not be a bad thing, even for a poor country.

In a rich country, Economic Democracy could easily work. Its internal economy would remain efficient and dynamic, and it could continue to trade peacefully with other countries, capitalist or socialist. However, because of the way workplaces and the investment mechanism are structured under Economic Democracy, there would be significant differences in the nature of the economic transactions. Above all, *there would be virtually no cross-border capital flows*. The enterprises within an Economic Democracy will not relocate abroad because they are controlled by their own workers. Finance capital will also stay at home, since funds for investment are publicly generated and are mandated by law to be reinvested domestically. Capital doesn't flow out of the country—apart from a presumably small flow of private savings looking for higher rates of return abroad. In the basic model, private savings earn no interest at all at home; in the expanded model, they do. (More on this below.) Capital doesn't flow into the country, either, since there are no stocks or corporate bonds or businesses to buy. The capital assets of the country are collectively owned—and hence not for sale. (As noted in the previous paragraph, there might be *some* foreign investment in worker-run firms, but the amount would doubtless be small. Government borrowing might still take place, although most countries would presumably strive to live within their means.)

The elimination of cross-border capital flows has two exceedingly important positive effects.

- There is no downward pressure on workers' incomes coming from company threats to relocate to low-wage regions abroad.
- Countries cannot cite the need to attract capital as an excuse for lax environmental standards.

Significant as these effects are, cooperative labor and a publicly generated investment fund do not completely negate international wage competition or the incentives to be soft with environmental regulation. *Free
trade* (i.e., trade regulated only by supply and demand, even when confined to goods and services) encourages such behavior. If trade is free, domestic goods produced by high-wage workers will not be as competitive
as comparable imported goods produced by low-wage workers. A similar
imbalance occurs with respect to environmental restrictions. To insulate itself from such detrimental tendencies, *while at the same time contributing toward a reduction in global poverty*, Economic Democracy should
adopt a policy of "fair trade," not "free trade." Free trade is fine so long as
the trading partners are roughly equal in terms of worker incomes and environmental regulations. However, when trading with a poorer country or
one whose environmental regulations are lax, Economic Democracy will
adopt a policy of *socialist protectionism*.

"Protectionism" is, of course, a dirty word in mainstream discourse—despite
the fact that virtually every economically successful nation of the capitalist era
has been protectionist. We needn't point to Japan. The record goes back much
further. Alexander Hamilton, in his 1791 *Report on Manufacturers*, argued
(successfully) that "the United States cannot exchange with Europe on equal
terms, and the want of reciprocity would render them the victim of a system
of reciprocity which would induce them to confine their views to Agriculture
and refrain from Manufactures."

Three-quarters of a century later, President Ulysses S. Grant observed,

> For centuries England has relied on protection, has carried it to extremes and
> has obtained satisfactory results from it. There is no doubt that it is to this sys-
> tem that it owes its present strength. After two centuries, England had found it
> convenient to adopt free trade, because it thinks that protection can no longer
> afford it anything. Very well, Gentlemen, my knowledge of my country leads me
> to believe that within two hundred years, when America has gotten all it can out
> of protection, it too will adopt free trade.[29]

In point of fact, a degree of protectionism can be good for a country, not
only to allow for the development of local industries (the concern motivat-
ing Hamilton and Grant) but to prevent the sort of competition that puts
downward pressure on domestic wages and on environmental regulations.

Economic Democracy's fair trade policy is motivated by two distinct considerations. On the one hand, it wants to protect its own workers from the
sorts of competition that are damaging to everyone in the long run. On the
other hand, it wants to contribute positively toward alleviating global
poverty. Both these goals can be met if trade policy is appropriately designed. (The drumbeat allegation that protecting domestic workers hurts
poor workers abroad is not true.)

The socialist conviction underlying fair trade is the moral conviction that one should not, in general, profit from, or be hurt by, the cheap labor of others. To the extent that inequalities are necessary to motivate efficient production, they are justifiable. However, consumers should not benefit because workers in other countries work for lower wages than home-country workers, nor should home-country workers be put at risk by these lower wages. This conviction suggests the following two-part trade policy:

- A "social tariff" will be imposed on imported goods, designed to compensate for low wages and/or a lack of commitment to social goals regarding the environment, worker health and safety, and social welfare.[30]
- All tariff proceeds are rebated back to the countries of origin of the goods on which the tariffs were placed.

As a first approximation, the social tariff raises the price of an imported commodity to what it would be if workers in the exporting country were paid wages comparable to those at home and if environmental and other social expenses were the same. This figure would then be adjusted downward to compensate for the fact that poor country workers may be using less productive technologies. (Unless some such adjustment is made, it will be almost impossible for poor-country manufacturing industries to compete with rich-country industries, since, given the relatively greater degree of labor-intensity in most poor country industries, a tariff that would equalize labor costs would make the poor-country good much more expensive than that produced by a rich-country competitor.)[31] The point is to allow for competition, but only of a healthy sort. This "protectionist" trade policy derives from the stance Economic Democracy takes with regard to competition in general. Economic Democracy is a competitive market economy, but it discriminates between socially useful kinds of competition—those fostering efficient production and satisfaction of consumer desires—and socially destructive kinds of competition—those tending to depress wages and other social welfare provisions and to encourage lax environmental controls. Social tariffs are meant to block the latter without interfering with the former.

These social tariffs do more than shield domestic industries from socially undesirable forms of competition because they are imposed on *all* imports from poor countries—foodstuffs and raw materials, as well as manufactured goods—even when the imports do not compete with domestic producers. Consumers will thus pay "fair prices" for goods imported from poor countries as opposed to the lower prices dictated by low wages abroad, whether or not these goods compete with those produced by local industries.

The second part of our "socialist protectionist" trade policy is the socialist part. Tariffs imposed on imported goods do not go into the general revenue fund of the importing country but are sent back to the poor countries doing the exporting. Thus, with socialist protectionism, harmful competition is constrained but the negative effect of the tariffs on poor countries is mitigated. Consumers in rich countries must pay "fair prices" for their imported goods—to protect their own workers from destructive wage competition, and to help alleviate global poverty.

To be sure, these higher prices will likely decrease the consumption of imports from poor countries, which will adversely affect certain workers in those countries during the transition period. However, the overall effect of the higher prices accompanied by tariff rebates is to allow poor countries to devote fewer of their resources to producing for rich-country consumption, and thus to have more available for local use. The long-run consequences here are favorable to both rich nations and poor nations alike.

Because the consumers in Economic Democracy are paying higher prices for consumer goods, in part to help alleviate global poverty, the rebates should be directed to those agencies in the poor country most likely to be effective in addressing the problems of poverty and attendant environmental degradation—state agencies where effective, labor unions, environmental groups, and other relevant nongovernmental organizations (NGOs).

To sum up briefly: Economic Democracy is a competitive market economy, but it is not a free trade economy. It will engage in free trade with countries of comparable levels of development, but not with poorer countries. With a poor country, fair trade is better than free trade—for both countries.

3.6 ECONOMIC DEMOCRACY: THE EXPANDED MODEL

The basic, simplified model of Economic Democracy is meant to highlight the fundamental institutions. It is a pure model, not only devoid of capitalists but lacking all institutions that allow one to make money with money. You can, of course, save a portion of your income, but only for purposes of consumption later. There is no way to make your savings grow, apart from continuing to make deposits. There are no private businesses in which to invest, no stock or bond markets; there are not even banks that will pay you interest on your savings.

A country structured along the lines of Economic Democracy need not adhere to so pure a model. It might want to retain certain institutions now associated with capitalism. These institutions are not necessary to a well-functioning economy, but the citizens of the country might want to retain them anyway, perhaps because they enhance the scope of individual choice or provide some additional economic benefits. If properly structured, these institutions need not conflict with the basic structure of Economic Democracy or undermine the ethical principles that underlie the system.

In this section, we will examine two such institutions:

- Cooperative banks that function as savings and loan associations.
- Some private ownership of means of production and some legalized wage-labor—that is, some capitalism.

3.6.1 Socialist Savings and Loan Associations

In principle, the payment of interest can be abolished under Economic Democracy. Since the economy no longer relies on private savings to generate investment capital, it has no need for the mechanisms that have developed under capitalism to encourage private savings. The economy can function quite well without any private savings at all.

Individuals may still want to save, but the well-being of the economy as a whole no longer depends on their doing so. Their own individual well-being should not depend on personal savings either. In keeping with the basic values of socialist solidarity (in this case, intergenerational solidarity), a publicly funded social security system should, as noted earlier, provide all retired persons with decent incomes. People may still want to save, but they don't have to. In any event, they don't need to receive back more than they've saved.

However, instead of eliminating interest altogether, it would not be unreasonable for an Economic Democracy to allow a network of profit-oriented, cooperative savings and loan associations to develop. These would function to provide *consumer* credit, not *business* credit. If a person wants to purchase a high-cost item for which she does not have ready cash, she can take out a loan from a cooperative bank, to be repaid over time with interest. Money for this loan would come from private savers, just as under capitalism, who would not only enjoy the convenience of having their savings protected, but would also receive interest on their savings. Housing loans (mortgages) would likely play the dominant role in this sector (as they did in the savings and loan sector in the United States prior to the disastrous deregulation that ushered in the savings and loan crisis of the late 1980s).

It should be noted that there is no *theoretical* reason why interest must be charged, even on consumer loans. Consumer credit *could* be supplied by public institutions, interest free. In this case, loan repayments could be recycled, making further loans available. Additional funds could come from savers—who appreciate a safe haven for their money, even though they get no interest on it. If loan repayments and private savings should be insufficient to cover the demand, additional funds could come from general tax revenues.

Society has a choice here: abolish interest payments to private individuals altogether and make consumer credit available interest-free through public savings and loan associations, or allow the "private sector" (i.e., the profit-seeking cooperative sector) to handle the matter. If society prefers cheap credit but no interest payments on savings, it can opt for the first solution. If it prefers more expensive credit, but also the possibility of earning interest on savings, it can opt for the latter. There are also intermediate positions that could be taken—public banks charging interest, or cooperative banks with supplementary funds supplied by the government—but we needn't consider these here. The point is, there are a variety of options available, none of which seriously conflicts with the values or institutions of Economic Democracy.

What should *not* be done is what capitalism does: merge the institutions that generate and distribute investment funds with the institutions that handle consumer credit. Business investment, as opposed to consumer credit, is too important to the overall health of the economy to be left to the vagaries of the market.

3.6.2 Capitalists under Socialism

Would capitalist acts among consenting adults be prohibited under Economic Democracy? This taunting question raised by conservative philosopher Robert Nozick deserves a response.[32] It should be clear from what has been presented so far that two of the traditional functions of the capitalist can be readily assumed by other institutions. We don't need capitalists to select the management of an enterprise (workers are quite capable of doing that) and we don't need capitalists to "supply capital" for business investment (such funds can be readily generated by taxation).

There remains the entrepreneurial function. As we observed in chapter 2, the class of entrepreneurs is by no means coextensive with the class of capitalists. Most of the income that flows to holders of stocks, bonds, and other income-entitling securities has no connection whatsoever with productive entrepreneurial activity on the part of the holders of those securities. However, it cannot be denied that *some* capitalists are entrepreneurs, and that *some* of the creative innovations such people have produced have been highly beneficial for society. Might it not be desirable to allow a sector of genuinely entrepreneurial capitalism to function under Economic Democracy?

In fact, some capitalism would certainly be permitted in any realistic version of Economic Democracy—or at least some wage labor. The complete abolition of wage labor would entail that the requirement that enterprises be run democratically, one-person, one-vote, be extended to *all* enterprises. In practice, such a rule would be too rigid. Small businesses need not be run democratically. Restaurants, repair shops, small family businesses—if the owners of these businesses, who in most cases, since they also have to work, aren't true capitalists, can persuade people to work for them for a wage, there is no need to prohibit such arrangements. The mere fact that most enterprises are democratically run would serve as a check on whatever authoritarian or exploitative tendencies the owner might have. Such small businesses would in no way threaten the basic structure of Economic Democracy. In fact, they would provide added flexibility. Such small businesses could raise their own capital privately, or they too could go to the investment banks. These banks, charged with providing investment funds to profitable enterprises that would increase employment, will not hesitate to make loans to such businesses.

But small businesses don't really address the entrepreneurial issue. Certainly, small businesses are often "entrepreneurial" in seizing specific opportunities: a new restaurant here, a new boutique there, a dollar-store on the corner—but such businesses contribute little in the way of technological improvement or new product design. The entrepreneurial talent that creates or exploits large technical or conceptual breakthroughs must be able to mobilize large amounts of both capital and labor. Being able to set up your own small business isn't enough.

As noted, the basic model of Economic Democracy encourages communities to set up entrepreneurial agencies—institutions that research investment opportunities and provide technical advice and bank capital to those individuals interested in setting up new worker cooperatives. In all likelihood, society would want additional, complementary institutions to encourage entrepreneurial activities that combine training and economic incentives. Business schools, for example, could instruct students in the art of setting up successful cooperative enterprises. Local employment agencies could aid prospective entrepreneurs in recruiting workers. Financial incentives—bonuses and prizes—could be awarded to individuals who set up successful new cooperatives.

It is my considered conviction that such institutions would be more than sufficient to keep the economy dynamic. The record of Mondragon is certainly impressive in this respect. I believe that there are more than enough people with entrepreneurial talent willing to exercise those talents in a democratic setting to maintain a healthy flow of new technologies and products. I think that the citizenry of the nation would be more than satisfied with the pace of change these "socialist entrepreneurs" would provide.

This pace may not be "maximal"—perhaps not as rapid as under certain periods of capitalism—but we shouldn't forget that new and faster is not always better. Few people who have experienced life in an economically dynamic society would want a static society, but no one can deny that too rapid change can be unsettling and sometimes destructive of genuine values. Small is often beautiful. Speed can be an unhealthy addiction.

We needn't fear that "falling behind" more dynamic neighbors would entail terrible consequences. Economic development need not be viewed as a race, wherein not to win is to lose. We can copy technological developments made elsewhere, if it seems appropriate to do so. We need not fear that our investment capital will flow to greener pastures, or that our workers will emigrate en masse. True, our export industries will be under pressure to keep up with technological innovation—but that's a healthy pressure. Imports that become cheaper because of technological innovation will threaten local industries, but here too the pressure is basically benign. We want our industries to keep abreast the latest developments. Since our industries have clear economic incentives to do so, there wouldn't seem to be a great need for additional entrepreneurial activity.

Since we have as yet no national experiments in Economic Democracy, this "considered conviction" cannot be regarded as definitive. In any event, the entrepreneurial problem need not become acute, for there is always the option in Economic Democracy to allow *some* large-scale capitalism. If the basic institutions of Economic Democracy provide the society with sufficient technological and product innovation, then there is no need for capitalist entrepreneurs. But if society should find the pace of innovation too slow, or if it just fancied the idea of letting those with entrepreneurial talent be given freer reign, the prohibition on private ownership of means of production and wage labor could be relaxed—for any *new enterprise* started by a single individual or small group of individuals. These firms could be privately owned. They could hire whatever workers they could attract. They could grow as large as market conditions permitted, without any legal limitation. The owners could retain for themselves whatever profits the firm generates.

They are also free at any time to sell their firms—but only to the state. The government will pay them a fair market price and turn the enterprise over to the employees. If a firm is not sold, it is turned over to the employees at the death of the founder, the fair market value being paid to the estate of the deceased.

These capitalist-entrepreneurs, should they be allowed to function, pose no threat to the basic institutions of Economic Democracy. The number of genuinely talented entrepreneurs who need the lure of great wealth to motivate their creative activity is surely small. Their ability to treat their workers in an exploitative manner is sharply curtailed by the presence of widely available democratic employment alternatives. As we shall see, the real damage done by capitalists under capitalism is not done by individual entrepreneurs acting creatively, but by their collective, non-entrepreneurial control of the investment process. Under Economic Democracy, even with entrepreneurial capitalists, this control remains securely in the hands of the democratically accountable deliberative bodies that oversee the distribution of the tax-generated investment fund.

So capitalist acts among consenting adults need not be prohibited under Economic Democracy—so long as other options are genuinely available.

NOTES

1. For the argument, see David Schweickart, *Against Capitalism* (Cambridge: Cambridge University Press, 1993), 315–19. See also my contribution to Bertell Ollman, ed., *Market Socialism: The Debate among Socialists* (New York: Routledge, 1998). In this book, James Lawler and I defend market socialism; Hillel Ticktin and Ollman oppose it.

2. See *Against Capitalism*, 73, for the calculation.

3. For an outline of institutions that would enable an economy to mimic the Japanese model, see Chalmers Johnson, *MITI and the Japanese Miracle: The Growth of Industrial Policy, 1925–1975* (Stanford, Calif.: Stanford University Press, 1982), 315–19.

4. For a discussion of various forms of efficiency, allocative, Keynesian, and X-efficiency, see *Against Capitalism*, 81. In a nutshell, allocative efficiency pertains to the division of resources among enterprises, X-efficiency pertains to their use within an enterprise, and Keynesian efficiency pertains to the human waste associated with unemployment. Technical efficiency comprises allocative and X-efficiency, but not Keynesian efficiency.

5. I am indebted to Bruno Jossa of the University of Naples for this justification. The idea of allocating funds for public services on a per capita basis comes more readily to mind to a European than to an American, since European countries tend to allocate educational and health care resources that way, whereas we in the United States (unfortunately) do not.

6. If you want to know how vast these sums really are, see Mark Zepezaurer and Arthur Naiman, *Take the Rich Off Welfare* (Tucson, Ariz.: Odonian Press, 1996).

7. Joseph Stiglitz, "Quis Custodiet Ipsos Custodes?" ("Who Will Guard the Guardians?") *Challenge: The Magazine of Economic Affairs* (November/December 1999): 27.

8. Citations in this paragraph are from U.S. Department of Health, Education, and Welfare, *Work in America* (Cambridge, Mass.: MIT Press, 1973), 112; and Derek Jones and Jan Svejnar, eds., *Participatory and Self-Managed Firms: Evaluating Economic Performance* (Lexington, Mass.: Lexington Books, 1982), 11. See also Alan Blinder, ed., *Paying for Productivity: A Look at the Evidence* (Washington, D.C.: Brookings, 1990), especially the contribution by David Levine and Laura Tyson.

9. Katrina Berman, "A Cooperative Model for Worker Management," in *The Performance of Labour-Managed Firms*, ed. Frank Stephens (New York: St. Martin's Press, 1982), 80.

10. Hendrik Thomas, "The Performance of the Mondragon Cooperatives in Spain," in *Participatory and Self-Managed Firms*, ed. Jones and Svejnar, 149.

11. For more on Weirton, see James Lieber, *Friendly Takeover: How an Employee Buyout Saved a Steel Town* (New York: Viking, 1995).

12. Harold Lydall, *Yugoslavia in Crisis* (Oxford: Clarendon Press, 1989), 69 (emphasis mine).

13. Lydall, *Yugoslavia in Crisis*, 96 (emphasis mine).

14. Henry Levin, "Employment and Productivity of Producer Cooperatives," in *Worker Cooperatives in America,* ed. Robert Jackall and Henry Levin (Berkeley: University of California Press, 1984), 28.

15. John Maynard Keynes, *The General Theory of Employment, Interest, and Money* (New York: Harcourt Brace and World, 1936), 161–62.

16. Amartya Sen, *Resources, Values, and Development* (Cambridge, Mass.: Harvard University Press, 1984), 103.

17. For more details concerning this fascinating experiment, the following English-language books are available: Henk Thomas and Chris Logan, *Mondragon: An Economic Analysis* (London: George Allen & Unwin, 1982); Keith Bradley and Alan Gelb, *Cooperation at Work: The Mondragon Experience* (London: Heinemann Educational Books, 1983); William Foote Whyte and Kathleen King White, *Making Mondragon: The Growth and Dynamics of the Worker Cooperative Complex* (Ithaca, N.Y.: Cornell University Press, 1988); Roy Morrison, *We Build the Road as We Travel* (Philadelphia: New Society Publishers, 1991); and George Cheney, *Values at Work: Employee Participation Meets Market Pressure at Mondragon* (Ithaca, N.Y.: ILR/Cornell University Press, 1999), as well as the works by MacLeod and Kasmir cited below.

18. For current financial data on the Mondragon complex, consult their Web page at www.mondragon.mcc.es. These figures are for the year 2000.

19. Greg MacLeod, *From Mondragon to America: Experiments in Community Economic Development* (Sidney, Nova Scotia: University College of Cape Breton Press, 1997), 91.

20. MacLeod, *From Mondragon to America*, 90.

21. Sharryn Kasmir, *The Myth of Mondragon: Cooperatives, Politics, and Working-Class Life in a Basque Town* (Albany: SUNY Press, 1996).

22. Kasmir, *Myth*, 173.

23. Kasmir, *Myth*, 154.

24. See Barbara Ehrenreich, *Fear of Falling: The Inner Life of the Middle Class* (New York: Pantheon, 1989) for an eloquent analysis of this anxiety.

25. Philippe Van Parijs, *Real Freedom for All: What (If Anything) Can Justify Capitalism?* (Oxford: Clarendon Press, 1995).

26. Michael Howard, *Self-Management and the Crisis of Socialism: The Rose in the Fist of the Present* (Lanham, Md.: Rowman and Littlefield, 2000).

27. Milton Friedman, *Capitalism and Freedom* (Chicago: University of Chicago Press, 1962), chapter 12.

28. Data from Robert Cherry and Max Sawicky, "And Now for Something Completely Different: Progressive Tax Cuts That Republicans Can Support," *Challenge: The Magazine of Economic Affairs* (May–June 2001): 47.

29. Both quotes cited by Andre Gunder Frank, *Dependent Accumulation and Underdevelopment* (New York: Monthly Review Press, 1979), 98–99.

30. The language here is from Thomas Palley, *Plenty of Nothing: The Downsizing of the American Dream and the Case for Structural Keynesianism* (Princeton, N.J.: Princeton University Press, 1998), 172. Palley suggests the second provision as well, although he does not call his proposal "socialist protectionism."

31. I thank Frank Thompson for this observation, which came up in his discussion of socialist protectionism with Cuban economists.

32. Robert Nozick, *Anarchy, State, and Utopia* (New York: Basic Books, 1974), 163.

4

Capitalism and Its Discontents

In essence, the grand comparative argument for capitalism (TINA) claims that there is no alternative to capitalism that is

- As efficient in the allocation of existing resources
- As dynamic in its innovative growth
- As compatible with liberty and democracy

Capitalism, so it is said, is optimally efficient, innovative, and free. In the preceding chapter, we saw that Economic Democracy, since it is a market economy, will also be efficient, perhaps even more so than capitalism, because workplace democracy motivates better than does wage labor. We also saw that there are many options open to Economic Democracy to nurture and reward the entrepreneurial spirit. (Whether or not the growth engendered by capitalism is all to the good is a matter to be considered more carefully later in this chapter. As we shall see, citizens of Economic Democracy may well want to develop differently.)

Thus far, we haven't considered the political framework within which an economy structured as Economic Democracy might be embedded, but there would seem to be no reason to think that Economic Democracy would conflict with liberty or democracy. Economic Democracy is a decentralized market economy. There is no central authority dictating consumption, production, or employment. Economic Democracy would seem to fit well with the structure of basic political liberties now well established in advanced capitalist societies. (This issue will be examined more fully in chapter 5.)

Before defending Economic Democracy, we need to examine some of the issues that TINA glosses over. TINA acknowledges that there are negative features to capitalism, but it avoids looking at them closely. In proclaiming "there is no alternative," TINA cuts short the discussion. Proponents of capitalism may extol its liberty, efficiency, and economic dynamism, but critics of capitalism are silenced.

TINA cannot be taken at face value. It cannot mean, literally, that there are no alternatives to capitalism. Of course there are—some of which have been tried and found wanting. What TINA means to assert is that there are no *preferable* alternatives. Can this be true? To decide this matter honestly, we have to consider the negatives of capitalism as well as the positives. Six in particular stand out:

- Inequality
- Unemployment
- Overwork
- Poverty
- The mockery capitalism makes of democracy
- Environmental degradation

This chapter will take up each of these issues. In chapter 5, we consider these same issues from the point of view of Economic Democracy.

4.1 INEQUALITY

Let us begin with some facts. Everyone knows that capitalism tends to generate large-scale inequalities of income and wealth, but unless you have a particularly acute mathematical sense, the exact contours of these inequalities are hard to grasp. Economists cite Gini coefficients or they compare the share of income going to the top 10 percent with the share going to the bottom 10 percent, but these measures don't do much for the imagination. Some years ago, I came across a useful devise for visualizing income distribution. I call it, following the economist from whom I borrowed the idea, "a parade of dwarfs and a few giants."[1]

Here's how it works when applied to the United States.[2] As of 1999, there were slightly more than 100,000,000 households in the United States. The average income of these households was $55,000. Let us imagine a parade involving a representative from each of these households. The parade will last one hour. Representatives will be lined up so that those of the poorest households come first, followed by the ever more wealthy.

Let us suppose that, through some feat of biological alchemy, we can make the height of each person proportional to that person's household income. Thus, poor people will be very short, rich people much taller. Let us assume the average height of an American to be six feet—somewhat an exaggeration, but it makes the calculations simpler. This represents a $55,000 annual income. Suppose you are of average height and are positioned along the parade route. What will you see? (Consult figure 4.1 for a graph of the story about to be told.)

As you would expect, the parade begins with a lot of very small people, many just inches off the ground. Indeed, nearly five minutes pass before the participants reach the one-foot level—representing an annual income of $9,200. There are some *eight million* households in the United States that make no more than $9,200. (By way of comparison, there are roughly five million millionaires in the United States—but that's getting ahead of the story.) After twelve minutes, the marchers have grown to slightly more than a foot and a half, representing an income of $15,000, the official poverty line for a family of four. Twenty million households make less than that—some forty-five million people, half of them children.[3]

This parade, you soon realize, is rather boring. There are lots and lots of small people, and they are not growing very fast. Twenty minutes have passed, a third of the parade has gone by, and you are still looking way down. The marchers at this point are only three feet tall. Their household incomes are $27,500.

Your attention begins to wane. You go off to buy a beer from a street vendor. You return to your spot ten minutes later. The parade is now half over, so you expect to see people your own height. But no, the marchers are still small, only three-quarters your height, the tops of their heads still lower than your chest.

A statistician, who happens to be standing next to you, notices your puzzlement. He explains to you the difference between "median" and "average." The median income is that which cuts the population in half. By definition, half the households make less than the median and half make more. In the United States, the median household income is $40,000—making their representatives four and a half feet tall. The *average* income (also called the "mean") is different from the median. You calculate the average income by taking the total income earned by all the households and divide by 100,000,000. Since the distribution of income is top heavy in the United States, the average income is considerably higher than the median.

The parade has been going on during this conversation. You look at your watch. Eight more minutes have passed. Now the average incomes, proud six-footers making $55,000 walk by, looking you straight in the eye. (These are household incomes; in most cases, that $55,000 is a combined income.)

Heights begin to increase more rapidly, although not dramatically so. At forty-eight minutes, the marchers have reached nine feet—representing incomes of $80,000. We're now at the lower end of the upper quintal (i.e., 20 percent). At the fifty-four-minute mark, we reach the top 10 percent. These people, with incomes of $110,000, are twelve feet tall—twice your height.

Data from 1999–2000: 100,000,000 households, with an average income of $55,000
One hour parade: average height = 6 feet = $55,000

5 min   = 1 ft = $9,200   8 million households make less

12 min   = 1.5 ft = $15,000   official poverty line (20 million households make less)

20 min   = 3 ft = $27,000   33 million households make less

30 min   = 4.5 ft = $40,000   median income (50 million households make less)

38 min   = 6 ft = $55,000   average income

48 min   = 9 ft = $80,000   lower limit of upper 20%

54 min   = 12 ft = $110,000   lower limit of upper 10%

57 min   = 15 ft = $142,000   lower limit of upper 5%

36 sec to go = 33 ft = $300,000   lower limit of upper 1%

30 sec to go = 44 ft = $400,000   salary of the President

Last few seconds:
        $1,000,000   = 110ft   ten-story building
       $12,000,000   = 1,300ft   tallest buildings on earth
       $50,000,000   = one mile
      $100,000,000   = two miles $50,000/hr
        $4.5 billion   = 90 miles   16x higher than Mt. Everest (Bill Gates)

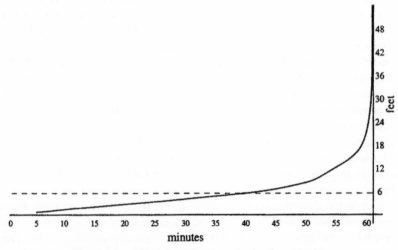

Figure 4.1   A Parade of Dwarves (and a Few Giants)

Three minutes later, the first members of the upper 5 percent appear, with incomes of $142,000. These people are much taller than you—fifteen feet tall, two and a half times your (proud?) six feet.

In fact, you hardly notice them, for suddenly the giants have come into view. Now the parade gets interesting. Now people start getting bigger faster. By the time the top 1 percent begins to pass by—36 seconds to go—heights have more than doubled. Incomes are now at $300,000, their bearers thirty-three feet tall. With thirty seconds to go, you are looking at $400,000—the salary of the president of the United States, the maximal government salary. (Prior to the year 2000, the president's salary was $200,000, a figure so pitiful by corporate standards that Congress doubled it.)

Even at $400,000, a presidential salary is not big money, not in the United States at the end of the century. In 1998, 172,000 individuals had adjusted gross incomes of a million dollars or more—two and a half times the president's salary. The smallest of these giants strides by at a 110 feet, the height of a ten-story building.

In the last seconds, the superrich pass by, among them various CEOs of major corporations. Those in the $10-million range tower above you at 1,100 feet. Well over a hundred CEOs of the Forbes 800 (top corporations) made more than $10 million in 2000. The $12-million heads reach to the top of the world's tallest office buildings, the 110-story Sears Tower in Chicago and the slightly taller Pentronas Towers in Kuala Lumpur. Disney's Michael Eisner walks by; he's taking home $50 million a year. His head is a mile from the ground—four times the Sears Tower—as are those of the 250 or so billionaires in the country. (A billion dollars put in a credit union that earned a modest 5 percent interest would generate a $50-million income annually.) The $100-million CEOs are two miles tall, among them Jack Welch of General Electric, Lewis Gernster of IBM, Steve Case of America Online, and Reuben Mark of Colgate Palmolive. (You do the math in your head—40 hours per week, 50 weeks a year—these guys are making $50,000 *per hour!*)

CBS's Mel Kormazin makes twice that much, $100,000 per hour—he's four miles tall. Charles Wang, of Computer Associates, made three times as much as Kormazin. He's twelve miles tall. The last person to come by, his head too far away to see, is ever-boyish William Gates. His income is not a matter of public record, but if his estimated wealth of $90 billion (in 2000) brought him a 5 percent return, he would have an income of $4.5 billion a year. Mt. Everest, the tallest mountain on Earth, is more than five miles high. Gates is more than sixteen times taller than Mt. Everest. (He's more than 10,000 times taller than a presidential salary would make him.)

Such is the distribution of income in the United States. Amazingly enough, this parade has actually *understated* the degree of inequality, for it depicts the distribution of income, not wealth. As all economists know, the distribution of wealth is *much* more unequal than the distribution of income. Income is your cash flow per year. Wealth is the value of what you own—your clothes, stereo, car, home, and all those stocks and bonds. For most people, "wealth" generates minimal income, but for the fortunate few, wealth begets wealth. Dividends and interest flow in, which are compounded into more wealth, which generates more income, onward and upward. Men become giants.

The difference in distribution is roughly this: If we divide the income of the United States into thirds, we find that the top 10 percent of the population gets a third, the next 30 percent gets another third, and the bottom 60 percent gets the last third. If we divide the wealth of the United States into thirds, we find that the top 1 percent owns a third, the next 9 percent owns another third, and the bottom 90 percent claims the rest. (Actually, these percentages, true a decade ago, are now out of date. The top 1 percent is now estimated to own between 40 and 50 percent of the nation's wealth, more than the combined wealth of the bottom 95 percent.) If we had a Parade of Wealth instead of a Parade of Income, the dwarves would be more numerous and much smaller, the giants fewer and much, much larger.

Such are the facts. What do we make of them? For some of us, such a distribution appears grotesque and makes us angry. So many millions a few feet from the ground, while the superrich tower above our tallest buildings, some soaring out of sight into the clouds. But for others, well, it's fun to imagine rising miles above the earth, too high up to even see those tens of millions of silly dwarves. Who's right? We can't just rely on feelings here. We have to ask the basic ethical question: What's *wrong* with inequality? As it turns out, this is not so easy to answer. Moreover, the correct answer has implications for the transition from capitalism to Economic Democracy. (The giants need not be lined up against the wall and shot, or even compelled to live like dwarves—however good that might be for their character. They will have to come down from the clouds, however.)

To get at this question, it is important to distinguish the issue of poverty from the issue of inequality per se. Would we be concerned about inequality if everyone in our society had *enough*? If the dwarves at the beginning of our parade weren't so small, would we worry about the giants? Wouldn't our objection to those giants be simply a matter of envy?

Plato voiced the two most common objections to inequality long ago. First of all, excess at either end of the economic spectrum is said to be corrupting. Excessive poverty corrupts, but so too does excessive wealth. Secondly, inequality is said to undermine the unity of society, the "community" of people. As Plato noted, within most societies there are really two societies, one rich and one poor, with decidedly different interests.[4] Harvard's liberal philosopher John Rawls echoes this argument in endorsing progressive taxation to head off what he calls "excusable envy."[5]

Neither of these objections, however, touches the deepest problem with inequality—with capitalist inequality, that is. I will argue that it is the *nature* of the inequality in our society today, rather than the mere fact of its existence, that is most problematic. (Later, when we consider how we might move beyond capitalism, it will be important to understand that it is not the sumptuous lifestyles of our upper class that are objectionable; it is the *source* of their income, and what they do with what they *don't* consume.)

If inequality were simply a matter of differing levels of consumption, I don't think we would have much cause to rail against it. If there were no desperately poor people in our society or in the world at large, and if the basic democratic ideals of our society were not compromised, then we would be hard pressed to find good moral grounds for objecting to the lifestyles of our giants. The lives of the rich (whether or not famous) would provide innocuous grist for our entertainment mills, a harmless source of fantasy, perhaps even some socially beneficial motivation.

However, there *are* desperately poor people both within our society and in the world at large, and our democratic ideals *are* being compromised. The structures that generate the massive inequalities endemic to capitalism are causally connected to both these phenomena. As we shall see, when we modify these structures, our giants will shrink—not to human size exactly, but they won't rise much above our walk-up apartment buildings. (These are big guys still, but not so big or powerful as to make a mockery of our democratic system. There will be small people, too—but not so small as to live in poverty.)

4.2 UNEMPLOYMENT

In Chicago we have a free weekly newspaper, *The Reader*, which runs along with a great number of ads for movies, music, theater, and phone sex, a syndicated weekly compilation, "News of the Weird," by Chuck Shepherd. Here's a telling entry from a few years back: "In November the city of Bombay, India, announced it had 70 job openings for rat catchers; it received 40,000 applicants—half from college graduates."[6]

Two weeks later, the United Nation's International Labour Organization released a report stating that 30 percent of the world's labor force, some 820 million people, are either unemployed or working at a job that does not pay a subsistence wage.[7]

Not so many years ago, reports such as these might have been greeted with indifference by most Americans—"Yes, yes, things are terrible in the Third World, but there's not much *we* can do about it, is there?" Today the response is different. Far more Americans than ever before are troubled by such news—because we now feel threatened. That vast pool of unemployed labor—some of it very smart and highly skilled labor—represents job competition. (A recent *Washington Post* poll revealed that 67 percent of

Americans worry that good jobs will move overseas and that workers will be left with jobs that do not pay enough.)[8]

It is fashionable these days to parrot "communism is dead" and "socialism is dead," but it is not often observed that the political-economic structures of Eastern Europe and the Soviet Union were undermined by the very developments that now make American workers tremble. Technological advances that allowed images of Western consumer society to penetrate the Iron Curtain have rendered *all* national boundaries porous. Innovations in communications and transport have given fierce new meaning to the concept "global competition."

In a sense, there's nothing new in any of this. Marx and Engels pointed out over 150 years ago:

> The bourgeoisie has through its exploitation of the world market given a cosmopolitan character to production and consumption in every country. . . . All old-established national industries have been destroyed or are daily being destroyed. They are dislodged by new industries, whose introduction becomes a life and death question for all civilized nations, by industries that no longer work up indigenous raw material, but raw material drawn from the remotest zones, industries whose products are consumed, not only at home, but in every quarter of the globe. In place of the old wants, satisfied by the production of the country, we find new wants, requiring for their satisfaction the products of distant lands and climes.[9]

It is true that the dislocations we are suffering, others before us have also suffered. However, for those of us born during or after World War II and who have lived most of our lives in the United States or Western Europe, what we are experiencing is new *for us*. For most of our lives, we have *benefitted* from low labor costs abroad. Such low wages translated into low-cost raw materials and mass-affordable coffee, tea, chocolate, and bananas. The workers of the Third World worked for us, not in competition with us. Now, for many in the West, the game has changed. As consumers, we still benefit; as workers, we are threatened.

Why has the game changed? I submit that the driving force behind the dislocation so many of us now experience or fear is the current *hypermobility of capital*. Recent technological developments now make it possible not only for "money capital" (i.e., investment funds) to flash almost instantaneously from one capital market to another but for up-to-date "real capital" (i.e., factories and machinery) to set up almost anywhere. Plants now "move." Shops "run away."

How are we to think about this hypermobility of capital? Is it right? Is it ethical? The usual procedure in ethics is to consider the matter from two perspectives. How does the situation look from the point of view of *rights* (the "deontological" approach)? How does it look from the point of view of *human happiness* (the "utilitarian" approach)? Are rights being violated? Is the principle, "the greatest happiness for the greatest number," being transgressed?

Well—it is hard to see any rights being violated if I decided to invest in the Singapore stock market, or even if I decide to move my toy factory from Chicago to Juarez. Workers might claim that they have developed certain employment rights with respect to the company that employs them, but it is hard to see how I can give these rights much credence, when honoring them might drive me out of business and leave them jobless anyway.

Things don't look much different from a utilitarian perspective. If we grant that unemployment hurts more in poor Mexico than in the rich United States, then shifting capital from where it is relatively plentiful to where it is less so would seem to be a *good* thing. It is hard to see how I can be faulted on utilitarian grounds if I provide employment to 300 Mexicans who would otherwise live in squalor, even if this comes at the expense of 300 Americans who can collect unemployment compensation and enroll in job-retraining programs.

The fly in the ointment of such ethical reasoning becomes visible only through the lens of economic theory—theory that many economists who should know better seem to have forgotten. The theory is basic Keynesian macroeconomics, elements of which were reviewed in chapter 2. Let us draw out the implications for globalized capital.

Nobody disputes the fact that capitalism is immensely effective at producing goods. Indeed, it is capable of producing far more goods than it is presently producing. Most plants have excess capacity, and many workers are out of work. Excess capacity and unemployment are *basic* features of real-world capitalism. Full employment of workers and resources (except during wartime) is a textbook fantasy.

As Keynes pointed out, the key to capitalist production is *effective demand*—needs or desires backed up by purchasing power. If the demand is there, goods will be produced. Rarely are there production shortages, and when there are, they are temporary. But if demand is not there, the economy will slump.

This effective demand comes from three sources: from private consumers, from private investment (*real* investment—building new factories, installing new technologies, and so on, not "investing" in the stock market, which, macroeconomically, is saving, not investing), and from government expenditures.

The variable upon which Keynes focused his attention was private investment. The health of a capitalist economy depends on "investor confidence," on the "animal spirits" (as Keynes liked to say) of the investors. Thus we get his famous policy prescription: When investor confidence flags, the government should step in and make up the difference. The government should spend more than it takes in, in order to provide the requisite stimulus to the economy. If necessary, pay people to bury cash in bottles and pay others to dig them up. Better that than nothing. (Keynes noted that one could probably find more useful things for them to do).

Keynes is certainly right that flagging investor confidence can throw an economy into recession. The 1997–1998 meltdown of the Asian "baby tiger" economies is a case in point. But why do investors lose confidence? Sometimes there are good reasons for this loss. Suppose consumers simply can't buy all the goods being produced. Then it makes no sense to keep investing.

We are looking here at one of capitalism's central contradictions. Wages are both a cost of production and an essential source of effective demand. Capitalist firms are always interested in cutting costs, expanding markets, and developing new products. But to the extent that the first of these goals, namely cost cutting, grows in importance relative to the other two, effective consumer demand will tend to be depressed—and hence also those "animal spirits" of investors. This can mean a stagnating economy and rising unemployment, perhaps on a global scale.

The logic is straightforward. If aggregate demand declines, which it will if average wages decline, which they will if the search for low wages dominates the movement of capital, then production—and hence employment—will also decline. That is to say, if the search for lower wages comes to dominate the movement of capital, the result will be *not only* a lowering of worldwide wage disparities (the good to which some economists point) but *also* a lowering of total global income (a straight-out utilitarian bad).

I do not claim that global stagnation or worse is inevitable under capitalism, but the possibility is ever present, and the likelihood seems to be increasing. Intense global competition exacerbates the problem of overcapacity, since each firm in each country is under pressure to upgrade its technology as fast as possible to avoid being left behind. With capacity rising, the threat of "overproduction" looms large today.[10] (Of course, "overproduction" here does not mean too many goods relative to human needs but too many goods relative to effective demand, that is, money-backed desires.)

In any event, Keynes's basic point is certainly valid. A laissez-faire capitalist economy has no tendency whatsoever toward full employment. It can stabilize at any level of unemployment. It is quite possible for a capitalist economy to marginalize large numbers of people, who, in the absence of governmental intervention, will remain permanently unemployed. In a globalized capitalism, large sections of the *world* can be so marginalized. In fact, they have been.

Keynes urged governmental intervention and his prescriptions were widely adopted after the Second World War, but they were not altogether successful. It is now clear why this was so. To the extent that the government engages in deficit spending to boost aggregate demand, and thereby succeeds in reducing the unemployment rate, the economy tends to "overheat." If labor markets become tight, workers demand higher wages. These extra costs are passed onto consumers, and inflation ensues. Workers, feeling cheated, demand still more, and so inflation accelerates—until the capitalist class decides enough is enough and slams on the brakes. (The "stagflation" of the 1970s set the stage for the conservative revival that brought Ronald Reagan to the presidency. The worst recession since the Great Depression, deliberately engineered by Federal Reserve chief Paul Volcker, quickly followed.)[11]

Liberal confidence in Keynesian full employment is not much in evidence today. Economists now speak of a "natural rate of unemployment," defined as that below which inflationary pressures set in. This, of course, is an utterly ideological manner of speaking, since there is nothing at all "natural" about unemployment. But the concept points to something real, something emphasized long ago by Marx but forgotten by Keynes: a healthy capitalism *requires* unemployment. It is precisely this "reserve army of the unemployed" that serves to discipline the workforce. If unemployment is too low, workers make wage demands that either cut into profits to the degree that future investment is jeopardized, or are passed onto consumers, thus generating inflationary instability.

We need to be clear on this point. Unemployment is not an aberration of capitalism, indicating that it is somehow not working as it should. Unemployment is a *necessary* structural feature. Capitalism cannot be a full-employment economy, except in the very short term. Unemployment is the invisible hand—carrying a stick—that keeps the workforce in line.

There is another problem with the Keynesian solution, which is more acute now than it used to be. Keynesian deficit spending depends on a "multiplier effect." The government spends $X more than it has, putting Y people to work. These people now have money, so demand for goods goes up, which generates more employment, which generates more demand, and so on—a virtuous upward spiral. Thus, an $X deficit generates many times $X of new effective demand. Hence, the deficit does not have to be excessive.

However, if an economy is wide open to imports, which contemporary capitalist economies increasingly are, then the multiplier effect is attenuated. A significant portion of those $X buys imported goods—which may increase employment abroad, but not at home. Hence, to reinflate the economy, a government must go much deeper into debt than in the past. Since the costs of this debt must be borne by the nation's citizenry, while the good effects spread globally, governments, not surprisingly, are now reluctant to apply the Keynesian remedy; when they do, it no longer works so well.

4.3 OVERWORK

If unemployment is a structural feature of capitalism that seems destined to become ever more severe, so too is its accompaniment, overwork. We have here a seeming paradox. A visitor from another planet would be perplexed to discover that in a purportedly free and rational society there are millions of people who want to work more, living in close proximity to millions who want to work less. The visitor would be even more perplexed to learn that new technologies allow us to produce ever more goods with ever less labor, and yet the intensity of work—for those who have work—has increased.

Of course, this paradox is no mystery to those of us who live here. The more precarious your job is, the more you must do everything possible to keep it. The more competitive the economy becomes, the more managers insist that they—and everyone under them—work harder. The treadmill effect: all must intensify their efforts just to remain in place.

The threat of job loss is real. Even once secure jobs in major corporations are now vulnerable. "Downsizing" is no myth. In the United States, for example, the 800 largest firms, whose assets comprise half of all corporate assets, employed a million and half fewer people in 1993 than they did twenty years before.[12] Clearly, not only income is distributed in a vastly unequal manner under capitalism; so too is leisure. Millions have more leisure than they want—the under- and unemployed. Millions more would love to slow down, work less, but can't—most of the rest of us, I suspect.

Neoclassical economists like to deny that such "Pareto-non-optimality" (i.e., inefficiency) can exist in a competitive economy. They like to say that those who are working long hours have chosen to do so. They have chosen consumption over leisure.

For some, this is doubtless the case. There are people who get into debt, then work a second job to get out. There are people who, given the option of overtime, leap at the chance. There are people who, given the choice between taking their "raise" in the form of fewer working hours or taking home a larger pay check, would opt for the money.

But "some of us" is not "all of us" or even "most of us." It is quite false to conclude that, by and large, capitalism has given us the consumption-leisure combination we really want. Two considerations call such a conclusion into question.

The first is obvious. For the vast majority of jobholders, the hours of work are fixed. Once hired, you do not have the choice of trading a bit of income for a bit more leisure. You can quit your job and try to find less demanding work that pays somewhat less, but you have virtually no chance of negotiating a consumption-leisure tradeoff with your current employer. (There are exceptions, but they are rare.)

The second consideration is subtler. Given the fact that leisure is not a real option, people adjust their consumption accordingly. You spend most of what you make (or more), since there is not much else to do with your money. You can save some of it, but that just means spending more later. Of course, you can always substitute a large increase in leisure for a large decrease in consumption by quitting your job, but that is a choice that few of us would want to make, and one altogether different from the marginal option—to substitute somewhat more leisure for somewhat less consumption. In the absence of the marginal option, you orient your life toward consumption; you search for happiness in things; you even go into debt in search of that fulfillment that consumption alone (you know in your heart) can never bring.

Harvard economist Juliet Schor has calculated just how much leisure our increased productivity could in fact support. Suppose, fifty years ago, we in the United States, happy with our standard of living (which was the envy of the world) had opted to take our productivity gains in leisure instead of increased consumption:

> We could now produce our 1948 standard of living (measured in terms of marketed goods and services) in less than half the time it took that year. We actually could have chosen the four-hour day. Or a working year of six months. Or, *every worker in the United States could now be taking every other year off from work—with pay.*[13]

Let us think about this for a moment. The year 1948 was not a bad time to be alive in America. People had washing machines, refrigerators, cars (not as many as today, but more buses and trams), telephones, record players, TVs (admittedly black and white), typewriters, lots of movie theaters. True, they didn't have cell phones, CDs, PCs, or VCRs, but life was hardly uncomfortable. (I'm thinking here of middle-class life. Life for poor people was miserable—as it still is.) Suppose we (current voters) were given a choice: either our current standard of living or a 1948 standard with a full-pay sabbatical every other year. Or perhaps a third option: a consumption mid-point between 1948 and now, say 1975, and a three-month summer vacation every year? (For everyone, not just schoolteachers and academics.) Is it so obvious that we would choose the present consumption-leisure tradeoff? *If* we were given the choice—which, of course, we are not.

Although our technologies might have given us more leisure, in fact, as Schor's research shows, the hours of work (for those who have work) have been steadily *increasing* since 1948. It is possible that we as a society prefer it that way, but the fact is, no choice was ever offered.

This is not an accidental feature easily remedied. A bias for consumption is built into the structure of capitalism. Even though workers in an enterprise might prefer to take a part of their productivity increase in leisure rather than income, the owner of an enterprise has nothing whatsoever to gain from such a tradeoff. A capitalist wants to get as much work from his workforce as possible. Unless it can be demonstrated that there would be a significant gain in worker productivity, the capitalist has no reason to consider such a proposal. The fact that workers might be happier is irrelevant.

From the perspective of the capitalist class as a whole, the undesirability of allowing leisure to substitute for consumption is even more striking. Capitalist firms make a profit only from selling. If profit rates are to remain high, then goods and services must be consumed in ever increasing quantities. Any kind of cultural shift that emphasizes leisure over consumption bodes ill for business. To be sure, individual businesses catering to the increase in leisure that people would have might profit, but if this leisure comes at the expense of income, overall aggregate demand will fall, profits will decline, the economy will stagnate or slip into recession. Consumption is good for business. Leisure—if not oriented toward consumption—is not.

4.4 POVERTY

The link between unemployment and poverty is more obvious than the link between unemployment and overwork. The vast majority of poor adults in advanced capitalist countries are able-bodied people who are unemployed or who work at minimum-wage jobs. (Working full time at a minimum-wage job garners $10,000 a year; the poverty line for a family of four is $15,000.) But the connection goes deeper than this straightforward observation because poverty is not simply a matter of material deprivation. An old radical song makes the point: "Hearts starve as well as bodies; give us bread but give us roses."

It is important to distinguish "living in poverty" from "being poor." The people of Cuba, for example, are poor. The per capita income of Cuba is but a fraction of that of the United States (one-twentieth, by one measure), yet there is little malnourishment or homelessness in Cuba, and everyone has access to basic health care. The striking result: infant mortality and life expectancy in Cuba are nearly identical to what they are in the United States. The people of Cuba are poor, but they do not live in poverty.

Grinding material poverty is a terrible thing: hunger and malnourishment, homelessness, pain, and sickness—bloated stomachs, teeth that ache and rot and go untreated, diseases that prey on weakened bodies. But poverty is not only a material phenomenon. Poverty can destroy the spirit as well as the body. (What is it like to be evicted from your home because you can't pay the rent? What do your children think of you? What is it like to watch your child cry from hunger or from a sickness you know can be cured, but you can't afford the treatment?)

Damage to the human spirit is particularly acute in a rich society that has removed the legal barriers to equality and preaches (whatever the practice) the ethos of meritocracy. If you don't make it, it's your own fault. Poverty becomes unbearable. It destroys self-respect. Is it any wonder that if you are poor and without prospects, you join a gang and wreak havoc? Is it any wonder that you seek relief in alcohol, crack cocaine, and other chemicals that dull the pain? Is it any wonder that you are tempted to deal the poison—your only chance, however slim, at the (false) happiness of big money? Sure, you'll likely go to prison, but so what? Inside is not so very different from outside. (The United States, during the past two decades, has seen its Dow Jones Industrial Average soar from under 1,000 to over 10,000—and its prison population quadruple. With 5 percent of the world's population, the United States now contains an astonishing 25 percent of the world's prisoners, some two million adults.)

The only real cure for the material and spiritual ravages of poverty is decent work. We all know that. Liberal and social-democratic welfare measures can never really solve the problem, and they sometimes make it worse—as conservatives delight in pointing out. Human beings need to work. Work— good work—gives structure and meaning to your life. Every living human being consumes, or else she would cease to be a living being. But if you consume, other people have worked for you. Self-respect demands that you contribute something in return.

Of course, a normal psyche can bear only so much shame and guilt, so defensive mechanisms kick in: self-deception, cynicism, a hardening of the heart, a brazen disregard for basic principles of human decency. Without the pride and self-discipline that good work instills, the human spirit shrivels.

Capitalism, as we have seen, cannot provide work for all, work, period, let alone good work. Unemployment is essential to a healthy capitalism. A healthy capitalism requires not only poor people but *poverty*, a painful, degrading, shameful condition that people will strive mightily to avoid. How else can employers keep those workers in line? You can beat slaves but not "free" men and women.

We have been considering poor people in rich countries. But as we all know, there are countries that are themselves poor, many desperately so. There are now an estimated one billion people on this planet who are malnourished, many severely so that they cannot function properly. There are many more who, while not technically malnourished, live in squalor, either in an impoverished countryside or in one of the teeming squatter settlements that are part of every Third World city. And the situation is getting worse, not better. The United Nation's Development Program reported in 1996 that 100 countries were worse off then than they had been fifteen years earlier. In 1995, people in well-to-do countries had average incomes eighty-two times higher than average incomes of the poor countries in which 20 percent of the world's population live—the gap having widened from thirty times in 1960.[14]

Proponents of globalized capitalism like to point out that the number of desperately poor people has declined in recent years. They fail to note that this is largely due to the success of well-protected, market-socialist China in lifting hundreds of millions out of poverty. On the other hand, the most precipitous drop in living standards ever witnessed in peacetime occurred in the ex-Soviet Union, following its renunciation of socialism. (Whether China still merits the label "market socialist" or should now be considered capitalist is a matter of some debate, to which we will direct our attention in chapter 6.) What is not debatable is the fact that huge increases in economic well-being for poor Chinese took place following the market reforms post-1978, during which time the vast preponderance of productive assets remained public, not private, property. Nor is the present state of the Soviet Union in dispute. As Princeton professor Stephen Cohen notes,

> Since 1991 Russian realities have included the worst peacetime industrial depression of the twentieth century; the degradation of agriculture and livestock herds even worse in some respects than occurred during Stalin's catastrophic collectivization of the peasantry in the 1930s; the impoverishment or near-impoverishment of some 75 percent or more of the nation; and more new orphans than resulted from Russia's almost 30 million casualties in World War II.[15]

What is so galling, tragic, heartbreaking, hideous (choose your adjective) about global poverty is how *little* it would take, in material terms, to eliminate it. So many human beings dying so young, so many people too famished or disease-ridden to function normally, so many members of our species without a chance at human happiness: how much would it cost to end this nightmare? Oxford economist Partha Dasgupta sums up his calculations thus:

> Resources required for eliminating poverty amount to approximately ten percent of their national income in sub-Sahara Africa and the Indian subcontinent. . . . Assuming a growth rate of income per head of one percent per year [a growth rate routinely exceeded in India and Pakistan], poverty in these parts could in principle be eradicated in ten years.[16]

Could be, but won't be—not as long as global capitalism prevails, not in ten years, not ever. The link between capitalism and the poverty of poor countries is more complex than the link between capitalism and the domestic poverty in rich countries, but is no less sure. As we have seen, domestic unemployment—and hence at least spiritual poverty—is necessary for a healthy capitalist economy. Labor must be disciplined. Third World poverty is more a byproduct of global capitalism than a structural necessity. (To be sure, poor-country capitalists need their workforces disciplined, but the extent of poverty in most poor countries far exceeds this structural requirement. Capitalism requires *some* poverty, but not an impoverished majority.)

Historically, most currently poor regions of the world were plundered by capitalist colonial empires and had their autonomous development blocked. The centers of capital wanted cheap raw materials and outlets for their surplus production. Force was employed to secure these ends. Exploitation enriched the powerful and impoverished the weak. (Whoever said crime doesn't pay?) As Marx observed,

> The discovery of gold and silver in America, the extirpation, enslavement and entombment in mines of the aboriginal population, the beginning of the conquest and looting of the East Indies, the turning of Africa into a warren for the commercial hunting of black skins, signalized the rosy dawn of the era of capitalist production.[17]

That was then. The centers of capital still want cheap raw materials and outlets for their surplus production, but force is not so necessary any more. Nor do rich-country capitalists stand to gain from an increase in global poverty. Quite the contrary. Poor people buy less than rich people. Capitalists like low wages, but they also like healthy workers and good consumers. Stark poverty is unattractive, even to capitalists. (It is no accident that the poorest poor countries attract only minuscule amounts of foreign direct investment apart from investment aimed at extracting their raw materials.) Nevertheless, the unintended effect of rational capitalist action is to increase global poverty rather than ameliorate it.

How capitalism can increase poverty is no mystery. In *Capital,* Marx notes the horrendous consequences to Indian textile workers that the opening of Indian markets to British textiles brought about. He quotes from the governor-general's report of 1834–1835: "The misery hardly finds parallel in the history of commerce. The bones of the cotton weavers are bleaching the plains of India."[18]

This scenario has been repeated countless times in poor countries: local agriculture and local industry wrecked by cheap imports. The technological advances nourished by capitalism that could, in theory, better the conditions of everyone without making anyone worse off, have, in practice, destroyed the livelihoods of millions, and torn apart the social fabric of vast regions.

God forbid that poor countries try to protect themselves! The British used their gunboats to bring the Chinese into line when they tried to block the importation of opium into their country—in the name of free trade, of course. (It should be noted that capitalism's first drug war, the Opium War of 1839–1842, was a war *in favor of* drugs.) Subsequently, the mechanisms became more subtle, but the goal has remained constant: keep all countries "open"—not necessarily to liberty or democracy, but certainly to Western capital and commodities.

Poor countries, most now firmly in the hands of pro-Western elites, go along, although now, with the income gap ever widening, they have become less important to global capitalism's dynamic. They continue to serve as a minor market for rich country production and as a source of cheap raw materials, but unemployed people in poor regions generate little effective demand, and so, apart from being a source of cheap labor (which now exists in near infinite abundance), most are of little interest to global capital. (For all the blather about "emerging markets," the vast majority of foreign direct investment goes to only a handful of countries, and these are far from the poorest.) In the coming decades, a few poor countries might make it into the ranks of the "middle-income" countries, but most will not. Most will sink even deeper into poverty, as cheap imports and new technologies render ever more workers superfluous. The younger ones, those who do not migrate to richer countries (younger males), will be ever more drawn into crime and internecine warfare, killing for crumbs and the brief thrill of violence. A few may decide to wreak a little havoc in rich countries—especially in the one that dominates all others.

Some of the world's superfluous poor will migrate to the advanced capitalist countries—large numbers, in fact. From the point of view of capital, this is a *good* thing: low-cost nannies and housekeepers, workers willing to work harder and for less than domestic workers, and a source of potent racial resentment to keep the working class divided. (Small wonder that the rich love the invisible hand. It acts so shrewdly on their behalf, while absolving them of all personal responsibility.)

The people left behind must go begging to international agencies that insist that their countries be made attractive to foreign capital. Their ruling elites comply, despite the fact that there will be few, if any, winners among these countries and lots of losers in this beggar-thy-neighbor game of fools. The elites know this, of course, but, so they say, "it's the only game in town."

The watchword becomes *suave qui peut*—every man for himself. The lucky among the elite will be able to siphon off a bit of that foreign capital for themselves. There are enclaves now in all of the world's capitals and other major cities where the poor-country rich can live a lifestyle not much different from their rich-country counterparts—and ignore the megaslums outside their walled and guarded compounds and the even more wretched countryside beyond. At least for now.

4.5 DEMOCRACY (LACK THEREOF)

The coexistence of political equality with material inequality has long been a conundrum of democratic theory. Plato thought, not unreasonably, that democracy would always degenerate, precisely because the demos (the people) would insist on redistributing the wealth, thus provoking a backlash, which would ultimately lead to tyranny.[19] All classical liberal philosophers during the rise of capitalism worried about the threat to property that an extension of democracy to the propertyless masses would entail. (Even so decent and progressive a thinker as John Stuart Mill proposed to give multiple votes to property holders to counterbalance the excessive influence of the propertyless.)[20] Why has this threat not materialized? How has it come to pass that political democracy now seems to be the natural concomitant of capitalism rather than its antithesis?

In its starkest form, the answer is simply this: capitalism is *not* compatible with democracy. What passes for democracy in advanced industrial societies is something else.

Some years ago, Yale political scientists Robert Dahl and Charles Lindblom proposed to distinguish between democracy and polyarchy.[21] A polyarchy is a system in which a broad-based electorate selects political leaders from competing candidates in elections that are reasonably honest. In Dahl's words, a polyarchy is a political order in which "citizenship is extended to a relatively high proportion of adults, and the rights of citizenship include the opportunity to oppose and vote out the highest officials of government."[22]

All the advanced industrial societies of the world are now polyarchies, and so are most other countries. Polyarchy (if not democracy) has spread rapidly throughout the world during the last two decades. Not only have the communist regimes of Eastern Europe and the Soviet Union crumbled but so have the military dictatorships of Latin America and racist rule in southern Africa.

Polyarchy is not a bad thing. It is better than tyranny. But polyarchy is not democracy. Following Dahl and Lindblom, let us keep "democracy" close to its etymological meaning, "rule by the people." Let us define democracy to be a system in which

- Suffrage is universal among adults.
- The electorate is "sovereign."

An electorate is "sovereign" if

- Its members are reasonably well informed about the issues to be decided by the political process and reasonably active in contributing to their resolution.
- There exists no stable minority class that is "privileged."

A class is "privileged" (this is the key concept) if

- It possesses political power at least equal to that of elected officials and unmatched by any other stable grouping.

In short, democracy is a system in which a universal electorate is reasonably well informed and active, and unobstructed by a privileged minority class.

I contend that the capitalist class in a capitalist society is a privileged minority class. It is a "stable minority class that possesses political power at least equal to that of elected officials and unmatched by any other stable grouping." Hence, we do not live in a democracy.

It is not fashionable to talk about class these days, certainly not about a "capitalist" class, but such a class exists. Author Gore Vidal, born into this class and thus well positioned to know, puts it this way:

> That is the genius of our ruling class. They're so brilliant that no one knows they even exist. The political science professors, perfectly sane men, look at me with wonder when I talk about the ruling class in America. They say, "You are one of those conspiracy theorists. You think there's a headquarters and they get together at the Bohemian Grove and run the United States." Well, they *do* get together at the Bohemian Grove and they do a lot of picking of Secretaries of State. But they don't *have* to conspire. They all think alike. It goes back to the way we're raised, the schools we went to. You don't have to give orders to the editor of *The New York Times*. He is in place because he will respond to a crisis the way you want him to, as will the President, as will the head of Chase Manhattan Bank.[23]

Vidal marks out the "ruling class" as the top 1 percent of society. This upper 1 percent is roughly the number of people comprising what we have defined as the "capitalist class"—namely, people who own enough productive assets that they can, if they so choose, live comfortably on the income generated from these assets. The wealth cut-off for the upper 1 percent is roughly $2 million, which would generate an annual income of about $100,000.

Is this class truly "privileged," in the technical sense of possessing power at least equal to that of all elected officials? If the capitalist class is a ruling class, how does this ruling class rule? Vidal says they all think alike. This may be too simple, and in any event, we need to know more. How are capitalist attitudes translated into public policy? What are the mechanisms by which a small and nearly invisible class in a "democratic" society exercises decisive power?

Some of these mechanisms are obvious, some less so. The most obvious, at least in the United States, is the provision of campaign contributions. Election campaigns have become exceedingly sophisticated in their techniques, utilizing focus groups and polling data to see what hot-button issues to push, selective mailings combined with television saturation to get one's carefully tailored "message" across. These campaigns are enormously expensive. (The average winning candidate for a House seat spent $816,000 in 2000; the average winning senator spent $7 million. Even local races require an astonishing amount of fundraising. One candidate for the Illinois House raised over $650,000 in 2000. A candidate for the Illinois Supreme Court raised $737,000.)[24] Hence, wealthy "contributors" must be courted and wooed. That is to say, they must be assured that their interests will be looked after. Of course, it is theoretically possible to raise large sums from small contributions, but consider: to raise $7 million, you would have to persuade 350,000 fellow-citizens to give you $20—or 350 to give you $20,000. Given that there are a million households for whom $20,000 is small change—the top 1 percent who owns nearly half the country's wealth—it is hardly surprising that rational politicians fish mostly in the pond with the big fish.

I hardly need to belabor the point that big money influences politics, since the evidence is all around us. Here's a typical example:

> In February, with customer complaints about air travel at an all-time high, the Senate Commerce Committee chairman John McCain, Republican of Arizona, took off on a passenger rights crusade. He filed an Airlines Passenger Fairness Act to force airlines to clean up their acts, then held dramatic hearings to spotlight tales of marooned, bumped and otherwise mistreated travelers. . . . In June, though, after the airline industry announced a voluntary plan to improve customer service—*and directed a hasty infusion of "soft money" donations to both parties*—the issue seemed to disappear. Mr. McCain replaced his bill with a much weaker version that simply encourages the airlines to follow their own plans, and his committee overwhelmingly approved the substitute.
>
> "We were stunned," said Peter Hudson, director of the Aviation Consumer Action Project. "This wasn't just a sweetheart deal; it was a giveaway."
>
> The week before the committee vote, the airline industry shelled out $226,000 in soft money. . . . In the first six months of this year, the airlines spent more than $1.3 million on political donations.[25]

It should not be supposed that individual contributors of large sums always get their way. All wealthy contributors want their interests protected, but these interests are not always harmonious. Wealthy contributors will have divergent feelings about many of the issues that come within the purview of elected officials, issues specific to narrow economic interest, but also issues of broad social significance. (They don't all think *exactly* alike.) So there is room within capitalism for genuine electoral competition—hence, polyarchy. Nevertheless, none of these big contributors, virtually without exception, will favor policies that might erode the basic structures by which they maintain their wealth, namely, the basic institutions of capitalism itself.

Effective control of campaign financing is not in itself sufficient to maintain class rule. In a capitalist polyarchy, where it is theoretically possible for a political party to challenge the basic institutions of the system, it is important that the interests of the capitalist class be well formulated and buttressed by argument and data that will make it appear that these interests coincide with the general interest. Among the most important means to this end are the large numbers of "private" (i.e., capitalist-funded) foundations, ranging from "liberal," that is, moderately conservative (e.g., Ford, Rockefeller, Carnegie) to rabidly right wing (e.g., Bradley, Schiafe, Olin). These foundations, in turn, fund various think tanks and roundtables, ranging from the moderately conservative Brookings Institute, Rand Corporation, and the Council on Foreign Relations to such right-wing bastions as the Hoover Institute, Cato Institute, and American Enterprise Institute. These institutes undertake policy research, draw up model legislation, bring together representatives from the business community, government officials, respectable (i.e., nonradical) academics, and members of influential media to debate, discuss, and refine such proposals. These institutes also provide a steady supply of reliable "experts" to testify before Congress and to appear on mass media news programs.

The major foundations have enormous quantities of assets under their control. To point to just the tip of the iceberg: the National Committee for Responsible Philanthropy has reported that between 1992 and 1994, twelve major right-wing foundations, with assets totaling $1.1 billion, gave some $210 million to promote conservative policy groups and educational efforts.[26] By way of contrast, during that period, the one national weekly news magazine still identifying itself a socialist, the highly respected *In These Times*, nearly went bankrupt, due to an outstanding debt of $100,000—one-tenth of 1 percent of what the top right-wing foundations devote to their causes each year. (*In These Times* did in fact survive, but it no longer calls itself socialist.)

Not only must class interests be well formulated but they must also be disseminated to the general public. Hence the importance of the major media—virtually all of which are privately owned, that is to say, controlled by the class that controls most the other productive assets of society. These media, moreover, depend for their own economic survival on advertising revenues, hence, on the good will of their corporate sponsors. In the United States, even "public" radio and "public" television are heavily dependent on corporate sponsorship, for which the producers "publicly" (i.e., after every broadcast) express their gratitude.[27]

Thus, it should come as no surprise that not a single major newspaper or television station in the United States features a regular commentator that will voice anticapitalist sentiments in a principled, consistent manner. Once in a while, if you pay close attention, you will encounter a Noam Chomsky or an Alexander Cockburn, but these are rare exceptions—and even these play a role in shoring up the dominant ideology. An occasional critical voice serves to "inoculate" the public, allowing us the illusion that all serious views are fairly represented. These dissenting views are sometimes challenged by the "respectable" experts and commentators that dominate news programming, but more often they are simply ignored. (I do not mean to suggest that leftist thinkers should avoid the mass media. On the contrary, a leftist presence will be crucial if we are to move beyond capitalism. The fact remains, however, when progressive forces are weak, such voices, while keeping hope alive in some quarters, also strengthen capitalism's immune system.)

Apart from these mechanisms—which ensure that the interests of capital will be well protected by elected officials—the capitalist class possesses another powerful weapon, perhaps the *most* powerful in its impressive arsenal, that can be brought into play should a government be elected that proposes policies deemed inimical to their interests. (With the possible exception of Franklin Delano Roosevelt—who was not *in fact* hostile to capitalism—this has never happened in the United States, although it has happened elsewhere.) Capitalists can engage in an "investment strike." This is a particularly formidable weapon, since it requires no planning or coordination to implement. Indeed, it will come into play automatically if a government should come to power deemed unfriendly to "business interests."

The mechanism is simple enough. Capitalism relies on the savings of the upper classes for a large portion of its investment. Since these funds are private funds, they may be disposed of in any manner their owners see fit. Now more than ever, investors have many options. They can invest in their own country, or they can invest elsewhere. They can play the Nikkei Stock Exchange or speculate in Latin American currencies. They can do whatever they want with their funds in this "free and open" world, for these funds are *their* money. So, if significant numbers of investors lose confidence in a government, they, not unreasonably, will move their funds abroad. This lack of confidence thus becomes a self-fulfilling prophesy, for the usual Keynesian reasons. When investors fail to invest, effective demand falls, layoffs ensue, demand declines further, triggering further cutbacks—the familiar downward spiral that constitutes a recession.

We know what happens next. In a polyarchic government, leaders are held responsible for the economic well-being of the nation. During bad times, every oppositional candidate proclaims some form of the same slogan, "It's the economy, stupid!" Since the point of polyarchy is to allow the electorate to remove officials who are not thought to be performing appropriately, governing politicians unloved by the business community will be removed—and those problematic programs will be reversed.

Clearly, as long as investment decisions remain in private hands, governments that want to survive—which is to say, *all* governments—have little choice but to cater to the sensibilities of the capitalist class.

The problem goes even deeper. It is not only elected officials whose self-interest is structurally bound to the interests of this class. So too are the interests of practically everyone else. When an economy slumps, private sector workers are laid off. Tax revenues decline, so public sector workers are also squeezed, as are people on welfare, whose benefits now seem too expensive.

We can see now why governments under capitalism will never attempt serious income redistribution, no matter how attractive the proposals might seem. To give an example: Andrew Hacker calculated that if a $200,000 cap were put on incomes in the United States and the excess redistributed to the bottom 20 percent of the population, this would allow some twenty million households to benefit substantially, their average income nearly doubling, while only one million would be made worse off.[28] At first glance, such a scheme might appear attractive to a sovereign electorate. Twenty percent of our poorest citizens would benefit, while only 1 percent would be made worse off—and even they would still be making five times the median income. Ninety-nine percent of us would be no worse off than before, and the poorest among us would benefit significantly. Why doesn't a political party, perhaps a new one, pick up on this issue and run with it—the capitalist class's nightmare scenario?

The answer should now be obvious. Almost everyone would soon realize, since the message would be loudly proclaimed by every political commentator in the country, that the middle 79 percent of us would *not* be unaffected. It would be pointed out, correctly, that any such radical redistribution attempt would provoke massive capital flight. We would get, not a more egalitarian prosperity, but a Great Depression.

So we see, a capitalist economy is ingeniously structured. Almost everyone has an interest in maintaining the spirits of its ruling class. This is one of the features that give capitalism its remarkable resiliency. *So long as the basic institutions of capitalism remain in place*, it is in the rational self-interest of almost everyone to keep the capitalists happy.

Of course, in a true democracy, the electorate could alter these basic institutions. They could, if they so chose, opt for a different system. Since the ways in which the interests of capital diverge from those of the great majority are not so hard to grasp, a sovereign electorate probably *would* want to try something else—which is why capitalism will tolerate polyarchy but not democracy. (Capitalist societies tend to be "tolerant" societies—unless the basic institutions of capitalism are threatened. Then the gloves come off, and we get death squads, military coups, and fascism. At least, that has been the historical record to date.)

4.5.1 A Note on Anticommunism

Looking back over the twentieth century, we cannot fail to notice how deeply the ideology of anticommunism shaped Western foreign policy. From the beginning, communism has triggered hostile passions among the upper classes. Long before the Russian Revolution, long before the Soviet Union had any sort of serious military capability, fear of communism was promoted by the dominant political, educational, economic, and religious institutions of society. Communism came to be hated with far greater intensity than fascism or Nazism or any other sort of nondemocratic rule. Indeed, the polyarchical Western powers not only did *not* intervene when democratic institutions disappeared in Italy, Germany, and Spain during the interwar years but were also quite "tolerant" of the new governments. After all, Mussolini's Italy, Hitler's Germany, and Franco's Spain were all vehemently and murderously anticommunist.

But *why* has capitalism been so profoundly opposed to communism, while tolerating all other kinds of repressive antidemocratic regimes? At first sight, the answer would seem to be straightforwardly economic: capitalism needs access to cheap raw materials, foreign markets, and cheap labor. Communism denies them all that. The problem with this answer, so plausible on the surface, is that communism has *not* denied capitalist corporations these things. Communist regimes have always wanted to trade with the West and have often been eager for foreign investment. It is the West, led by the United States, that has imposed trade sanctions, embargoes, and blockades.[29]

It is true that capitalist enterprises, when allowed to operate in communist countries, have been more closely regulated than they would doubtless have preferred, but foreign corporations have been tightly regulated in other capitalist countries as well (in Japan, for example) without provoking a hostile response, let alone a cold war that a slight miscalculation could have turned annihilatorily hot.

In my judgment, the real motivation behind anticommunism runs deeper. It's the profound worry on the part of the capitalist class that the communists could in fact be *right*: that capitalism is not the end of history, that there is a brighter future beyond capitalism, and that sooner or later their own workers (i.e., the vast majority of their fellow citizens) will come to realize this and take appropriate action. Recall the dominant metaphor. Communism is a *disease*. It spreads. Infected countries must be quarantined. No country is safe from the deadly germ, no matter how healthy and prosperous. It must be mercilessly fought at home and abroad.

Which it has been. To grasp the magnitude of this relentless war, try to imagine what the history of the twentieth century might have been like had Western foreign policy been guided by the ideals of democracy instead of anticommunism. To confine ourselves only to the most important player, let us suppose that the United States had been truly committed to democracy. Then:

- It would not have sent troops into Russia in 1918 to oppose that revolution.

- It would not have looked so kindly on Mussolini's seizure of power in Italy, or supported so readily a policy of "economic appeasement" of Hitler.
- It would not have endorsed the coming to power in the 1930s of the patriarchal dictatorships in Central America and the Caribbean (Hernandez Martinez in El Salvador, Somoza in Nicaragua, Ubico in Guatemala, Carias in Honduras, Trujillo in the Dominican Republic, Batista in Cuba).
- It might have aided Republican Spain in its fight against Franco's antidemocratic revolt (which was supported materially and with personnel by both Hitler and Mussolini).
- It would not have supported the brutal, corrupt rule of Chiang Kai-shek in China, supplying his government with some $6 billion in aid during its civil war with a Communist insurgency that eventually triumphed.
- It would not have supported the efforts of the French to regain control over Indochina after World War II.
- It would not have insisted on partitioning Korea after World War II, or supported the installation of a brutal right-wing dictatorship in the South (and hence would have avoided the Korean War).
- It would not have engineered the overthrow of the Iranian government and the installation of the shah in 1953 (and hence would not be regarded today as the Great Satan by the government that drove the shah from power a quarter of a century later).
- It would not have orchestrated the destruction of democracy in Guatemala in 1954, nor encouraged the spread of military rule (with death squad supplements) there and elsewhere in Central America.
- It would have recognized the right of the Cambodian, Laotian, and Vietnamese people to choose their own future, and hence avoided the war that claimed some fifty thousand American lives and as many as four million Indochinese.
- It would not have opposed until the very last moment the black liberation struggles in southern Africa.
- It would not have looked the other way (to put the best face on the matter) when the Indonesian military seized power in 1965 and massacred a million "communists."
- It would not have aided and abetted the establishment of military rule of monumental savagery throughout most of Latin America in the 1960s and 1970s, among other places in Chile, where it deliberately undermined Latin America's most deeply established democracy.
- It would not have embraced the Marcos dictatorship in the Philippines from its onset in 1972 until its next-to-the-last moment in 1986.
- It would not have bankrolled murderous armed struggles against the popular governments that came to power in the 1970s after overthrow-

ing a hated dictator or a colonial power in Angola, Mozambique, and Nicaragua.

- It would not have given the green light to our trusted anticommunist ally, General Suharto of Indonesia, to invade newly independent East Timor and begin a reign of terror that has claimed the lives of a third of the population.
- It would not have worked ceaselessly, to this very day, to destroy the one society in Latin America that has eliminated starvation and homelessness, namely "communist" Cuba.

This is by no means an exhaustive list. The United States has backed many more antidemocratic regimes than enumerated here. Nor has the United States stood alone in its anticommunist crusade. Most of the major European countries have backed most of these policies. Body-count comparisons have an obscene feel about them, but still it should be noted: the wars, coups, killings, terror, and torture that have been justified in the name of anticommunism have destroyed at least as many people as did Hitler or Stalin.

It didn't have to be that way. Had we been a democracy and not merely a polyarchy, it would not have been.

4.6 ENVIRONMENTAL DEGRADATION

Marx has remarked that humanity never sets itself problems until the material conditions are at hand for their resolution.[30] Could this strikingly optimistic assertion be true? It *is* true that we have pulled back from the brink of nuclear holocaust. At the point when it became possible for us to put a quick end to our species, we grabbed the emergency brake, proving false (at least for now) the age-old adage that new weapons are always used. (Lest historical amnesia allow us to think that it was the collapse of communism that saved us, we should remember that it was the huge popular movement for nuclear disarmament coupled with Mikhail Gorbachev's remarkable proposal to eliminate all nuclear weapons by the year 2000, both occurring in the early 1980s, that called decisively into question the ever-more-dangerous arms race. It now appears that the collapse of the Soviet Union has slowed rather than hastened the disarmament process. Had Gorbachev remained in power and the Clinton administration responded appropriately, we might now be living in a world largely free of nuclear weapons.)

We have pulled back from nuclear destruction, but there is another time bomb ticking. Concern for our natural environment has developed rapidly over the past several decades. We are now more than ever conscious of the threats posed to the natural infrastructure of the planet by our current ways of living. This concern has mobilized millions of people around the globe, and has freed up funds for large-scale scientific investigations of almost all aspects of the various dangers we now face.

Marx may again be proven right. These researches have borne fruit—at least at the level of knowledge. The fact of the matter is, we know enough now to deal with the problems that are upon us. We know both the proximate behaviors and deep structures that are intensifying ecological stress, and we can see clearly what changes need to be made if we are going to preserve our planet in its basic integrity. This is the good news. The bad news is, our knowledge will not be put into effective practice so long as capitalism remains dominant.

Let's first look at the good news: our basic problems have solutions.

4.6.1 Overpopulation

The world had 1.6 billion human inhabitants when the twentieth century began. It has six billion today. Most of the increase, 3.5 of the 4.4 billion, has occurred since 1950. If present trends continue, there will be twelve billion humans on earth by 2050 and twenty-four billion by the end of twenty-first century. Of course, present trends will not continue because they cannot continue. The question is, *how* will these trends be reversed—by warfare, famine and disease, or by our acting reasonably and humanely?

Clearly, population growth is not an uncheckable biological phenomenon. The populations of the industrialized nations, apart from immigration, are flat or declining. We have the technical means to limit population increase. Why are these means ineffective in large parts of the world? Why do people living in poverty produce so many children? The answer is straightforward: among the poor, especially in poor countries, children constitute an economic resource for their parents. They are an important source of income even when they are young, and they provide a measure of social security for their parents when the parents get old. Moreover, given the high infant mortality rates in most poor countries, a woman must have many children to ensure that enough survive. Of course, other factors interact with these purely economic considerations—lack of education, lack of access to means of family planning, and above all, male dominance. (Men and women both share in the economic gains from having children, but men tend to gain disproportionately, whereas the costs are borne overwhelmingly by women.) Poverty exacerbates all these conditions. It can be safely said that poverty is the root cause of the population problem.

The distinction drawn earlier in this chapter between being poor and living in poverty has relevance here. A country does not have to be rich to satisfy the conditions for population stability, at least not "rich" as measured by GDP per capita. To cite the best-known example: China has a per capita GDP of about one-tenth that of the United States; its fertility rate has dropped *below* that of the United States. Or to cite a case that hasn't involved coercive measures: Cuba's rate of population increase is identical to that of the United States, although its per capita income is even less than China's. The Indian state of Kerala might also be cited. In Kerala, social programs have given the citizens of one of the poorest states of India near–First World rates of literacy, infant mortality, and life expectancy, and a rate of population increase only slightly above that of the United States (and falling faster).[31] A country can be poor and have population stability—but not if the majority of its people live in poverty.

Poverty need not persist. As we have seen, it wouldn't take much in terms of basic resources to eliminate it. The fact is—and this is an important fact—the steps that need to be taken to enable all the citizens of a country, men and women alike, to have an education, basic health care, and significant economic security are not particularly expensive. Both education and public health, for example, are labor-intensive services—and there is no shortage of labor in poor countries. As China, Cuba, and Kerala have all demonstrated, the population problem is not intractable.

4.6.2 Food Scarcity

If people aren't the problem, perhaps resource shortages are. The most serious potential resource shortage is the most basic: will we run out of food? Although agricultural productivity has increased greatly since the 1950s, faster than population growth, these gains have slowed considerably during the last decade. Moreover, large amounts of cropland are giving way to urban development and even more is being degraded by overuse. It would seem that global food production is approaching capacity.[32]

The global food supply can still be increased, but it seems clear that the fundamental solution to the food question must come from the demand side of the equation—the quantity and composition of the food consumed. What kinds of food are produced, in what quantities, and for whom will be determined by distribution of effective demand within countries and by the structures that regulate international trade.

It is an important and hopeful fact that at present, on the supply side, there is no food problem at all. Even the neoliberal *Economist* concedes that "if all the world's grain were distributed evenly, there would be more than enough for everyone's needs."[33] Lester Brown offers some numbers:

The average American requires 800 kilograms of grain a year, the vast bulk of it consumed indirectly in the form of beef, pork, poultry, eggs, milk, cheese, yogurt and ice cream. The average Indian, in contrast, gets by with about 200 kilograms of grain a year, almost all of it consumed directly. . . . With a diet of 400 kilograms of grain per person, roughly what the Italians eat each year, 2 billion tons of grain per year [a plausible increase from the 1996 harvest of 1.82 billion tons] would support 5 billion people.[34]

So we see, the malnourished need not always be with us. Current resources exist to feed everyone at a level only slightly less than the average Italian. But only if current consumption and distribution patterns are radically altered and population growth is checked. Once again, we see what needs to be done. We needn't pin our hopes on new technologies (although some of these might help). There is enough to go around—but we have to make it go around.

4.6.3 Pollution

It might well be argued that the most serious environmental threat to our future comes not from what we consume, but from what we *don't* consume—the effluents we discharge daily into our rivers, seas, ground waters, and atmosphere. It is clearly within our reach to bring our population growth to a halt, and there is clearly enough food available for everyone to eat. But is the regenerative capacity of our planet sufficient to handle the unwanted by-products of our overall production and consumption?

Let us consider two specific cases involving atmospheric pollution. The general lesson to be drawn will apply to other forms of pollution as well.

First, a success story: In 1987, the Montreal Protocol on Substances That Deplete the Ozone Layer went into effect, having been negotiated by representatives of countries rich and poor, East and West. It was signed on the spot by twenty-four countries and the European Community. It has since been ratified by some 150 nations. The protocol calls for strict restrictions on the production and use of chemicals that damage the ozone layer, principally chlorofluorocarbons.[35] These restrictions have been obeyed, and the results have been impressive. By 1995, production of ozone-depleting chemicals was down 76 percent from its 1988 peak. Recent scientific estimates suggest that if all countries comply with the Montreal Protocol, the ozone shield will begin to heal, and might fully recover by the middle of this century.

Given the complexities of the factors involved, we cannot be certain that the ozone layer problem has been definitively solved, but the success of the Montreal Protocol is surely a life-affirming event. At least with respect to one ecological disaster, our species seems to have again confirmed Marx's optimistic assessment.

Can such a success be repeated with respect to the other major global atmospheric problem, the carbon dioxide emissions that are causing the "greenhouse effect," and hence global warming? In 1992, a Framework Convention on Climate Change was established at the Earth Summit in Rio de Janeiro (and signed there by, among others, then-President George Bush). In

1997, the United States and 100 other countries signed the Kyoto Protocol, requiring the industrialized nations—which are overwhelmingly responsible for existing carbon dioxide levels—to reduce their emissions of greenhouse gases 5 to 7 percent below 1990 levels by 2012.

How is this to be done? In two ways—by increasing energy efficiency, so that less overall energy is required, and by shifting from high-carbon energy sources to low-carbon or no-carbon sources. How do we motivate producers and consumers to make these changes? The basic, multipart answer is clear enough:

- Stop subsidizing coal and oil production (globally, fossil fuel subsidies currently run to more than $120 billion a year).[36]
- Set strict emission limits for automobiles, power plants, and other heavy polluters.
- Impose a stiff carbon tax on all fossil fuels (to provide financial incentives for cutting back high-carbon usage).
- Use some of these funds to subsidize research and development of cleaner technologies.

Can the Kyoto targets be met? It would seem so—if the effort is made. Germany and Great Britain are close to their targets. In fact, we can do even better than that. A sustainable world economy based solely on renewable, non–carbon-based energy would seem not beyond our reach. Bent Sørensen, at the University of Roskilde, has put together scenarios for achieving this happy state by 2050. As Seth Dunn of the Worldwatch Institute reports,

> The Roskilde study concludes that a combination of dispersed and more centralized applications—placing solar PVs and fuel cells in buildings and vehicles, and wind turbines adjacent to buildings and on farmland, plus a number of larger solar arrays, offshore wind parks, hydro installations—would create a "robust" system capable of meeting the world's entire energy demand.[37]

4.6.4 Optimism, Pessimism, Growth, Development

Unfortunately, this optimistic projection now seems unlikely. As most readers know, George W. Bush, son of the president who signed the Rio Convention, reneged on his campaign pledge and withdrew from the Kyoto agreement. Since the United States is by far the largest producer of greenhouse gases (more than a quarter of the world's total), its withdrawal has probably killed this crucial global-warming protocol. (Less than a year earlier, the Russian icebreaker *Yamal* discovered an expanse of open, calm water at the North Pole, the first such occurrence, scientists estimate, in fifty million years—yet more evidence for the near-consensus that global-warming is real.)[38]

Why did the United States pull back from the protocol signed with much fanfare by then–Vice-President Al Gore in 1997? It would be a mistake to think that this is a mere partisan disagreement. The obstacles to a global warming agreement are vastly more formidable than those to an ozone treaty. The Montreal Protocol should not lull us into thinking that capitalism can readily accommodate all sensible environmental solutions. The phasing out of chlorofluorocarbons has been relatively costless to the companies that produced them. The major chemical companies did not oppose the treaty, since chemical substitutes were available or at least on their drawing boards. In 1988, DuPont Chemicals announced that it was phasing out its $600 million chlorofluorocarbon business altogether to concentrate on developing and marketing alternatives, which it has successfully done.

Any attempt to radically reduce carbon emissions will encounter far stiffer resistance, as recent events have demonstrated. Some of the world's most powerful industries, oil and automobile among them, are massively implicated in the problem, and they are prepared to fight. (In 1998, under the headline, "Industrial Group Plans to Battle Climate Treaty," the *New York Times* reported on the multimillion-dollar effort then underway. The effort was successful. Kyoto is, for all intents and purposes, now dead.[39]) There are cleaner ways of generating energy than burning oil, and cleaner ways of transporting people than relying on private automobiles, but it is hard to envisage the transition to these cleaner modes that preserves the status and incomes of these giant industries.

The problem goes deeper than just corporate resistance. The phasing out of chlorofluorocarbons had no direct impact on consumption habits. A transition away from carbon-based energy most certainly would. Whatever good things might be said about bicycles, buses, trams, and trains, it is more convenient to have your own car—particularly on a rainy day, particularly if you have children, particularly if the nearest bus stop is a long walk away.

An additional complication: not only must people in rich countries cut their oil-based energy consumption drastically, but people of poor countries must be induced not to imitate the consumption habits of rich countries—no easy task, particularly since so many in poor countries are being encouraged to do just that. Given the titillating images of rich-country life and the relentless propagandizing on behalf of consumption that now constitute the essence of mass media everywhere, Austrian journalists Hans-Peter Martin and Harald Schumann are probably not wrong when they write:

> If the nearly six billion inhabitants of the planet could really decide by referendum how they want to live, there would be an overwhelming majority for the kind of middle-class existence lived in a suburb of San Francisco. A qualified,

informed minority would opt in addition for the social standards of the Federal Republic of Germany before the Wall came down. The luxury combination of a Caribbean villa with Swedish welfare protection would be the dream to end all dreams.[40]

This is an impossible dream—and a dangerous one. In Martin and Schumann's apt phrase, "everything is everywhere"—but most of "everything" is tantalizingly, maddeningly out of reach of most members of our species, and must forever remain so. Our planet cannot sustain universal consumption at that level.

Can we really imagine solving all or even most of our environmental problems? It would seem that although we may know how to solve environmental problems taken one at a time, we cannot possibly solve them altogether, since they are interrelated in contradictory ways. To solve the population problem, we must eliminate global poverty. But if we eliminate global poverty, then people will consume even more than they do now, thus intensifying both the food problem and the carbon emission problem. If we try to reduce the energy consumption by imposing energy taxes, then higher food and energy prices will make the problems of poverty worse. If we try to redistribute food and energy by means of some sort of rationing scheme . . . well, who would (or could) draw up a coherent plan? How would it be administered? How would it be enforced? (The United States, for example, contains 5 percent of the world's population, but generates 25 percent of the world's carbon emissions. Is the United States going to be told that it will henceforth be allowed to consume one-fifth of the oil it now uses? Who will do the telling? Who can force compliance?)

In fact, it *is* possible to envisage feasible comprehensive solutions to global ecological problems, provided we think in dynamic, developmental terms, rather than static, redistributionist terms. This is not to say that we can *grow* our way out of our problems. Economic growth is *not* the answer. We must distinguish between "growth" and "development." "Growth" means growth in consumption as measured by standard GDP. By "development," let us mean rational movement over time toward a sustainable future.

To understand "development," we must understand "overdevelopment." Herman Daly, one of the leading theoreticians of environmental economics, offers a concise definition: "An overdeveloped country is one whose level of per capita resource consumption is such that if generalized to all countries could not be sustained indefinitely."[41] Looking at carbon emissions, for example, and assuming the amount of carbon dioxide released globally into the atmosphere is now at or beyond what is sustainable, we see that the United States is producing *five times* its sustainable share. Since carbon emissions tend to correlate with general levels of consumption, the United States can be said to be overdeveloped by a factor of five. China, by way of contrast, although the second-largest producer of carbon emissions after the United States, is generating less than two-thirds of its per capita share; India is generating a quarter of its share.[42]

We can now identify the two basic causal factors at work in undermining our environmental security: *overdevelopment* and *poverty*. Some countries are consuming more than their sustainable share of the world's nonreplaceable resources and are contributing more than their sustainable share of pollution. Such economies need to contract, not expand. (Of course, it is theoretically possible for a country's overall GDP to grow while its consumption of nonrenewable resources and its contribution to global pollution declines. However, given the sheer magnitude of contemporary overdevelopment, it is wishful thinking bordering on self-delusion to suppose that materials substitution and cleaner technologies will allow rich countries to continue, and even increase, their current levels of consumption while the poorer countries catch up.)[43]

If we think in terms of rational development, it is clear that the primary environmental-developmental goal of overdeveloped countries should be to bring down their levels of material consumption so that they use no more than their sustainable share of resources and contribute no more than their sustainable share to global pollution. Most underdeveloped countries (those consuming and polluting at less than their sustainable share) must confront mass poverty as their basic problem, and must have alleviating that poverty as their fundamental environmental-developmental goal. These economies do indeed need to grow, although in a manner more respectful of the environment than rich countries have grown, and with the aim of achieving sustainable, not overdeveloped, levels of consumption.

It is evident that we need an array of national development plans. One size does not fit all. Countries that are overdeveloped must devise green taxes and other restrictions to bring their pollution and resource consumption down to sustainable levels. A significant quantity of the society's investment must be allocated for the transition. Overdeveloped societies are "addicted" to overconsumption. Withdrawal will not be easy.

This is not to say that the consumption changes necessary for sustainability must bring down the quality of life in overdeveloped countries. Indeed, if the transition is properly managed, the quality of life—and the level of human happiness in such societies—can be markedly improved. Addiction does not, in general, contribute to overall well-being, however difficult it is to break.

For poor countries, the developmental priority should be to eliminate poverty, but this "poverty" should not be understood solely, or even primarily, in terms of national income. As already noted, the provision of universal education and basic public health care are labor-intensive services that are not terribly expensive. To eliminate poverty, poor countries needn't depend much on external aid (as the examples of China and Cuba make clear). For sustainable development, some assistance from rich countries should be expected (and indeed, elementary justice would demand it), but in truth material aid is not what is most needed for long-term development. What poor countries need from rich countries, above all else, is genuine autonomy and freedom from exploitation (i.e., debt relief), control over locally based foreign enterprises, and higher prices for raw materials and other products exported to rich countries. Beyond that—not much else. (More on this in the next chapter.)

4.6.5 Why Capitalism Can't Save Us

If we know how to solve our basic environmental problems, why don't we set about seriously to do so? The answer is straightforward. The fundamental environmental problems cannot be resolved under global capitalism.

At first glance, this claim may seem implausible. After all, thanks to the efforts of determined environmental activists in virtually every advanced capitalist country, air quality is better now than it was two decades ago, and rivers and lakes are cleaner. Environmental protection laws have been passed and "green" taxes imposed in many countries—so that, for example, the per capita carbon emissions in Germany are now only half those of the United States; those of Japan are even less. Is it really so unreasonable to imagine a future in which similar restrictions and taxes are applied the world over, thus stimulating the introduction of ecology-friendly technologies worldwide? If such taxes and restrictions are compatible with capitalism in Western Europe or Japan, why shouldn't they be compatible with global capitalism?

It won't do to say that the fundamental problem is the market. To be sure, unregulated market prices do not reflect true costs. This fact is universally accepted, even among the most neoclassical of economists. When a market transaction imposes costs on parties other than those engaged in the exchange (pollution being the paradigmatic example), the price that brings supply and demand into equilibrium will be lower than it should be. The price should be higher, high enough to fully compensate the affected third parties. Thus, green taxes should be imposed on commodities and production processes that have negative environmental effects. These taxes, which can be varied to account for differential impact, discourage the production and consumption of ecologically damaging products and, at the same time, generate funds for health compensation and clean up. They also motivate the development of cleaner technologies and more ecologically friendly consumption substitutes.

Such price regulation is fully compatible with capitalism. Indeed, it is mandated by standard neoclassical theory as well as by common sense. Certainly, it is difficult to put a price tag on pollution or to the loss to future generations of certain irreplaceable natural resources, but such calculations will have to be made in *any* society, market or nonmarket, that aims at ecological sustainability. Any such society will have to devise a mixture of qualitative restrictions, quantitative restrictions, and pricing policies to bring production costs and benefits into sustainable balance.

If income inequalities in society are equitable and if commodity prices are adjusted by a suitable system of green taxes, then using the market to allocate resources will not be environmentally problematic. Of course, if income inequalities are all out of proportion to what is necessary for efficient production—as is the case under capitalism—then the market allocation of resources will not be optimal. But capitalism's use of the market for allocating goods and services is not the fundamental structural feature that pushes it to transgress ecological limits. To concentrate on market failure is to miss the real story.

There are three features of capitalism which, taken together, give the system its ecologically destructive dynamic, each of which we have encountered before in different contexts:

- Capitalism's expansionary dynamic
- Its peculiar crisis tendency deriving from its basis in wage labor
- The unrestrained mobility of its defining element, "capital"

Let me tell the story a little more fully than before, connecting it to the environmental problematic. Capitalism is enormously productive. Every year, enormous quantities of commodities are produced that, when sold at anticipated prices, generate enormous profits, a large fraction of which are reinvested back into the economy in anticipation of still greater production and still more profits. Every enterprise within a capitalist system is under competitive pressure to behave in exactly this fashion: to produce, make a profit, reinvest, and grow.

The ever-present danger to system stability is deficient demand. When supply outstrips demand, the economy falters. If goods can't be sold, production is cut back, workers are laid off, and demand declines further. A contracting economy, as we know, is bad all around. Businesses go bankrupt, unemployment rises, and tax revenues fall off. Economic growth is in the immediate interest of virtually every sector of society—growth in the straightforward sense as measured by GDP. Whether or not such growth makes people happier or enhances the overall quality of life is quite beside the point.

Under capitalism, you get either growth or recession, and nobody wants a recession. How is this growth to be achieved? Two parallel strategies develop: on the one hand, the stimulation of domestic demand via easy credit and an ever-more-sophisticated sales apparatus; and, on the other hand, an ever-increasing orientation toward production for export. The strategies soon come together, since exports must be sold. Where demand does not exist, it must be created. So the sales apparatus of modern capitalism, honed to near perfection in the domestic market, is unleashed abroad. The culture of consumption spreads throughout the world.

But enterprises in the core capitalist countries are not content to merely sell abroad; they also want to produce abroad. New opportunities thus arise for capitalists and entrepreneurs in poor countries to join forces with the transnational elites of the advanced capitalist countries. Barriers to capital flows are removed. Labor-intensive manufacturing blossoms in (some) poor countries, with production aimed at rich-country markets.

The race is now on. Every poor country now strives to become rich, rich through the mechanism of export-led growth, rich in precisely the same sense that the advanced countries are rich. They are encouraged in this pursuit by the business press, by most respectable economists, by the governments of the rich countries, by international lending agencies, and by their own (usually Western-trained) technocrats. Whatever doubts might arise are quickly swept aside. It's a globalized economy. Not to grow is to stagnate, regress, slide into chaos. TINA.

From an ecological point of view, this is madness. Environmental sanity requires that overdeveloped countries cut back on consumption and poor countries target their resources to eliminating poverty—the exact opposite of what globalized capitalism demands. From the perspective of globalized capitalism, overdeveloped countries must consume ever more, because they are the key markets for the "lesser-developed" ones, whereas poor countries must cut back public spending, keep wages low, open up their economies, look the other way when ecological issues surface, because they must, above all else, attract foreign investment.

So long as the structures of global capitalism remain in place, there is no alternative to this madness. If rich countries continue to grow, poor-country elites will emulate the consumption patterns of their rich-country counterparts, and will target their countries' resources to rich-country markets—putting ever more pressure on our planet's limited supplies of food and natural resources, and subjecting the environment to ever increasing quantities of toxic wastes. If rich countries cease to grow, their own economies will implode—and so will the economies of poor countries, increasing the level of poverty, increasing the level of environmental degradation that poverty entails, and decreasing the amount of funds available for environmental damage control.

It's no wonder that environmental economists tend to be a gloomy lot.

NOTES

1. Jan Pen, *Income Distribution: Facts, Theories, Policies* (New York: Praeger, 1971).

2. The data that follow have been derived from the U.S. Census Bureau, Current Population Reports, *Money Income in the United States: 1999* (Washington, D.C.: Government Printing Office, 2000); Bureau of Labor Statistics and Bureau of the Census, *CPS Annual Demographic Survey: March 1999 Supplement* (http://ferret.bls.census.gov/mcro/032000/hhinc/new01_001); and the *Forbes*, 15 May 2000, issue on executive pay.

3. For a first-person account of what it's like working at low-end jobs and trying to survive, see Barbara Ehrenreich, *Nickel and Dimed: On (Not) Getting By in America* (New York: Metropolitan, 2001), a record of her two-year odyssey as a waitress and hotel maid in Florida, a nursing-home aide and house cleaner in Maine, and Wal-Mart "associate" in Minnesota.

4. Plato, *The Republic*, books 3 and 8.

5. John Rawls, *A Theory of Justice* (Cambridge, Mass.: Harvard University Press, 1971), 534.

6. *Chicago Reader*, 14 January 1994.

7. *Chicago Sun-Times*, 3 February 1994. More recent data: if those people who work substantially less than full time but wish to work more are included, then one-third of the world labor force of about three billion is either unemployed, underemployed, or earns less than is needed to keep their families out of poverty. *World Employment Report 2001: Life at Work in the Information Economy* (Geneva: International Labour Office, 2000): section 1.1.

8. Cited in Andrew Kohut, "A Disquiet about Globalization among Americans," *International Herald Tribune*, 4–5 December 1999.

9. Karl Marx and Frederick Engels, *The Communist Manifesto* (London: Verso, 1998), 39.

10. See William Greider, *One World Ready or Not: The Manic Logic of Global Capitalism* (New York: Simon and Schuster, 1997) and Paul Krugman, *The Return of Depression Economics* (New York: Norton, 1999) for recent statements of concern.

11. See William Greider, *Secrets of the Temple: How the Federal Reserve Runs the Country* (New York: Simon and Schuster, 1987) for details.

12. Andrew Hacker, *Money: Who Has How Much and Why* (New York: Simon and Schuster, 1997), 46.

13. Juliet Schor, *The Overworked American: The Unexpected Decline of Leisure* (New York: Basic Books, 1992), 2; her emphasis.

14. United Nations Development Programme, *Human Development Report 1998* (Oxford: Oxford University Press, 1998), 29.

15. Stephen Cohen, *Failed Crusade: America and the Tragedy of Post-Communist Russia* (New York: Norton, 2000), 28.

16. Partha Dasgupta, *An Inquiry into Well-Being and Destitution* (Oxford: Clarendon Press, 1993), 80. Extreme poverty, he notes, could be eradicated in four years.

17. Karl Marx, *Capital*, vol. 1 (New York: International Publishers, 1967), 751.

18 Marx, *Capital*, 432.

19. Plato, *The Republic*, book 8.

20. John Stuart Mill, *Considerations on Representative Government* (Indianapolis: Bobbs-Merrill, 1958), 94ff.

21. See Robert Dahl and Charles Lindblom, *Politics, Economics, and Welfare* (New York: Harper, 1953); Charles Lindblom, *Politics and Market* (New York: Basic Books,

1977); Robert Dahl, *Democracy and Its Critics* (New Haven, Conn.: Yale University Press, 1989).

22. Dahl, *Democracy and Its Critics*, 220.

23. *Playboy* interview, December 1987, 53.

24. Figures for national elections from Joseph Cantor, "Campaign Financing," Government and Finance Division of the National Council for Science and the Environment (6 April 2001); http://www.cnie.org/nle/rsk-36.html.

25. *International Herald Tribune*, 21 October 1999. Emphasis mine.

26. Vince Stehle, "Righting Philanthropy," *The Nation* (30 June 1997), 15.

27. For an important treatment of the media question, see Robert McChesney, *Rich Media, Poor Democracy*. (Champaign: University of Illinois Press, 1999.)

28. Andrew Hacker, *Money: Who Has How Much*, 56. Hacker's calculation is based on mid-1990s data. The cap could now be raised to $300,000.

29. Carl Lesnor makes this point and draws out its implications, unsettling to orthodox Marxist theory, in his "War: The Health of the State," *Radical Philosophy Review* 2, no. 1 (1999): 41–49.

30. Karl Marx, "Preface to a Contribution to the Critique of Political Economy," in Erich Fromm, *Marx's Concept of Man* (New York: Ungar, 1966), 217.

31. For an account of this remarkable state, see Bill McKibben, *Hope, Human and Wild* (St. Paul, Minn.: Hungry Mind Press, 1995), chapter 3; and Richard Franke and Barbara Chasin, *Kerala: Radical Reform as Development in an Indian State* (San Francisco: Institute for Food and Development, 1989).

32. My discussion of food shortage draws primarily on the data and analyses of Lester Brown, "Facing the Prospect of Food Scarcity," and Gary Gardner, "Preserving Global Cropland," both in Lester Brown, et al., eds., *State of the World 1997* (New York: Norton, 1997), 23–41 and 42–59 respectively, and from Lester Brown, "Struggling to Raise Cropland Productivity," *State of the World 1998*, 79–95. See also Lester Brown, "Eradicating Hunger: A Growing Challenge," *State of the World 2001*, 43–62.

33. "Survey of Development and the Environment," *The Economist* (31 March 1998), 14.

34. Brown, "Facing the Prospect of Food Scarcity," 34. See also, *State of the World 2001*, 181–84.

35. My account here draws on Hilary French, "Learning from the Ozone Experience," *State of the World 1997*, 151–72.

36. Seth Dunn, "Decarbonizing the Energy Economy," in *State of the World 2001*, 90.

37. Dunn, "Decarbonizing," 95.

38. *New York Times*, 19 August 2000.

39. *New York Times*, 26 April 1998.

40. Hans-Peter Martin and Harald Schumann, *The Global Trap* (London: Zed Books, 1997), 14.

41. Herman Daly, *Beyond Growth* (Boston: Beacon Press, 1996), 106.

42. Calculations from *State of the World 2001*, figures on p. 20.

43. An interesting example of such delusional thinking—which nonetheless contains much valuable, hopeful information—is Paul Hawkins, Amory Lovins, and L. Hunter Lovins, *Natural Capitalism: Creating the Next Industrial Revolution* (Boston: Little, Brown, 1999). It is not altogether surprising that then-President Bill Clinton endorsed this book.

5

Economic Democracy: Why We Need It

I have argued that capitalism is plagued by insurmountable difficulties: staggering inequality, systematic unemployment that globalization will almost surely make worse, an unnecessary and undesirable intensification of work, poverty that wrecks minds as well as bodies, a perversion of the democratic process, and an inherent ecological destructiveness. But would things be significantly different under Economic Democracy? Is it plausible to think that such deep-seated problems will miraculously disappear if we simply democratize workplaces and socialize investment?

In fact, these problems will not disappear, not all of them, not all at once. Capitalism has imprinted itself everywhere—on our political institutions, our built habitats, our natural environment, our private lives, our souls. It has shaped our desires and expectations. It has broken a lot of people, many of whom will never recover. But it has also opened up possibilities that did not exist before, possibilities for human fulfillment and human happiness on a truly universal scale. I am convinced that Marx's double insight remains valid: Capitalism has made a truly human world possible, but we cannot reach that world without transcending capitalism.

I am also convinced that we can now see what basic economic structures need to be put in place if we are to move closer to that truly human world. If we make these changes, the problems we have elaborated in the last chapter will not "miraculously" disappear, but intractable problems will become tractable. We will be in a position to resolve difficulties that cannot be resolved so long as capitalism remains dominant.

Will it be a simple matter to institute genuine democracy and end unemployment, overwork, poverty, and environmental degradation? No, of course not. Will new problems appear? Doubtless they will. But our present

historical task would seem to be set: to move beyond capitalism to something like Economic Democracy, humanity's next stage, where it is *possible*
to solve the huge difficulties we now face.

How we might make such a move will be discussed in chapter 6. This
chapter makes the case for the desirability of such a move. Here we examine the claim that the problems we have seen to be unresolvable under capitalism become manageable under Economic Democracy. We will try to understand how the relatively simple structural changes required by Economic
Democracy can make such a difference. Economic Democracy will not usher
in Utopia, but if we make a few structural changes, a far better world becomes possible than most of us can now imagine.

Before examining, one by one, the "discontents" of capitalism discussed in
the last chapter, we need to consider some of the differences that altering the
internal structure of firms will make to their individual and collective behavior. Democratizing the workplace can be expected to increase the technical
efficiency of a firm, but it will also give it certain behavioral characteristics
that are different from those of a comparable capitalist firm. These behavioral differences will in turn give an economy composed largely of such
firms a different economic dynamic (different "laws of motion," if you will)
than we find in a capitalist economy.

5.1 WORKPLACE DEMOCRACY: SOME BEHAVIORAL
CONSEQUENCES OF STRUCTURAL CHANGE

At first glance, it might seem that democratizing enterprises should have little macroeconomic impact. Firms will still seek to make a profit. They will
still be concerned to satisfy consumer demand and to produce efficiently. It
might seem reasonable to suppose that an economy of such firms would ex-
hibit pretty much the same characteristics as a capitalist economy. Whatever
differences there might be between capitalism and Economic Democracy
would be due to the difference in the investment mechanism, not to workplace democracy.

Not so. In fact, democratic firms do not behave like capitalist firms in all
respects. For one thing, since labor is not a cost of production in a democratic firm, *democratic firms have no interest whatsoever in lowering labor
costs*—since those "costs" are precisely the incomes of the workers. Technology will not be introduced, for example, so that a firm can reduce its
workforce or replace skilled workers by unskilled workers. Worker-run enterprises, unlike their capitalist counterparts, have no interest cutting their
workforce or in "de-skilling" their workers.[1] Of course, it is theoretically possible for a majority of workers to vote to lay off some of their colleagues or
to replace a minority of higher-paid workers with lower-paid ones, but the

natural solidarity engendered by democracy sharply mitigates against such behavior. In practice, democratic firms almost never vote to reduce the incomes of some so that others will have more. They rarely lay off workers at all, apart from circumstances of financial exigency, and even in these cases, the tendency is to share the burden as much as possible and to let retirements and voluntary departures bring down the size of the workforce. In general, employment is significantly more secure in a democratic firm than in a capitalist one.

There is a second behavioral difference, distinct from a reluctance to reduce labor costs, that has far-reaching consequences: *Successful worker-run firms, unlike their capitalist counterparts, do not possess an inherent tendency to expand.* There are two distinct reasons for this, each serving to inhibit expansion. The first has been often noted by economists. Although both capitalist and democratic firms strive to make a profit, what exactly is maximized is different. Roughly speaking, capitalist firms strive to maximize total profit, whereas democratic firms strive to maximize profit per worker. This difference translates into a different expansionary dynamic.[2]

Consider a simple example. I set up a small business, employing twenty workers at $10,000 per year, and, using traditional capitalistic management techniques, make a profit of $100,000. I sense that demand for my product is strong, so I hire another twenty workers and double production. My company now produces twice what it did before, and assuming I was right about demand, my profit doubles to $200,000. If demand remains strong, the incentive to grow is immediate, palpable, almost irresistible.

Now consider a twenty-person worker-run enterprise, producing the same product in exactly the same environment. Suppose you are one of the workers. You will make more the first year than one of my workers—the $10,000 she is being paid, plus another $5,000, your share of the $100,000 profit. You and your fellow workers also sense that demand for your product is strong. Will you press to double production? Well—why should you? Assuming no change in technology or work intensity, this would entail taking on twenty more workers. Sure, this would double the firm's profits—*but these profits would have to be shared with twice as many workers.* Each individual worker, you included, would make exactly what you made before. So there is no incentive to expand.

The logic of this example does not imply that a democratic firm will *never* vote to take on new workers and expand production. So long as there are sufficient economies of scale involved, the firm will expand—to the point of optimal efficiency. But not beyond that. It will not keep expanding when returns to scale are merely constant, whereas a capitalist firm will keep expanding throughout that range, continuing until demand is saturated or further expansion drives down efficiency (decreasing returns to scale).

The second reason why a democratic firm lacks the expansionary dynamic of a capitalist firm has to do with the nature of democracy itself. As a rule, democratic polities are not expansionary because increasing the size of the polity dilutes the political significance of the existing members. Look at the above example again. Twice as many workers would mean twice as many participants in the democratic process, hence the weight of your own voice and vote would be halved. In general, a democratic firm will resist expansion unless the financial gains are clear and palpable, and when it does expand, it will prefer to expand gradually rather than rapidly, so as not to alter too radically the existing culture of the institution. (This is true of cities, states, even nations, as well as democratic firms. Increased size must promise significant gains to voters if the natural reluctance of a democratic polity to take on new members is to be overcome.)

There are a number of important corollaries to this difference in expansionary dynamic:

- Firms under Economic Democracy will tend to be smaller than comparable capitalist firms. Once a firm reaches the optimal size for technical efficiency, it will stop growing. If demand for the product remains strong, new firms will come into being to satisfy this demand, sometimes "hiving off" from parent firms. (This dynamic was observable among the Mondragon cooperatives prior to their consolidation into a single corporation.)

- Firms under Economic Democracy will be less intensely competitive than capitalist firms. Competition is more defensive than offensive. A firm does not want to lose market share, since that would cut into each worker's income, but it doesn't want to expand rapidly either, not unless a technological development allows for expansion without the employment of more labor. A democratic firm has little interest in driving a competitor out of business, buying it out (which is impossible anyway), or even merging with it (unless the economies of scale are significant).

- Monopolistic tendencies will be less pronounced under Economic Democracy than under capitalism, since monopolies generally arise when successful firms drive their competitors to the wall or buy them out or merge with them. (Note the paradox: The economy of an Economic Democracy is at once less competitive and more competitive than a capitalist economy. Firms tend to be less cutthroat in competing with one another, while at the same time they are less likely to become monopolistic. Capitalism exhibits an analogous, though less benign, paradox—what Marx called a "contradiction": the more intensely competitive the economy is, the more likely it is that the big fish will swallow the small fish, with monopoly—the antithesis of competition—the end result.)

Although firms under Economic Democracy will tend to be smaller than their capitalist counterparts, since they lack an inherent expansionary dynamic, it cannot be assumed that large firms will not exist. Firms will sometimes find it advantageous to combine into a larger entity, as did the Mondragon cooperatives. But these larger entities will likely be structured differently than large capitalist enterprises. Large firms under Economic Democracy will tend to be confederations of smaller firms, each of which preserves a degree of autonomy. As in a political democracy, there will exist a creative tension between centralized authority and local control. It may make economic sense for a number of enterprises to pool their resources so, as to fund research and development facilities or marketing departments, but individual units will want to preserve a degree of autonomy. (The Mondragon Cooperative Corporation has such a structure. Individual units sign a contract with the corporation that binds them to certain conditions, but they may withdraw at any time if they so choose.) It has long been recognized that overcentralization can be detrimental to efficiency; hence, large capitalist corporations tend to give a degree of autonomy to their divisions. Economic Democracy can be expected to carry this decentralization even further.

With these differences in mind, let us now turn to those deep defects of capitalism that were analyzed in the last chapter. The "comparative" argument now begins in earnest.

5.2 INEQUALITY

There will be inequality under Economic Democracy. There will be inequalities within firms, since enterprises employ financial incentives to acquire and hold qualified workers. (Individual financial reward may not be the only motive for a person choosing to work at a particular firm, but it would be naive to assume that money won't matter.) Workers may also find it desirable to insist on seniority differentials, to give tangible credit to loyalty and service over time. The workplace will not be a site of strict equality unless the workers in a particular firm choose to make it so. Probably they won't, although, over time, as the democratic culture deepens and the work itself is restructured so as to be more intrinsically rewarding, income differentials will likely diminish.

There will also be inequalities among firms. Economic Democracy is a competitive market economy. Some firms will do better than others. Skill and hard work will account for some of these differences. Luck will also be a factor—being at the right place at the right time when demand shifts in your direction or guessing right as to what new products people will want. Luck will always play a significant role in a market economy; hence, certain inequalities will always be "undeserved." This fact should be acknowledged and accepted.

It does not follow that the structure of inequalities within Economic Democracy will be the same as under capitalism. Workplace democracy tends to keep intrafirm inequalities in check. In Mondragon, for example, the differential between the highest paid worker in a firm and the lowest was for many years held at 3 to 1. More recently, as competition with capitalist firms, particularly the European multinationals, has intensified, the allowable spread has been raised to 4.5 to 1, and in some cases even more. Still, even though MCC is now a multinational corporation in its own right, it has nothing like the 100 to 1 or more differentials typical of large capitalist firms.

It is to be expected that democratic firms will be more egalitarian than capitalist firms. Democracy is always a check to inequality. When managerial incomes have to be justified to the workers themselves, they will tend to be less than when CEOs and other upper administrators are free to determine their own salaries (perhaps in consultation with major stockholders, who are themselves very rich and not averse to being generous to those whose duty it is to keep them that way). Even in the United States, where ideological justifications of inequality are largely unquestioned, the highest salary of a government official is only $400,000—a fraction of top private-sector salaries. (The fact that democratic firms tend to be smaller than capitalist firms also enhances equality. The larger the firm, the more extensive the hierarchy; the more extensive the hierarchy, the larger, in general, the income gap, since managers are almost always paid more than the managed.)

How much inequality can be expected *between* firms? Given the variables involved, no hard and fast answer to this question is possible, but structural differences point to less inequality than under capitalism. As we have seen, in Economic Democracy successful firms do not expand rapidly and drive their competitors out of business. Hence, successful innovations in product design or production techniques will likely diffuse to competitors, and reestablish, over time, intra-industry equality. To the extent that certain industries themselves are more profitable than others, market forces will encourage a shift of resources from less profitable sectors to more profitable, increasing supply in the former, decreasing it in the latter. Prices should adjust accordingly, coming down in the more profitable sectors, rising in the less profitable sectors—the standard equalizing mechanism of the market. The investment banks can be expected to assist this transition. Since firms are smaller and competition less intense under Economic Democracy than under capitalism, it should be easier for a new start-up firm—or a retooled existing firm—to enter the more lucrative industry.

If we make the rough estimate that in Economic Democracy the strongest firms will pay their workers three times what the weakest firms pay, and if we assume that without the pressure of capitalist firms trying to lure away top personnel, income differentials within a firm will also be about three to one, we can say that in Economic Democracy the overall spread between top incomes and bottom incomes will be about ten to one. If we further assume that under Economic Democracy, the minimum wage is high enough to keep you out of poverty (say, in the United States, $10/hour), this would put the range between $20,000 and $200,000. This is far from total equality. It is the difference between someone in the United States now making twice the minimum wage and Bill Clinton's White House salary. But it is nothing like the inequality under capitalism. In terms of our parade, we are looking at dwarves a little over two feet tall and giants of twenty-two feet. We don't see dwarves just inches from the ground or giants with their heads in the clouds. It's a different world.

It should be noted that it is not against the law under Economic Democracy to accumulate great wealth. The system has no ideological bias against wealth per se. It is just that the structures that define Economic Democracy make accumulation at once more difficult and less necessary. Without the ability to make money with money, it is impossible to accumulate the multi-million-dollar fortunes that members of our capitalist class have accumulated. You *might* make it to a million (small potatoes by capitalist standards), but not easily. Do the math. To become a millionaire without the magic of compound interest, you would have to save $20,000 per year, each and every year, for fifty years. You *could* do this, I suppose, if you had a decent job and started saving early—but why would you want to? Since Economic Democracy is a socialist society, we can assume that its citizens enjoy publicly funded benefits comparable to those provided under the best of existing social democracies, that is, quality education, quality health care, and decent pensions. So there is little point to saving, other than to accumulate funds for a down payment on a home or to supplement your pension when you retire. You do not need to save, not for your own good, or society's, although you are free to do so. (Society, recall, generates its funds for investment from taxation, not private savings, so the health of the economy in no way depends on the rate of private savings.)

It is not strictly true that under Economic Democracy, it is impossible to make money with money. For example, in the expanded model, there are savings and loan associations that will pay you interest on your deposits. It is also true that some capitalism might be permitted, so that highly skilled entrepreneurs can build up a company, then sell it (to the state) and walk away with a windfall. But details make a difference. So long as interest rates are kept low, savings do not compound rapidly. At 4 percent, for example, a $10,000 deposit takes eighteen years to double. Under Economic Democracy, only modest interest is paid to savers—and only modest interest charged to borrowers. Savers do not become rich at the expense of borrowers. No giants will spring from such ground. As for our capitalist entrepreneurs (if we decide to have any), some might become giants, but since these individuals would be few and highly visible, their wealth would not easily translate into political power, nor—more importantly—could their investment decisions put the economy at risk.

Under Economic Democracy, greater equality is a by-product of structures introduced for other purposes rather than a matter of direct design. Be that as it may, this equality can be expected to have some highly positive effects. Above all, it should enhance our sense of community, our sense of having interests in common, our sense of the common good. The fact of the matter is, common purpose is hard to come by in a society riven by deep inequalities. It is difficult for a person making fifty, a hundred, two hundred times more than another person to find much common ground with the poorer person—even if the poorer person isn't poor.

It is curious that, although there is much discussion these days about "community"—our declining sense of it, what can be done to remedy this—little attention is paid to the connection between community and equality. Perhaps this is because Americans don't care much about equality anymore. (European social democracies would seem to care more, but these feelings are being attenuated as Europe becomes more "Americanized.") Ordinary working people are rarely celebrated on film or television, as they once were. Fanfares are no longer composed "for the common man." Wealth is a source of endless fascination and perhaps some envy, but it is rarely resented.

Leftists often bemoan that lack of class consciousness among the working class, but at this historical juncture it may be just as well that class antipathy is not widespread, and that ordinary people do not despise the wealthy. A movement for Economic Democracy can avoid a politics of resentment, which, although potent in the past as an organizing strategy, has often been brutalizing. What we want (we who want Economic Democracy) is not equality per se, but a genuinely democratic, full-employment, ecologically sustainable society without overwork or poverty. If we get in the process a degree of equality that enhances our sense of community, that is a welcome bonus. If there are still a few giants among us, even after a full transition to Economic Democracy, that is no cause for concern, since their existence is consistent with our fundamental values, and poses no threat to our basic institutions.

I do not mean to imply that the counterproject should not strive to recover the lost memories of heroic struggles on the part of ordinary working people to build collective institutions that would better their lives and the lives of their children. It should. There is much work to be done here. Contemporary capitalism has pretty much effaced these memories. As we know from the efforts of women and minorities to recover their lost histories, such projects need not be fueled by resentment.

5.3 UNEMPLOYMENT

The analysis of unemployment in chapter 4 demonstrated that capitalism has no automatic tendency toward full employment, or even toward some relatively benign "natural" level of unemployment. Unless there is specific government intervention, the economy can stabilize at *any* level of unemployment, and even with government intervention, full employment cannot be maintained, since low unemployment undermines worker discipline and generates inflationary instability. Moreover, recent "globalizing" trends reducing barriers to trade and capital flows have reduced the effectiveness of the traditional Keynesian mechanisms for bringing unemployment down, so the unemployment problem is likely to get worse, not better.

What about Economic Democracy? Does it possess an automatic tendency toward full employment or will it be caught up in precisely the same set of difficulties? At first glance, the prospect does not look promising. An economy of worker self-managed enterprises has no stronger tendency toward full employment than does a capitalist economy. If anything, the tendency is weaker, for, as we have noted, worker-run firms are actually less inclined to take on new workers than comparable capitalist firms. Insofar as firms aim at maximizing profit per worker rather than total profits, they will not increase employment under conditions of constant returns to scale, whereas capitalist firms will. Moreover, since workers once hired are rarely let go, there is a reluctance to take on new workers even when there would be gain all around by doing so, if it looks like this gain might be only temporary. In this respect, an economy of worker cooperatives would be similar to many Western European economies today, where work rules (strongly fought for by labor movements) make it difficult to lay off workers. Such countries tend to have higher rates of unemployment than do countries with "more flexible" work rules.

An economy of worker self-managed enterprises will not in and of itself tend naturally to full employment. All else equal, it will fare worse than unfettered capitalism at job creation. However, all else is not equal. The other structural feature distinguishing Economic Democracy from capitalism, namely social control of investment, serves to mitigate this defect. It also serves to block those patterns of cyclical, recessionary unemployment so typical of capitalism. Moreover, Economic Democracy allows the government to assume the role of employer of last resort, something a capitalist government cannot do. Let me elaborate each of these claims.

As to the first, that the "social control of investment" mechanism of Economic Democracy enhances job creation, recall that investment banks under Economic Democracy are public institutions, specifically charged with expanding employment whenever possible. These banks are not unconcerned about the profitability of the projects they fund. Unprofitable projects will not be funded. However, the degree of profitability is not the decisive criterion. Funds will be more readily granted to firms willing to expand production by taking on more workers, or to groups of workers with a promising idea, than to existing firms wanting to keep their workforce constant. (These latter firms are not denied all access to investment funding; they have their depreciation funds at their disposal, and they may seek additional funding from the investment banks, but their requests will be given lower priority than those of firms wanting to increase employment.) Banks also have entrepreneurial departments, always looking for new ways of generating profitable employment. Economic Democracy recognizes that, like capitalism, it does not naturally gravitate toward full employment. Unlike capitalism, its banking system is specifically designed to counter this defect.

Social control of investment also counters capitalism's constant vulnerability to recession. As we have seen, if investors for whatever reason lose confidence, a capitalist economy slumps: workers are laid off, demand decreases—the downward spiral. Economic Democracy is not so vulnerable to this perverse dynamic, for three reasons:

- Most importantly, Economic Democracy does not depend on private investors. There is no class of people who can "lose confidence" in the economy, and either park their funds in a savings institution or send them abroad. If demand for new business investments slackens under Economic Democracy, the excess surplus accumulating in the investment fund will be returned to the firms as a tax rebate, to be refunded immediately to the workers, who now have more money to spend. There need be no reduction at all in overall effective demand.
- The policy of socialist protectionism also keeps recessionary tendencies at bay. Not only does capital *not* flee the country when investment opportunities decline but socialist protectionism blocks the downward pressure on wages that imports from low-wage countries exert under free-trade capitalism. Jobs are more secure. Effective demand remains high.
- Finally, there is the positive flip side of a democratic firm's reluctance to take on new workers. It is also reluctant to let workers go when times turn bad. This reluctance puts a brake to the downward spiral.

It will be observed that although the above-mentioned factors point to lower unemployment under Economic Democracy than under capitalism, they do not guarantee *full* employment. Full employment can be assured in a market economy only by having the government function as the employer of last resort. In Economic Democracy, the government assumes this role. A universal "right to work" has long been a socialist demand. It will be honored. As we all know, work is crucial to a person's sense of self-respect. All but the most severely disabled should have the opportunity to engage in productive labor. If the market sector of the economy does not provide sufficient employment, the public sector will.

Even if it would be cheaper to simply provide people with welfare checks (capitalism's "solution" to the unemployment problem), our sense of social solidarity demands more than that. Economic Democracy is committed to providing decent work for all who want to work—which means the government will provide jobs for people who cannot find work elsewhere.

It was noted in chapter 3 that Economic Democracy embraces the principle of intergenerational solidarity: citizens regard care for children and the elderly as a public responsibility, not a wholly private matter. Our children are *our* children, our collective responsibility, to be cared for by us when they are young, to care for us in turn when we are old. Since the caring professions—child care and care for the elderly as well as health care—are labor-intensive, the commitment to intergenerational solidarity dovetails nicely with the commitment to full employment. Economic Democracy will make quality day care available to all who need it. Unemployment is thereby reduced, and the national quality of life enhanced. (Day-care centers can be public institutions, like public schools, or they can be worker cooperatives, financed by vouchers, or perhaps a mix of each. Economic Democracy does not automatically favor one system over the other. It does, however, insist that child care is a public responsibility, and so these institutions will be subsidized.) In general, the caring professions, which contribute so much to quality of life, are labor-intensive; there is therefore considerable scope for increased employment, publicly subsidized if necessary, in these areas.

Full employment is not an impossible dream—as the experience of the past century's socialist experiments, for all their faults, has shown. It has perhaps been forgotten that there was a time when governments of capitalist countries—forced to compete ideologically with socialist societies—also aspired to full employment. In the United States, for example, the Humphrey–Hawkins Act of 1978 committed the federal government to a full-employment policy. The original formulation of the proposal went so far as to include the provision we have incorporated into Economic Democracy—that the government be the employer of last resort. That provision, however, proved to be too much for Congress, which cut it—thus turning the act into an empty platitude.

In a sense, it is hard to fault Congress for excising the key provision; as we have seen, capitalism is fundamentally incompatible with full employment. The threat of job loss remains the basic disciplinary mechanism of the system. Under capitalism, workers cannot see their own interests as being in fundamental alignment with the interests of their enterprises because they are not. A capitalist enterprise is structured to serve the interests of the owners, not the workers. Lowering skill requirements, reducing wages, intensifying the pace of work—none of these familiar capitalist strategies benefit the workforce, so worker allegiance to company interests will not be sufficient to maintain work discipline. Fear of unemployment is essential.

Not so with Economic Democracy. Unemployment is *not* required to maintain work discipline. The fundamental incentive is positive. You work hard because your income, and that of your fellow workers, is tied directly to your company's profits. You also know that incompetent or irresponsible behavior on your part affects the well-being of your coworkers and will not be suffered by them lightly. The large, crude stick, fear of unemployment, is replaced by the carrot of profit sharing and the more subtle stick of social disapproval.

Since unemployment is not necessary to Economic Democracy as it is to capitalism, full employment is possible under the former, but not the latter.

5.3.1 A Note on Inflation

The importance of unemployment in keeping capitalism healthy is well known to the capitalist class and to the business press that articulates their concerns, although the issue is never stated to be a matter of worker discipline. Instead, it is phrased as concern about inflation. When labor markets are tight, workers push for higher wages. They have more bargaining power when unemployment is low, and they use it. So wage concessions are granted, which are then passed on to consumers in the form of higher prices.

Inflation is widely viewed to be a menace. Newscasters signal red-alert when the Consumer Price Index goes up. This is curious since, from a societal point of view, it is not so obvious that inflation is a terrible thing. If prices are going up, but wages are going up also, not much is lost. Yes, there is some "noise" introduced into the price mechanism, making long-range planning more difficult, but this isn't usually substantial. Most economists concede this fact privately, although they rarely say so in public. Paul Krugman is an exception: "It is one of the dirty little secrets of economic analysis that even though inflation is universally regarded as a terrible scourge, most efforts to measure its costs come up with embarrassingly small numbers."[3]

Krugman understates the issue. Inflation has often accompanied quite positive economic performance. In Japan, for example, consumer prices increased twenty-five-fold from 1946–1976, a huge rate of inflation, but its *real* economy grew an astonishing fifty-five-fold during this same period.[4]

Of course, working people don't like inflation; they feel robbed of their wage gains. But there are other things that hurt working people more—high unemployment, work speed-ups, benefit cuts, none of which are viewed with comparable alarm by politicians or the media. In point of fact, working people tend to come out ahead during periods of relatively high inflation

and lose ground during periods of low inflation, since periods of low inflation are usually periods of high real interest rates, which hit working people
especially hard.

Why then so much fear of inflation? The answer is simple enough, although not often discussed. The people who *really* don't like inflation and
who are well positioned to do something about it are finance capitalists. To
be sure, people on fixed incomes are squeezed by inflation, as are those
working people whose wage gains do not keep pace with rising prices, but
the people who take the biggest hit are the money-lenders. The logic is
straightforward. When I borrow $X during a period of inflation, the $X I borrow buys more than the $X I repay. If the rate of interest lags behind the rate
of inflation, I gain by borrowing—and whoever loaned me the money loses.
Since people with money to lend tend to have more of it than people who
borrow, inflation tends to redistribute income downward—not a welcome
prospect for the upper classes, or one they will accept without resistance.

Once again, we must be impressed by how well capitalism works for capitalists. Since everyone feels the adverse effects of inflation, it is not hard to
convince the general public that inflation is a scourge. People didn't laugh
when President Ford proclaimed, "Our inflation, our public enemy number
one, will, unless whipped, destroy our homes, our liberties, our property,
and finally our national pride, as surely as any well-armed enemy."[5] Instead,
they nodded their approval. What most of those nodding didn't realize—
since "responsible" opinion makers weren't telling—is that the capitalist solution to inflation is unemployment. So, after the Jimmy Carter interlude, inflation still high, the voters elected Ronald Reagan, who quickly engineered
the worst recession since the 1930s—to discipline labor, bring inflation
down, and allow real interest rates to rise.

To say that inflation is not a great evil is not to say that it is good. Innocent people do get hurt. Savings are eroded. People on fixed incomes suffer. Although there is a general transfer of wealth downward, those who
benefit the most are not the worst-off members of the working class, but
the more privileged sectors, who have the strength to negotiate the wage
increases that get passed on to consumers. It is preferable to live in a world
of price stability—if the price for such a world is not too steep. Unfortunately, under capitalism, the price is often steep indeed: serious unemployment and rising inequality—not a bargain. (The late nineties—a period
of low inflation *and* relatively low unemployment—might seem to contradict the analysis just given, but a closer look shows this not to be the case.
As all commentators have noted, inflation remained low despite low unemployment because workers, uncharacteristically, did not press for
higher wages. Why not? The answer is straightforward: fear of job loss.
With trade barriers coming down, companies were able to argue that they
could not pass wage increases onto consumers because their international

competitors would gain the edge. Workers, rightfully fearful of downsizing or plant relocation, went along. Fear of unemployment remains the disciplinary stick, even in the "new economy.")

Can we expect price stability under Economic Democracy? To the extent that the economy is competitive, inflation shouldn't be a problem. Workers can't simply press for higher wages—since workers don't receive wages but a share of the profits instead. Workers could insist on raising the prices of the goods they are producing, but if they do so and their competitors don't, they stand to lose, not gain. Of course, democratic competitors will be tempted to collude so as to set prices, just as capitalist firms do, so antitrust laws prohibiting such behavior must be kept on the books. Since firms tend to be smaller in Economic Democracy and, therefore, in a given industry more numerous, collusion is more difficult, and should be easier to detect. If antitrust laws prove ineffective, some price controls might be in order.

5.4 OVERWORK

We have observed that although labor-saving technologies can in principle be put to either of two uses, producing more or working less, capitalist self-interest much prefers the former, since profits can be increased by producing and selling more, not by allowing workers to work less. When a capitalist firm does "opt for more leisure," it does so by laying off a portion of the workforce, while intensifying the work of those remaining.

It is true that the length of the working day has declined since the mid-nineteenth century (having massively *increased* during the early phases of capitalism). But this decline, effected in steps, is anything but natural to capitalism. The reductions have always been the result of class struggle. Workers in the mid-nineteenth century fought for a ten-hour day. The first working-class May Day demonstration (Chicago, May 1, 1886) pressed further, for an eight-hour day—a demand not granted in the United States until half a century later. (The forty-hour week was signed into law in 1933, but then was promptly thrown out by the Supreme Court, not to be reinstituted until 1938. It is not *easy* to pry more leisure out of capitalism.) There has been no reduction since in the United States. Indeed, in recent years, working hours have increased. Overtime work in manufacturing, for example, has increased from 2.2 hours per week in 1982 to 4.5 today. Overall, nearly three-quarters of the American workforce now puts in more than forty hours a week.[6] (European workers, more highly organized than their American counterparts, have been more successful at continuing the fight for worktime reduction. French workers have succeeded in gaining a thirty-five-hour workweek, to be fully implemented in 2002, although they've had to grant capitalists considerable flexibility in work scheduling to get it. The thirty-five-hour week is on the agenda now in most European countries. The struggle continues.)

In principle, a laborsaving technological improvement introduced into the workplace can be used to increase either production or leisure. Do we want more goods with the same labor or the same goods with less labor? In a worker self-managed firm, this choice translates into a choice between consumption and leisure. Since democratic solidarity forestalls the option of laying off a part of the workforce, the choice is either to produce more (and hence make more money) or to spread the work around so that everyone works less. There would seem to be no systemic bias to the choice. Making more money is always attractive, but so too is working less. It is generally easier to increase production than to rearrange work. However, increasing production means more things have to be sold, so it is safer to produce the same amount as before and take more leisure. (Productivity gains can also be used to enhance the quality of the working environment. Since the logic here is identical to that of opting for more leisure, I will only discuss the former. Like leisure, meaningful work is a good workers might want, even if profits aren't increased—which means it is a real option under Economic Democracy, but rarely so under capitalism.)

Under capitalism, laborsaving technology does *not* provide workers with a choice between increased consumption and more leisure. The option for "leisure" means workers are laid off—hardly a voluntary choice. The option for consumption is the decision to increase production to increase profits—for the owners. Over time, this increased production may result in lower prices and hence more worker consumption, but there is nothing in this process that resembles a conscious choice.

Since choices between consumption and leisure can be freely made under Economic Democracy, we would expect to see, over time, various patterns develop, some firms opting for more leisure, some for higher incomes. Indeed, workers within a given firm could opt for different leisure-income packages, so long as overall production can be effectively coordinated. Raises and bonuses might be formulated in terms of choices between more income and more leisure. Reduced-time work, earning the same hourly rate as full-time work, could be readily offered.

We, as a society, might want to press enterprises to choose leisure over consumption rather than stay politically neutral and see what develops. There are at least two common-good reasons for opting for shorter working hours over increased personal income. First, there is the problem of unemployment, which, as we have seen, does not disappear under Economic Democracy. In theory at least, cutting the workweek by X percent should increase employment by X percent while maintaining output at the same level. The work is spread around. Leisure is redistributed—from the unemployed, who had too much, to the employed, who now work less. Second, substituting leisure for consumption makes sense from an ecological point of view. As we saw in the previous chapter, the capitalist drive to keep consumption ever expanding is putting severe, perhaps unbearable, strain on our natural environment. Rich-country consumption needs to be restrained. Choosing leisure over consumption is a step in that direction.

These considerations might seem to point to an across-the-board, mandated, shortening of the workweek. Indeed, the first of these, reducing unemployment, was a key rationale given by the leftist government in France for implementing a thirty-five-hour workweek. (In fact, this workweek may not have much effect on unemployment. Historical experience suggests that cutting the hours of work will almost surely result in an intensification of work during the remaining hours, so that few new jobs will be created. Nonetheless, in my view, trading some work intensification for more free hours is good for workers. The pressure to intensify work is ever-present anyway. Better to get something for giving into it than nothing. It is also important to shift the public perception as to what constitutes a "normal" working day, so that "after capitalism" a better balance between leisure and consumption can be more readily obtained.)

Actually, the case for an across-the-board workday-reduction mandate is less compelling under Economic Democracy than under capitalism. Since firms in the market sector under Economic Democracy already have a clear consumption-leisure tradeoff available to them, what they need is encouragement, not a command. So, let the government set the example. Cut the hours of government jobs by X percent and hire X percent more people to pick up the slack. The government is not constrained by market imperatives, so it can more readily hire new workers. This reduction can be phased in by giving all current employees the option of lower pay with less work (with the pay reduction proportionally less than the work reduction to make the offer attractive), and requiring all new jobs to have the shorter hours. With so large a sector of the economy shifting to a more-leisure, less-consumption pattern, the unforced force of the good example would almost surely affect the market sector.

Is it plausible that a democratic citizenry will choose to trade consumption for leisure in order to expand employment opportunities for their fellow citizens and to live more harmoniously with their environment? I think so, although it will be incumbent on environmentalists and other citizens concerned with the common good to persuade their fellow citizens to make such a choice. There are several reasons for being optimistic that such efforts at persuasion will bear fruit.

- We know that increasing consumption does not, as a general rule, make people happier. Every religious tradition tells us this, and so does everyday experience. Poverty is painful and degrading, but once you have reached a certain level of material comfort and security, consuming

more does little for your overall sense of well-being. In fact, it may contribute to the opposite. (Robert Lane has documented "the loss of happiness in market democracies" in his recent book of that title. On such
questions as "Are you very satisfied with your job?" "Are you pretty well
satisfied with your financial situation?" "Taking all things together,
would you say you are very happy?" Americans were significantly more
negative in 1994 than they had been twenty years earlier, despite a dou-
bling of real per capita income. Various objective indicators correlate
with these findings. For example, youth and adolescent suicide rates are
up, as are rates of depression. "Severe depression is ten times more
prevalent today than it was fifty years ago. It assaults women twice as
often as men, and now it strikes a full decade earlier in life on average
than it did a generation ago.")[7]

- We know that large numbers of people, perhaps most of us, feel
  squeezed for time. To do the things that give a human life texture,
  meaning, and real pleasure, apart from work itself, requires real leisure:
  to cultivate friendships, to sustain intergenerational family ties, to engage in community service, to develop our artistic or musical or literary
  or dramatic abilities, to devote ourselves to a hobby or a sport, to read,
  to go to movies or concerts or dances, to listen to all the CDs we've purchased, to play with our computers. Time has become a highly precious
  commodity.

- Finally, there is the ethical appeal of living a life more consonant with
  the demands of planetary fairness and ecological justice. It is not right
  to use far more than our share of the Earth's scarce resources or to contribute far more than our share of sustainable pollution. We do, after all,
  have certain obligations to other members of our species and to future
  generations. Deep down we know this, most of us do, however much
  capitalism tries to blind us to this basic ethical imperative.

It may not be obvious to everyone in the advanced industrial parts of the
world that we need to slow down, consume less, opt for more leisure or
meaningful work as the fruits of our technology, but it is obvious to many
people, and it would be more obvious still, if meaningful choices between
consumption and leisure were widely available. Unfortunately, so long as
capitalism remains dominant, they won't be.

5.5 POVERTY

In treating this issue, let us distinguish two sorts of poverty: that which afflicts large numbers of people in rich capitalist countries and that which
afflicts even larger numbers of people in poor countries.

5.5.1 Poverty in Rich Countries

I have argued that poverty in rich capitalist countries is structurally intractable because it plays a vital role in keeping the system healthy. Capitalism requires unemployment that is unpleasant in order to maintain workplace discipline and to prevent inflationary instability. A full-employment policy that guarantees a decent job to every citizen who is willing and able to work cannot be implemented under capitalism, nor can unemployment allowances be too generous. If the penalty for job loss isn't sufficiently steep, workers will be tempted individually to slack off and collectively to press for higher wages, generating both inefficiency and inflation.

A full-employment policy *can* be implemented under Economic Democracy. This was the principal conclusion of the previous section. It doesn't follow that such a policy will be easy to design and carry out, particularly during the transition. Capitalism will have left a lot of human wreckage in its wake. Since, under capitalism, investments flow only to where profitable opportunities are greatest, whole regions of the country (I'm thinking here of the United States, but the same is true of most rich countries) and large sections of most cities have been left indefinitely impoverished. Various "cultures of poverty" have emerged that have left many inhabitants bereft of the skills, habits, and attitudes necessary for productive work. It will doubtless take a societal commitment that calls on the resources of many dedicated people to undo the damage that has been done. We should have no illusions about the magnitude of the problem we will have to confront, but it is a worthy task, one that can be accomplished under Economic Democracy but not under capitalism.

5.5.2 A Note on Racism

In ethnically mixed rich countries, poverty tends to fall disproportionately on minorities. This is vividly true in the United States. In 1999, the median income for black families was $28,000; that of white families was $44,000—a ratio that has remained essentially unchanged over the last thirty years.[8]

But why should poverty be concentrated among minorities? As we have seen, capitalism needs unemployment, and it needs that unemployment to be unpleasant, but these requirements would seem to have nothing to do with race. To be sure, capitalism is historically linked to racism. Racism provided the ideological justification for the European colonization of the non-white world and for the immensely lucrative commercialization of slavery, factors that gave vital impetus to capitalism's takeoff.[9] But that was a long time ago. We are speaking here of mature capitalism. Might it not be one of the progressive features of capitalism that it should, over time, eliminate racism—just as it eliminated feudal serfdom and (eventually) the very slavery that had initially proved to be so valuable to it?

Free-marketeers are fond of claiming that capitalism is inherently antiracist. Capitalists, they say, want the best workers they can get; hence, anything that artificially restricts the labor pool runs contrary to their interests. To the extent that racism persists under capitalism, it is white workers, not capitalists, who are to blame, since these workers have an interest in restricting competition for better paying jobs.[10]

Our own analysis suggests a second argument that questions the link between capitalism and racism. Capital requires that its "reserve army" of unemployed be uncomfortably poor, but it wants them well equipped to work. When poverty is racially concentrated, it is more difficult to escape, and so subcultures develop that are deficient in the values, attitudes, and skills that capitalism needs. (Cultures of poverty need not be racialized, but when they are, their effects are more severe because the effects of poverty are compounded by the effects of other forms of racism.)

These arguments are not wholly specious. It is true that workers want to keep job competition to a minimum. When jobs are in short supply—as they almost always are under capitalism—an objective basis for working-class racism exists. It is also true that certain interests of the capitalist class are ill served by racism. Capital does want its various labor pools to be large and well qualified. Racial barriers to employment restrict these pools. Capital does want its reserve army to be well equipped to work. Racially concentrated poverty does not serve this end.

However, against these "disadvantages" to capital occasioned by racism, we must set a huge "advantage." *Racism keeps the working class divided*. In the United States, from post–Civil War reconstruction onward, southern business interests fought hard—by any means necessary—to prevent transracial class alliances from forming. Meanwhile, northern industrialists imported black strikebreakers from the South to foil early attempts at labor organizing, thus exacerbating racial animosities. Methods now are more subtle, but it is no accident that the political party most closely identified with business interests (i.e., the Republican Party) is the one that plays the "race card" most blatantly. Working people do not spontaneously identify their interests with the interests of business—for good reason. Hence, those politicians representing business interests most nakedly must make their appeal to voters on other grounds. No better ground exists than racism. Here the racialization of poverty works to their advantage. Politicians need not appeal to race directly, which would now alienate many voters, but can take their stand against "crime" and against "welfare." Their policies, when implemented, make matters worse, but no matter. This merely gives their next round of appeals for "law and order" all the more force—so much so that the opposition Democratic

Party must distance itself from its "liberal" past and also promise more toughness on crime and "an end to welfare as we know it."

Since racism is so effective at short-circuiting class solidarity, you will never find the capitalist class (i.e., the ruling class) exerting themselves collectively to eliminate racism. Certain segments of that class will be concerned with ameliorating the uglier aspects of racism—particularly those that interfere with workplace efficiency or adversely affect the business climate of a community, region, or the nation. (Race riots are not good for business.) But the wealthy can shield themselves from most of the social consequences of racial stratification. And they know that should a class-based political movement emerge that seriously calls corporate (or capitalist) interests into question, they will need to galvanize voters into opposition. They (the politically active elements) know from long experience how useful racism can be in this regard.

If it is unreasonable to expect racism to be eliminated under capitalism, can we be any more optimistic about Economic Democracy? The answer is yes, for two reasons:

- Job competition will not be so fierce under Economic Democracy, so the objective basis for racism among workers is much weakened. Economic Democracy will be a full-employment economy. Capitalism cannot be.
- There will not exist a politically powerful class with a vested interest in keeping the working class divided; hence, a political commitment to end racism faces fewer obstacles.

It does not follow that racism will disappear automatically with the advent of Economic Democracy. Neither of its two basic institutions, workplace democracy and social control of investment, guarantees that minority interests will not be sacrificed to majority interests. The elimination of racism becomes objectively possible under Economic Democracy, but it will take conscientious effort to make that possibility a reality.

Thus, we see how important it is for anyone hoping for a future beyond capitalism to confront the problem of racism *now*. The struggle against racial injustice cannot be postponed until "after the Revolution" (nor the struggle against sexism and homophobia either, to which at least some of the above analysis would also apply). Of course, the main reason to oppose racism is its inherent evil. The human suffering occasioned by racism has been massive and it persists.

But there is also an instrumental reason. Socialism in general and Marxism in particular have always embraced the concept of global solidarity: Workers of the world unite! To combat the appeal of this universalizing vision, powerful psychic energies have had to be mobilized. Nothing has worked so well as racism. As long as racism remains deeply rooted, white workers will be tempted into racist blind alleys, and the appeal of Economic Democracy to minorities will be weak. (After all, how excited can you get about workplace democracy if your coworkers are likely to be racist, or about democratic control of investment if voters cannot be expected to see the eradication of racialized poverty as a major priority?) Clearly, the struggle for Economic Democracy cannot be divorced from the struggle against racism. The struggle against racism will not likely succeed, so long a capitalism persists, but unless antiracism is an integral part of the counterproject, the effort to get beyond capitalism will not succeed either.

5.5.3 A Note on Immigration

We should be careful not to confuse the issue of racism per se with issues surrounding the large-scale immigration of people from poor countries to rich countries, which is now fanning the fires of racism in many parts of the world. Obviously, the rights of people who enter a country legally should be fully respected. Under present conditions, the rights of "illegal" immigrants must also be protected. But we shouldn't lose sight of three important points.

- *There is nothing inherently wrong or inherently racist about a country's wanting to restrict the flow of immigration.*

A sense of common identity and common culture is vital to a healthy society. Taken to excess—with no allowance for diversity within a shared framework—this sense can become ugly and chauvinistic, but the radical individualism that constitutes the other pole of the community-individual dialectic is not desirable either. (Do I really have the "right" to settle in whatever country I so choose, regardless of the wishes of the people living there, who have, after all, created the culture into which I wish to transplant myself and who must bear the effects of my leaving my homeland and relocating to theirs?) Controlled immigration can contribute to invigorating a society, but uncontrolled immigration has negative consequences that are by no means equally shared. As noted in chapter 4, such immigration is good for the capitalist class and others in the upper-income brackets who reap the benefits but bear little of the costs. The costs, however, are real—and are borne largely by the lower classes: downward pressure on wages, upward pressure on rents, and an additional burdening of already meager social services. (It is often said that immigrants are willing to do the work that local workers won't do. This is a half-truth. Local workers may not be willing to work *for the same low wage* as immigrant workers, but if labor is in short supply, wages will rise or the jobs will be redesigned. That is the way a market economy works.)

- *Large-scale emigration impacts negatively on poor countries.*

The term "brain drain" has gone out of fashion, but the reality remains. Poor countries lose large numbers of their best and brightest—not only their educated "best," but young people generally who have the most courage and initiative. After all, it is neither *easy* when you are poor to make your way to a foreign land, nor is it easy for you when you get there—a land where the customs, laws, and language are different from your own, and where many people are positively hostile to your presence. Typically, these emigrants remit large amounts of their earnings home, which cushions the loss, but the fact remains, they are no longer on hand to contribute their energy, intelligence, and skills to resolving the problems of their own country.

- *So long as the heavy weight of globalized capitalism presses down on poor countries, the pressure to emigrate will intensify.*

Few poor people undertake the arduous trek from their home country simply because rich countries are rich. Usually they are driven by desperation. More often than not, conditions have become desperate because of the dynamics of global capitalism, which we analyzed in chapter 4. (It has been estimated that the per capita income gap between the richest and poorest countries has widened from about three-to-one in 1820 to seventy-to-one in 1990.[11]) The free flow of goods and capital, so beloved by global corporations and their allies in government, academia, and the media, exacts a terrible price. Small businesses are destroyed. Labor-intensive subsistence agriculture is replaced by more capital-intensive cash-crop farming. We are told that these "disruptions" will only be temporary, but not even those doing the telling really believe that line any more. No one really expects those mysterious flows of capital, guided by the invisible hand, to revitalize south Asia, sub-Sahara Africa, or Latin America. A few lucky countries might make it—although the dearth of good examples, despite decades of trying, does not inspire much hope. If capitalism continues, our children and grandchildren will almost surely live in a world where millions of desperate people, fleeing from poverty, disease, and social disintegration, will be trying to find a salvific niche in a rich country—where they will *not* be met with open arms.

5.5.4 Poverty in Poor Countries

Would it be different if all or a large part of the world were structured along the lines of Economic Democracy? Can we really imagine a world *without* poverty?

This is not the place nor am I the person to outline a full-blown plan for global economic reform, but the analysis developed so far points to some basic prescriptions. Let us consider the question from two points of view. What should rich countries do to help poor countries? What should poor countries do to help themselves?

Suppose a rich country were restructured as an Economic Democracy. If this transformation came about as a result of a social movement inspired by deep humanistic ideals (which is the only way it will ever come about), it would want to do something to alleviate the global poverty that capitalism both profited from and exacerbated. The first order of business would thus be to stop the exploitation. Three steps would take us a long way toward that end.

Our government will:

- *Forgive all debts owed its banks.*

It is criminal for poor countries to be drained of scarce resources to pay interest on loans that can never be repaid, loans, moreover, the proceeds from which were usually squandered in graft or used for projects (often recommended by rich country advisors) that made lives worse for the majority of the citizenry. Individuals and businesses in advanced capitalist countries are allowed to declare bankruptcy when things get too bad, and start over with a clean slate. The same privilege should be extended to poor countries. Since banks under Economic Democracy are public, not private, and get their funds from the capital assets tax, debt forgiveness will have little or no negative impact on the forgiving country's economy.

- *Reconstitute the subdivisions of its multinationals that are located in poor countries as worker self-managed enterprises.*

Ownership of these enterprises will remain with our government—which technically owns all the enterprises of our own country as well—for a specified time period, say ten years, after which ownership is transferred to the government of the poor country. The newly constituted company will enter into a contractual agreement with the parent company to continue to supply whatever goods or services it currently supplies as a subsidiary, so as to minimize economic disruption. The workers in the new company will, in lieu of the capital assets tax, pay rent for the use of the assets. This rent will stay in the poor country and be used to assist local businesses, with preference given to worker cooperatives.

- *Phase in a policy of socialist fair trade.*

Fair trade works to the benefit of poor countries by assuring them higher prices for their exports. (Recall, fair-trade tariffs are placed on imported goods so that they sell in the domestic market at the prices high enough to prevent wage- and other destructive forms of competition, and to ensure poor countries a fair price for their goods; these tariffs, paid by the importers, are then rebated to the exporting countries.) As a result, fewer local resources need be devoted to export-production; more will be available for local use. Fair trade should be phased in gradually, to give rich countries time to adjust their consumption patterns in response to higher-priced poor-country imports, and poor countries time to adjust their own productive capabilities in accordance with the resulting altered demand.

Apart from ending the mechanisms of exploitation inherent in capitalist financial, production, and trade relationships, what else might a rich Economic Democracy do that would be helpful to poor countries? Such countries would doubtless welcome free technology transfer—an exemption from the patent restrictions, for example. They would also benefit if rich countries would redirect a meaningful portion of their research and development budgets toward dealing with poor-country problems, and would incorporate poor-country researchers into the process. (Malaria kills well over a million people each year and debilitates millions more, and yet a paltry $80 million is spent each year, worldwide, on malaria research. By way of contrast, a single American university (MIT) received nearly $400 million from the Pentagon in 1997 to do military research.)[12]

These steps should be taken, regardless of the internal structure of the poor countries themselves. Suppose the poor country is itself an Economic Democracy. What should *it* do to address the issue of poverty? Clearly, the government should make basic education and basic health care a top priority. Both of these areas are labor intensive and not terribly expensive. We know from the experience of Cuba, Kerala, and elsewhere that large gains can be made at a modest cost if the right sorts of institutions are put in place. A poor country could use some aid from rich countries to help with this process and to develop its economic infrastructure, but it should view this aid as temporary. It would want to avoid relationships of economic dependency that could impede its own autonomous development—whether that dependency is called "foreign aid," "foreign direct investment," or "reparations." Its leaders know that large infusions of cash and credit can be corrupting, and can often make bad problems worse. Moreover, such money transfers feed the illusion that rich-country models of development and patterns of consumption are optimal, which they most surely are not.

In all likelihood, well-governed poor countries, individually or in confederation with countries at similar levels of development, will aim at basic sustainable self-sufficiency. Some international division of labor may be in order, but since new technologies have tended to make possible the production of almost anything almost anywhere, countries and regions can aim at "import substitution," using resources locally available and technologies appropriate to their specific environments. These countries know that they will need to develop their own models of development and their own patterns of consumption. In doing so, they may well teach rich countries some important lessons. (For an inspiring account of what local scientists, engineers, and artisans working together with peasants, urban street kids, and indigenous peoples can accomplish even under extremely adverse conditions, see Alan Weisman's report on Gaviotas, an experimental, sustainable, beautiful community in the harsh savannas of eastern Colombia. To see what progressive city planning can do when conditions are right, one can look to the imaginative innovations that have made Curitaba in Brazil a model city.)[13]

5.6 DEMOCRACY

We have seen that capitalism thrives under polyarchy, but is not compatible with genuine democracy. The massive inequalities of income and wealth that invariably arise under capitalism allow the upper classes to dominate the electoral processes by providing huge amounts of campaign financing, by funding the foundations and think tanks that develop policy agendas, and by controlling the major media. Should these mechanisms prove insufficient, the economy can be thrown into crisis with an investment strike.

Economic Democracy, as its name suggests, greatly expands the role of democratic institutions in society. It does so in four ways:

- The most obvious and dramatic extension of democracy is to the workplace. The cornerstone authoritarian institution of capitalism is replaced by one-person, one-vote democracy. This is small-scale democracy, comparable in scale to that of the ancient Greek city-states. (Even large companies are small in comparison to most towns and cities.) Although most enterprises will have representative worker councils, this form of democracy is not far removed from the ancient ideal of direct democracy.
- "Market democracy" (that is, the ability of individuals, by their purchases, to "vote" for what they want the economy to produce) is preserved under Economic Democracy, but in such a way that the most objectionable feature of market democracy is removed. Market democracy is one-dollar, one-vote, not one-person, one-vote. It remains so in Economic Democracy, but since the degree of income inequality is vastly reduced under Economic Democracy, this feature is now harmless. Indeed, if the inequalities in society are to serve their motivational purposes, we want our productive output to be determined by monetary demand. (There is no point in allowing some people to make more money than others, if there is nothing worth buying with the extra money.)

- Representative political democracy of the familiar sort is also extended under Economic Democracy, in that matters of common concern that do not come up for a vote under capitalism are regularly considered by the national and regional legislatures. How much economic investment should the nation undertake this year? How much of this investment should be for projects of national and regional scope? How should investment be allocated between public capital expenditures and the market sector within our community? These decisions, which strongly affect our economic future, will be made by accountable elected representatives, and not by the invisible hand of the market.
- There is yet another sense in which democracy deepens under Economic Democracy. By law, every community receives its per capita share of the national investment fund. Local politics suddenly becomes more interesting. Citizens have a chance to shape the general structure of their community without having to worry that their decisions may inhibit fresh capital from coming in or cause local businesses to flee. We can anticipate a higher degree of participation by the citizenry in public matters under Economic Democracy than is typical under capitalism.

These are the pluses. Economic Democracy also avoids or greatly reduces the negatives associated with capitalist polyarchy. The much greater degree of economic equality lessens the degree of distortion that money has on the electoral process. Control of the media will no longer be in the hands of the economic elite.[14] Most important of all, there no longer exists a small class of people who, when displeased with government policy, can throw the economy into recession by staging an investment strike. If we recall our original definition of democracy—universal suffrage, a reasonably active and well-informed citizenry, no privileged class—we see that Economic Democracy is, in fact, a democracy and not merely a polyarchy.

5.6.1 A Note on Liberty

Economic Democracy may be more democratic than capitalism, but what about liberty? Political theorists are fond of pointing out that democracy in and of itself does not guarantee that other cornerstone value of modernity. Political freedom—freedom of conscience, freedom of religion, freedom of speech, freedom of assembly, *habeas corpus*, the rule of law, and so on—can be abridged by an overzealous majority as well as by a tyrant. Might not Economic Democracy be *too* democratic?

The historically developed check to majoritarian abuses is a constitution guaranteeing basic civil and political rights to all citizens. There is no reason why such guarantees cannot be provided under Economic Democracy. Doubtless they will be. A mass movement dedicated to establishing real as opposed to pseudo democracy is not going to trample on the genuine advances the previous order has achieved.

Political theorists also point out that civil and political rights are hollow if individuals do not have the ability to exercise them. Specifically, if the government controls all the media and all the employment in society—as it did in Soviet-style societies—then formal freedoms remain empty, since dissident views cannot be promulgated.[15] We see at once that this argument has no force against Economic Democracy, since the government of such a society does *not* control all the media or all the employment. Economic Democracy is a market economy. There are many employment opportunities in the market sector, and there are many forms of profit-oriented media. Therefore, if there is a significant market for your ideas, there will be publishing houses willing to publish them. If you have difficulty finding a publisher, you and your friends can start your own publishing company, with your own funds or with the help of an investment grant from one of the community banks, all of which are on the lookout for possibilities to fund new, employment-generating businesses.

Another objection to the alleged compatibility of Economic Democracy with liberty concerns the *size* of government. It will be asserted that since Economic Democracy extends the scope of governmental activities, it will give rise to a massive bureaucracy that will inevitably erode our meaningful freedoms.

This assertion rests on two false assumptions. It assumes that Economic Democracy greatly increases the power of government. However, Economic Democracy does not so much increase the power *of* government as redistribute the power citizens have *over* government—by greatly curbing the political clout of money. The claim also assumes that the bureaucracy under Economic Democracy will be significantly larger than under capitalism. This need not be the case. Certain government functions will be cut back under Economic Democracy. Since it will no longer be necessary to make the world safe for capitalist investment, the truly grotesque military budgets of the world can be drastically scaled back. So can those bureaucracies now in place to control that portion of the population constituting capitalism's "reserve army of the unemployed" and those people rendered more or less permanently redundant by the system. Governments will remain large, since there is much for government to do, but there is no reason to think that a large government, suitably held in check by a system of constitutional guarantees and accountable to the electorate, will pose any threat to political freedom.

5.6.2 A Note on Political Parties

Political parties under capitalism have historically represented different class interests: slave owners versus employers of wage labor, landed capital versus industrial capital, farmers versus urban dwellers, capital versus labor. Of course, parties must always cast themselves as representing universal interests and must appeal to an electorate beyond the narrow bounds of class, but the longevity and stability of political parties, when they are long-lived and stable, have depended on their representing distinct and enduring class interests. (In the absence of such interests, religion or ethnicity often substitutes—as we have witnessed so often and so tragically in recent years.)

If political parties tend to be class based, it is not altogether clear that political parties—as opposed to temporary and shifting voter alliances—would remain a feature of politics in postcapitalist society. This is not to say that political parties should be banned, but the class-based nature of traditional political parties suggests that various functions served by political parties in capitalist societies might be better served by other means.

What functions? What exactly do political parties do? Two functions stand out. First of all, political parties raise money for electoral campaigns. It would be more compatible with the democratic ideals of Economic Democracy to rely on public funding for electoral contests and free and equal access to media time—as is already done to some extent in many European polyarchies. (One way of proceeding might be as follows: Public funds, sufficient to run a decent campaign, would be made available to any individual who wished to challenge an incumbent, provided that individual showed evidence, via collected signatures, that s/he has significant support among the electorate. Each signatory would be required to contribute a minimal sum, say $5, to the candidate's campaign to ensure that the signature is more than perfunctory. Incumbents would be provided with equivalent funding. Campaign expenditures on the part of both incumbents and challengers would be strictly limited. Only a small amount of privately raised money could supplement the public funding.)

The second function is less obvious but equally important. Political parties provide a safety net of sorts for people interested in a political career. Electoral politics under capitalism is hazardous. Not only must you devote considerable time and energy to campaigning (to say nothing of money raising), but if you lose the election, you get nothing. (This prospect is particularly distressing to incumbents, who have perhaps given years of their lives to politics. It should surprise no one that incumbents try to rig the rules to ensure their own reelection and try to make deals while in office that can be parleyed into lucrative private-sector employment, should they lose an election.) Political parties lessen the insecurity, since, if all else fails, the party will find a place for you.

Clearly, the party system dovetails nicely with interests of capital. It is good to have individual candidates for office always in need of campaign funds, and ever on the lookout for a comfortable private-sector place to land if an election turns sour. Moreover, the political parties themselves—

employers of last resort for defeated candidates—are also beholden to wealthy contributors, so all the bases are pretty much covered.

Economic Democracy will have to face the career-risk problem squarely, if it is to draw good people into politics. A first step seems clear: If you decide to run for public office, you should be guaranteed a safe return to your former place of employment if your attempt fails. If you win the election, the option should always remain of returning to your former place of employment whenever you please, and at an income and position comparable to what you would likely have had, had you remained with the enterprise. Your former place of employment may have to make some adjustments to find a suitable spot for you, but such difficulties would seem a small price to pay toward ensuring good government. (Governments during wartime often make such arrangements for employees called to active duty.)

5.6.3 Democracy and Imperialism

I asserted in chapter 4 that the history of the twentieth century would not have been so blood-soaked had the United States been a true democracy and not merely a polyarchy. Is that claim plausible? Or—to look forward instead of back—is it reasonable to assume that a country structured as an Economic Democracy would pursue a more benign foreign policy than has been typical of capitalist polyarchies?

There are two reasons to think so. First of all, to the extent that anticommunism has served as a mere pretext for capitalist expansion, optimism is warranted. Investment funds under Economic Democracy do not flow abroad in search of higher profits, so there is no need to make the world safe for foreign investment. Of course, an Economic Democracy will still need access to critical raw materials not produced at home, but producing countries will be eager to sell to it, since they are guaranteed a fair price for their resources. There might be some friction in the other direction. Poor countries might wish to impose import restrictions to protect their domestic industries, pointing out, correctly, that all currently rich countries used protectionist policies to further their development. Since Economic Democracy is a socialist society that embraces the principle "fair trade, not free trade," it cannot object too strenuously. There won't be any Opium Wars under Economic Democracy.

The second reason for thinking Economic Democracy would be more benign in its foreign policy than capitalism derives from its being more democratic. Political theorists are fond these days of pointing out that "liberal democracies" do not make war on one another. Not one case in 200 years, they say.[16] True enough, although the celebratory tone of most such assertions is hardly warranted, given how much actual killing these "liberal democracies" (i.e., capitalist polyarchies) have in fact presided over from their inceptions to the present. The more important empirical point is that *democratic electorates* rarely press for war against anyone—or even for covert counterinsurgency. Policymaking elites, well shielded from the public, are the ones who decide such matters. If we turn back to the list of wars and interventions in support of nondemocratic regimes catalogued in chapter 4, we observe that *not a single one* was in response to pressure from an aroused electorate. In virtually every case, the general public was either lied to or kept ignorant concerning what was actually going on. (The primary reason for keeping an intervention "covert" is to keep it hidden from the electorate; it is rarely "covert" to those targeted.) When we study the documents of the policymaking elite, particularly the classified ones, we encounter over and over expressions of concern that ordinary people are not "sophisticated enough" to appreciate the "national security" need for antidemocratic policies.[17] We never find policymakers trying to hold back the voters from supporting dictators or marching off to war.

5.7 ECOLOGY

We have seen that there are two parts to the environmental problem, underdevelopment and overdevelopment. We have already addressed underdevelopment—the problem of poverty. In a world of Economic Democracies, poor countries will have the autonomy to develop in accordance with their own priorities. They will work to develop appropriate technologies. They will devote resources to undoing the profound damage done to their societies by the maldevelopment due to their incorporation into the system of globalized capitalism. They will employ their creative energies to invent ways of living that are healthy and humane, but do not put the unbearable stress on the local and global environment that overdevelopment does. Rich countries can help in this process by making available their scientific and technical resources, and some material aid, but poor countries, in federation with similarly situated countries, will mostly employ their own human and material resources to restructure their societies. There is no reason to think that this cannot be done. The constraints to eliminating poverty in poor countries are for the most part social and institutional, not material or technological.

The process will not be easy, but it is perhaps less daunting than the process of weaning overdeveloped countries away from their consumption addictions. It must be said that the structures of Economic Democracy do not guarantee success here. Economic Democracy is a market economy. Hence, stimulating consumer demand is in the immediate interest of every enterprise—just as it is under capitalism. No firm, worker run or not, wants its customers to consume less of its product. All firms want to keep demand strong.

Economic Democracy is no environmental panacea. However, several features of Economic Democracy make ecological sustainability vastly more feasible than under capitalism. The most important difference is that capitalism *requires* economic growth for stability, whereas Economic Democracy does not. Each capitalist firm—and capitalism as a system—operates under the imperative "Grow or die." Firms under Economic Democracy are not under this imperative, neither is the system itself. As we have seen, the primary motivation of a healthy worker-run firm is to avoid losing market share. It is less concerned with expansion, especially if this means taking on more workers. A capitalist firm is far more aggressive because there are great gains to be had (to the owners of the firm) if competitors are vanquished and their markets seized. A worker self-managed firm can be quite content with zero growth, particularly if it is utilizing new technologies to increase leisure and make work itself more interesting. What is true of the parts is true of the whole. A steady-state economy, with consumption patterns that are stable over time, is perfectly compatible with Economic Democracy.

Economic Democracy does not have the same underlying growth imperative as does capitalism, but ecological sustainability would seem to call for more than that, at least on the part of rich countries. The sustainability at which we aim is a *just* sustainability, meaning that no country consumes more than its per capita share of nonreplaceable resources or contributes more than its per capita share of sustainable pollution. This must entail, ultimately, a scaling back of consumption.

It is here that social control of investment becomes significant. The scaling back of consumption is not something that can be done quickly—at least, not without severe social disruption. Consumption habits, and the production facilities that satisfy these habits, must be given time to adjust. Moreover, much of our excessive consumption has become "necessary," given the structure of our built environment. It will take *investment* to alter these various patterns and structures.

To take but one example, consider the automobile in America. Every environmentalist knows that the private automobile is hazardous to planetary health, one of the prime culprits in atmospheric pollution. But we have designed our communities so that many people *must* use cars to carry out the functions of daily living. Communities needn't be designed that way. We could have better public transportation, more bicycle paths, more small, local markets near our residences, and more decent, affordable housing close to our work sites. But to redesign and reconstruct our communities, we must have the investment funds to do so.

Under Economic Democracy, such funds are available. Each year, the national, regional, and community legislatures make decisions as to investment fund priorities—the allocation of the investment fund between the public sector and the market sector, and what public sector projects to undertake. These decisions can be taken without worrying about how the "financial markets" will react, or whether businesses will flee. (To the extent that local industries will be adversely affected by certain decisions, investment funds can be made available to help them retool or otherwise adjust.) The process of redesigning our communities to bring them into compliance with rational standards of ecological sustainability may not always run smoothly, but serious attempts can be made, the more successful serving as models.

Of course, it cannot be said with certainty that a sustained attempt at ecological sanity will even be made. Economic Democracy is, after all, a democracy—and hence the quality of its "general will" is dependent on the particular wills of the individual citizens. Thus, the importance of a strong and determined environmental movement that strives to persuade us that our lives must be lived differently if our fragile planet is to recover from the terrible illnesses it now suffers and avoid those in the future that promise to be even worse.

I don't think it overly optimistic to think that the vast majority of our planet's inhabitants would agree—if they are secure in their basic necessities and can imagine a future of increased leisure and more meaningful work. Neither condition is plausible under capitalism. Both can be realized under Economic Democracy. Therein lies our hope.

NOTES

1. For the classic treatment of the de-skilling tendency under capitalism, see Harry Braverman, *Labor and Monopoly Capital: The Degradation of Work in the Twentieth Century* (New York: Monthly Review Press, 1974).

2. For a fuller, more technical account of the argument than is given below, see David Schweickart, *Against Capitalism* (Cambridge: Cambridge University Press, 1993), 91ff.

3. Paul Krugman, *The Age of Diminished Expectations: U. S. Economic Policies in the 1990s* (Cambridge, Mass.: MIT Press, 1990), 52.

4. Thelma Leisner, *Economic Statistics 1900–1983* (New York: Facts on File Publications, 1985), 116.

5. Quoted by Alan Blinder, *Hard Heads, Soft Hearts: Tough-Minded Economics for a Just Society* (Reading, Mass.: Addison-Wesley, 1987), 46.

6. Data from the Bureau of Labor Statistics and from the International Labour Organization, cited by Lonnie Golden and Deborah Figart, "Doing Something about Long Hours," *Challenge* (November/December 2000): 25, 17.

7. Robert Lane, *The Loss of Happiness in Market Democracies* (New Haven, Conn.: Yale University Press, 2000), 20–25.

8. U.S. Census Bureau, Current Population Reports, *Money Income in the United States: 1999* (Washington, D.C.: Government Printing Office, 2000), viii, xi.

9. Anyone unconvinced as to the centrality of racism to modernity should consult Charles Mills, *The Racial Contract* (Ithaca, N.Y.: Cornell University Press, 1997).

10. For a classic statement of this argument, see Milton Friedman, *Capitalism and Freedom* (Chicago: University of Chicago Press, 1962), chapter 7.

11. Angus Maddison, *Monitoring the World Economy, 1820–1992* (Washington, D.C.: OECD, 1995).

12. The figure on malaria research is from *The Economist* (14 August 1999): 19; that on MIT's defense contracts is from *The World Almanac and Book of Facts, 1999*, 205.

13. Alan Weisman, *Gaviotas: A Village to Reinvent the World* (White River Junction, Vt.: Chelsea Green Publishing Company, 1998). For a nice account of Curitaba, see Bill McKibben, *Hope, Human and Wild* (St. Paul, Minn.: Hungry Mind Press, 1995), chapter 2, or Paul Hawkins, Amory Lovins, and L. Hunter Lovins, *Natural Capitalism* (Boston: Little, Brown, 1999), 288–308.

14. For a thoughtful account of media restructuring under Economic Democracy, see Michael Howard, *Self-Management and the Crisis of Socialism: The Rose in the Fist of the Present* (Lanham, Md.: Rowman and Littlefield, 2000), chapter 11.

15. Milton Friedman presses this point in *Capitalism and Freedom*, 16–21.

16. See John Rawls, *The Law of Peoples* (Cambridge, Mass.: Harvard University Press, 1999) for a repeated invocation of this claim.

17. For a meticulous examination of one of the most famous examples, see Noam Chomsky's analysis of the Pentagon Papers in his *For Reasons of State* (New York: Random House, 1973).

6

Getting from Here to There

According to the criteria set out in chapter 1, successor-system theory must not only specify and defend an alternative economic model, it must also employ that model to help us make sense of the present world and to suggest a reform-mediated transition to a different world, a world "after capitalism." The previous three chapters described and defended a model of Economic Democracy. This chapter will employ that model in the two ways just noted—to make sense of the present and to suggest a reform-mediated transition to a qualitatively different future. Of necessity, the presentations here will be more schematic than what has come before. The issues are too large and complex to be handled adequately in a short chapter in a short book, but the topics are too important not to be broached at all.

6.1 ECONOMIC DEMOCRACY AS AN ORIENTING DEVICE

The twentieth century, especially the latter half, has been a time of remarkable large-scale economic experiments, whole countries reorganizing their economies, always in response to felt contradictions, hoping to create a new and better way of life. Without exception, these experiments have generated their own contradictions, leading to either hopeless dead-ends or further creative adjustments. If we look at these experiments through the lens of capital, we see all paths converging on the model of neoliberalism—the glorious or inglorious (choose your adjective) "end of history." But if we look at these experiments through the lens of Economic Democracy, we see something rather different.

Let me offer a sweeping, oversimplified illustration of this second perspective. (See the accompanying tree-diagram, figure 6.1.) The extent to which this sketch helps us see things in new and fruitful ways is a measure of the orienting power of the concept of Economic Democracy.

This diagram is essentially about the post–World War II period, although the great split in the twentieth century occurred in 1917. Socialism for the first time moved from theory to practice. A socialist "Second World" came into being to challenge a capitalist "First World" that had by then colonized most of the planet.

The economic disruption and insane destructiveness of World War I rendered the First World highly vulnerable. Workers and peasants everywhere began to stir. By way of reaction, we got fascism in Italy, and (when the

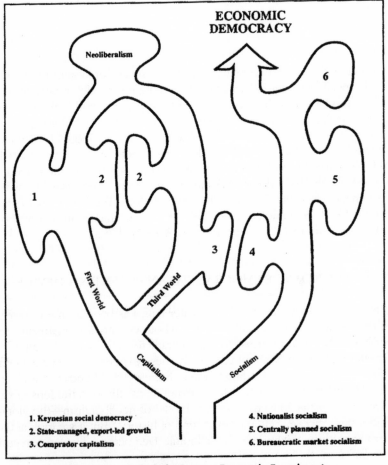

Figure 6.1   Twentieth–Century Economic Experiments

Great Depression made the situation even more acute) "National Socialism" in Germany—experiments in militarized capitalism aimed at preventing the radical left from coming to power. As economic experiments, fascism and Nazism failed. They were too aggressively militaristic to avoid self-destructive war—but they did buy capitalism needed time to find a better solution. The threat (and example) of fascism-Nazism justified a much larger role for government in economic affairs than laissez-faire orthodoxy countenanced, as well as the massive amounts of deficit spending that managed to pull the Western economies out of the deep Keynesian hole into which they had fallen. (World War II not only saved democracy from fascism; it saved capitalism from itself.)

Let us pick up the postwar story and trace the capitalist branch of the diagram. Following the great decolonization movements of the postwar period, the capitalist world split into two parts, as newly independent "Third World" countries broke away from their colonial masters. If we trace the development of the First World branch, we find two distinctive forms of capitalism making their appearance. The first form is "Keynesian liberalism," so called because it takes its theoretical orientation from Keynes's radical revision of neoclassical orthodoxy. This form became dominant in the United States, Canada, Australia, New Zealand, and Western Europe. A large state is deemed necessary to ensure the social security of the citizenry, and to mediate the conflicts between ever-more-organized labor and ever-more-concentrated business. High levels of government spending and high wages counteract the Keynesian problem of deficient demand.

For several decades, this model was solidly successful—high growth, rising real wages, low unemployment, economic stability. (This period is often referred to now as capitalism's "Golden Age.") However, as time passed, the internal contradictions of the model began to intensify. Since negotiated wage settlements could be passed on to consumers by near-monopoly enterprises, inflationary pressures began to build. Moreover, as these enterprises became hard pressed to sell all the goods they were producing, they became reluctant to engage in large amounts of new investment. Western countries found themselves strapped with "stagflation"—rising unemployment *and* inflation.

Laissez-faire conservatism, seemingly buried forever by Keynesian liberalism, came roaring back (under the auspices of Margaret Thatcher and Ronald Reagan) with its proposals to privatize, deregulate, cut back the welfare state, and open up domestic economies to more globalized competition. This new-old set of policy prescriptions, which we now call neoliberalism, eclipsed Keynesian liberalism and soon became what it remains today, the dominant economic ideology of Western policymaking elites.

The other great postwar experiment in advanced capitalism took place in Japan. In this second alternative to laissez faire, the state also plays a much larger role than neoclassical orthodoxy would allow, but of a different nature than under Keynesian liberalism. Here the state makes a conscious decision to pursue a policy of export-led growth. Consumer credit is kept tight, and pensions and other welfare provisions are kept low, both measures aimed at securing a high rate of private savings. The government then targets certain industries for global expansion and provides them with easy access to these savings, while at the same time engaging in heavy protectionism to allow the less-favored sectors of the economy to survive.

This model also proved to be remarkably successful. The world witnessed a "Japanese miracle"—a rate of growth that resulted in a fifty-five-fold increase in GDP over the space of thirty years (1946–1976). By the late 1980s, there was concern in the West that "Japan, Inc." would soon become globally dominant. However, this was not to be. The Japanese economy stalled—and remains stalled. Japanese exports now have to compete globally with lower-cost exports from other Asian countries. Their banking system has become overloaded with bad loans. Domestic demand, despite increased government expenditures, has been insufficient to pull the economy out of its doldrums. So the pressure is on Japan to reform: deregulate, open its markets to foreign competition, reduce the role of government planning—in short, to also adopt the neoliberal agenda.

If we look now at Third World capitalism during the postwar period, we also see two basic models. The first is the one most widely adopted in the wake of formal decolonization. A local elite takes the reins of political power and opens their country to transnational penetration. A regime of "comprador capitalism" is established. The local elite form domestic monopolies and connect to transnational capital. The country serves primarily as a market for First World goods and as a source of raw materials and exotic foodstuffs for First World buyers.

For a while, comprador capitalism embraced "import-substitution" as an economic strategy. Local industries were to be developed to supply what was currently being imported. But given the low level of domestic demand, the lack of access to requisite technologies, and the insistence on the part of First World countries that poor-country markets be kept open, this recipe failed. A few countries experienced spurts of economic growth, but even in these cases the wealth did not "trickle down." The mass poverty endemic to all comprador-capitalist countries intensified.

There were protests. When these protests threatened to become insurrectionary—as they often did—martial law or outright military rule was established. These Third World equivalents of the fascist-Nazi experiments, heavily assisted by the United States and utilizing all the means of torture and terror at their disposal, were usually able to check the revolutionary movements, but these militarized-capitalist regimes, like their First World predecessors, failed as economic models. So, when the Left's threat receded, most of them were overturned and replaced by more "democratic" governments. These new regimes, currently in place, are now advised, cajoled, and often heavily pressured (notably by the international lending agencies) to jump onto the neoliberal bandwagon.

The second model of Third World capitalism was considerably more successful than the comprador model. Taiwan and South Korea, the "baby tigers" of Southeast Asia, are the key examples. We have here a Third World version of the Japanese model. (Hence this model's placement next to the Japanese model on the diagram.) Since these countries were to serve as showcase alternatives to Chinese and North Korean communism, they were not only given substantial financial support by the United States, but they were also allowed a degree of economic independence uncommon in the Third World. The political elites of Taiwan and South Korea (in both cases, newly established) used this independence to institute large-scale land reform (thus breaking the power of the older elites) and to discipline capital as well as labor. Protectionist barriers were set up to shelter local industries, allocation of capital was overseen by the state, and production for export was emphasized.

Late in the game, numerous other Third World countries began to embrace export-led growth as their developmental strategy (although without as much regulation as Taiwan or South Korea). Then came the Asian meltdown of 1997–1998, which rocked South Korea as well as Indonesia, Thailand, Malaysia, and the Philippines. All countries are now being told to cut back on governmental expenditures, governmental regulation, governmental direction, and cast their lot with the wholly free market.[1]

Thus, all roads lead to neoliberalism, at least in the view of our global policymakers. For the first time in history, a single strategy is being pressed on First and Third World countries alike. All are being urged to cut social spending, deregulate, privatize, and reduce as many barriers as possible to the free flow of goods and capital.

But the neoliberal road is surely a dead-end. As the analysis of the previous two chapters makes clear, it is lunacy to entrust the health of the global economy to the animal spirits of private investors. Regional boom-bust cycles will intensify, as unregulated capital shifts rapidly from one country to another, looking for a quick fix, fleeing in panic when alarm bells go off. Long term, the Keynesian problem is bound to appear in ever more serious form. Competitive pressures compel enterprises everywhere both to cut costs, thus attenuating global effective demand, and to introduce the newest technologies, thus expanding productive capacity. The supply–demand gap will grow ever wider. The threat of a globalized overproduction crisis will grow ever more serious.

It is by no means clear that globalized capitalism can pull back from the trap it has set for itself. Stagnation, together with gradually rising global unemployment and steadily worsening inequality within and among countries, may be the best that can be hoped for—short of radical transformation. Or the roof might cave in. A deep and enduring global depression is a real possibility, as most serious analysts now realize.

Let us now look at the socialist branch of our tree. Shortly after the Second World War, various experiments in non-Marxist "nationalist socialisms" (not to be confused with Hitler's "National Socialism") were attempted—Egyptian socialism, Algerian socialism, Indonesian socialism, Guyanian socialism, and so forth. In this model, widespread nationalization of private businesses takes place, and large state bureaucracies are created. The party in power attempts to direct the economy.

Unfortunately, little in the way of genuine development occurred under regimes of this sort. These experiments soon enough came to resemble, or revert to, comprador capitalism (hence their placement on the diagram).

Far more important—and far more successful—is the model of centrally planned socialism pioneered by the Soviet Union, then imposed on Eastern Europe. This became the developmental model for China, Cuba, North Korea, and Vietnam, and inspired Third World revolutionary movements everywhere. The Soviet Union changed its status from semifeudal backwardness to global superpower in four decades. China moved from being the "sick man of Asia" to a great power in even less time. Cuba proceeded to eradicate illiteracy and poverty in so short an order that its example became a hemispheric "threat," against which the United States mobilized (and continues to mobilize) its vast resources.

But, as noted in chapter 1, this model too ran up against its internal contradictions. Bureaucratic planning is able to provide for basic needs, but its incentive structures are too perverse to yield efficient and dynamic development. Hence, reformers began to experiment with ways of combining market mechanisms with collective ownership of means of production, first in Yugoslavia, then elsewhere. In Eastern Europe and Russia, these experiments were cut short by the events of 1989–1991. (These experiments did not spontaneously abort as a result of the political upheavals. Local elites and Western advisors had to work hard to discredit market socialism as a viable option.)[2] In China, however, they have borne remarkable fruit. Not all of it has been sweet, particularly in recent years; the fact remains, however, that the Chinese experiment with market socialism, begun in 1978, dramatically raised the standard of living for most of its 1.2 billion inhabitants and sustained a growth rate over the past two decades that is unmatched by any other country on the planet. Over the past twenty years, real per capita income has more than tripled, housing space has doubled, the infant mortality rate has been cut by more than 50 percent, the number of doctors has increased by 50 percent, and life expectancy has gone from sixty-seven to seventy. In 1978, there were 262 million people living in poverty in China.

Twenty years later there were 74 million.[3] Whatever the shortcomings of the Chinese experiment—and there are many—it cannot be denied that never before in human history have so many people been lifted out of poverty so quickly.

The Chinese experiment is enormously complex and its trajectory is far from certain. At present, I think it best to regard it as a form of bureaucratic market socialism. There is at present much theorizing and much practical experimentation going on in China. There are factions pushing for capitalist restoration while others remain committed to a "market socialism with Chinese characteristics"—as the economic structure is officially described. There is considerable concern about rising unemployment—a problem that capitalism cannot resolve. There is considerable concern about increasing regional inequalities, a problem that market-determined investment flows will only exacerbate. There is considerable experimentation with various forms of workplace organization, including those that give ownership rights to workers. It is possible that the next move forward will be toward something like Economic Democracy.

Successor-system theory does not allow us to make confident predictions about the actual evolution of the Chinese Revolution or the reforms underway now in Cuba and Vietnam, but it allows us to be hopeful. It also suggests that in Russia, or perhaps elsewhere in Eastern Europe, a market-socialist evolutionary trajectory might be resumed, now that the huge costs and meager benefits of the attempted capitalist restoration have become apparent. In most of these countries, the ruling class lacks legitimacy, since everyone knows that the successful "capitalists" are mostly criminals who have looted the national patrimony. Successor-system theory suggests that there are more possibilities latent in that part of the world than conventional wisdom would allow.

6.2 AN ECONOMIC DEMOCRACY REFORM AGENDA

The diagram discussed above is a heuristic device that oversimplifies the real world, and hence might be misleading in certain respects. For example, it might be read as indicating that there is no path from capitalism to Economic Democracy. Successor-system theory does not draw that conclusion, although it does suggest that the transition to Economic Democracy might be easier for a country that had earlier taken a socialist road.

The diagram also leaves out an important consideration: the degree to which elements of Economic Democracy have been established within capitalism itself. Marx liked to speak of the institutions of the new society developing within the womb of the old. These institutions are perhaps best considered within the context of a reform agenda for an advanced capitalist society.

I have proposed that an adequate successor-system theory should be suggestive of concrete reforms that push in the direction indicated by the conceptual model. These reforms, if implemented, would fall short of full Economic Democracy, but they can be seen as steps along the way—much as the rather mild reforms proposed by Marx and Engels in their historic *Manifesto* fall short of their hoped-for communism. Let me advance a short list (not intended to be definitive), grouping them under the headings suggested by the institutional framework of Economic Democracy. Marx and Engels listed ten reforms. I will list nine, with brief comments, grouping them under three headings. I should say, as Marx and Engels did of their list: "These measures will of course be different in different countries. Nevertheless, in most advanced countries, the following will be pretty generally applicable."[4] In constructing this list, I am thinking of the United States.

6.2.1 The Extension and Deepening of Workplace Democracy

Since the goal of Economic Democracy is to have all enterprises worker run, let us offer assistance to those workers trying to set up such enterprises today. Even more important, let us push to extend the two basic tenets of worker self-management, participation and profit sharing, to workers in existing enterprises. Hence, two proposals:

- *Public financial and technical support for producer cooperatives and for worker buyouts of capitalist firms.* A worker buyout usually becomes feasible only when the capitalist firm is in economic difficulty, so the risk here is high. At the same time, the damage a plant closing can do to a local community is also high, and so there will often be strong local support for the endeavor, particularly in light of various success stories that can be told.[5]
- *Legislation mandating or at least encouraging more worker participation in capitalist firms and profit sharing.* Current Employee Stock Ownership Plan (ESOP) legislation in the United States encourages firms, by means of tax breaks, to provide employees with stock in their company, but it does not guarantee workers control over the company commensurate with their degree of ownership. A reform of this legislation is in order, to develop further its progressive potential. "Codetermination" along German lines, requiring worker representation on corporate boards, should also be pushed.

6.2.2 More Social Control of Investment

To replace private control over investment with social control is a key tenet of Economic Democracy. There are various reforms we might undertake that move us in that direction. Let me proceed from the least controversial (under present conditions) to the more so.

- *Green taxes and other strict environmental legislation.* Green taxes are mandated by neoclassical economic theory, since they force consumers to bear the full costs of their consumption habits; hence, they are supported in principle even by conservative economists—although not, of course, by the special interests that might be adversely affected. Such taxes and other environmental restrictions will encourage companies to invest in technologies and product development that satisfy public goals of environmental protection. Thus, the "natural" flow of investment funds is redirected in accordance with democratically determined priorities.
- *Reregulation of transnational capital flows.* Beginning with a "Tobin tax" (i.e., a small tax) on all transnational financial market transactions, we need reforms aimed at discouraging the rapid, speculative, destabilizing movement of massive amounts of funds from one market to another.[6] There are many voices being raised in support of such regulatory reforms, including that of billionaire financier George Soros.[7] Our ultimate goal is to *halt* market-driven cross-border flows, not merely slow them down, but reregulation is a step in the right direction. An important side benefit of a Tobin tax would be the generation of substantial revenues, which could be used to fund other parts of the reform agenda.
- *Democratization and reregulation of the banking system, to make the Federal Reserve System more accountable to the electorate, and local banks more accountable to their communities.* The Federal Reserve, like central banks in almost all capitalist countries, is now run primarily for the benefit of the financial class—hence, the obsessive concern with inflation. The Federal Reserve (and eventually all banks) should be managed so as to enhance the well-being of the democratic community. The ultimate goal is to separate the function of providing consumer credit from business investment, so that the latter function can be taken over by community-based *public* banks.
- *Democratization of pension funds, so that individual members and society at large can have some control over what is done with their money.* This is a large and complicated issue. Intermediate reforms should aim at making pension funds inclusive, so that everyone is covered, and at ensuring that they invest in a "socially responsible" manner. Ultimately, pension funds, at least in some countries, might be a key mechanism whereby workers, collectively, gain control over capital.[8]
- *Implementation of a capital assets tax, the proceeds to be used for community capital investment and to increase employment.* This tax can be justified as redressing a current imbalance. Currently, companies are

taxed for the labor they employ (payroll taxes) but not for the capital they use. Thus, companies use relatively less labor relative to capital than they otherwise would. Taxing capital to redress this imbalance reduces the incentives companies have to replace workers with machines. In addition, introducing a capital assets tax, small at first, sets the institutional basis for generating, ultimately, the entire investment fund this way.

6.2.3 Toward Fair Trade

Make no mistake: free trade is a fool's game for the underdog—for workers in contest with capitalists, for poor countries when dealing with rich countries. Not all anti-free-trade programs are progressive, but progressives should not cede protectionism to the reactionaries. Properly constructed fair trade can greatly benefit working people of all nations. To this end, we should adopt the following:

- *Tariff-based fair trade, not free trade, when there are significant wage and environmental-regulation disparities between the trading countries.* Tariffs should be imposed to make it impossible for countries to gain competitive advantage simply by paying their workers less or being less stringent with environmental regulations. To avoid displacing the burden of trade reduction onto the workers of poor countries, this reform should be coupled with the next one.
- *All proceeds from the fair-trade tariffs rebated to poor countries.* Free-trade advocates love to argue that tariffs are selfish, hurting both consumers and poor-country workers. Poor-country trade representatives often concur. It is important to undercut this argument. Rich-country consumers will indeed pay more for poor-country products—but higher prices will help, not hurt, poor countries, and will protect our own workers as well.

It should be noted that these reforms fall short of the full-bodied "socialist protectionism" of Economic Democracy, since it only targets those commodities that compete with locally produced ones. Under Economic Democracy, all commodities from poor countries would be subject to a tariff (which is rebated to the poor country), so as to ensure them a fair price (higher than the world market price) for their goods.

6.3 FROM REFORM TO REVOLUTION

The reform agenda outlined above, even if fully implemented, would not be Economic Democracy. These reforms would give us a kinder, gentler capitalism, but it would still be capitalism. It would be an unstable capitalism, however. With it becoming ever clearer that workers could run enterprises effectively and that expansionary funding could come from the state, the role of the capitalist class would be subjected to increased scrutiny. Workers would likely become ever more assertive, capitalists ever more nervous. With worker participation and profit sharing widespread, a capital assets tax in place, and with capital's freedom of investment ever more circumscribed, the stage would be set for a decisive confrontation. But how can we imagine such a confrontation working its way through to a happy ending? How can we imagine "revolution"?

Let me tell two stories. The first I'll call "radical quick"—an imaginary, abrupt transition from contemporary capitalism to Economic Democracy. The second story modifies and complicates the first by taking into account the fact that, at least in the United States, millions of ordinary citizens now have ties to the financial institutions that would be abolished in the "radical quick" transition. In both cases, the result is Economic Democracy—the successor-system to capitalism. In both cases, I am thinking of the United States.

These stories are not meant to be prescriptive or predictive. There are other ways of getting from capitalism to Economic Democracy. Nevertheless, it is important to understand that if conditions are right, a peaceful, relatively nondisruptive transformation could be made.

One of the "conditions," if there is to be a relatively peaceful transition from capitalism to socialism, is the coming to power of a leftist political party with a radical agenda. This condition will be presupposed in the two stories I will tell. (I will elaborate a bit more on this condition in the final section of this chapter.)

6.3.1 Radical Quick

Suppose, perhaps as a result of a severe economic crisis that destroys the credibility of the existing ruling class, a leftist political party is swept into office in a landslide election, and is thus empowered to enact whatever reforms it deems necessary. Let us set aside concerns about constitutional protections of property rights. We have an overwhelming mandate to move beyond capitalism to something better, to this "Economic Democracy" we have been promising. What would we do?

Let me say at the outset that I do not propose this as a realistic scenario. The "revolution" is not in fact going to happen this way, at least not in the United States. However, imagining an abrupt transition will give us a simple model, which can later be complicated and made more credible.

In fact, the basic institutional reforms are not hard to specify, nor is it hard to imagine their peaceful implementation. We don't have to talk about seizing the estates of the wealthy or replacing capitalists by dedicated cadre or creating hosts of new institutions. We do not find ourselves in Lenin's predicament, trying to figure out how to create a wholly new society. Four simple reforms would bring us to Economic Democracy.

- *First, we issue a decree abolishing all enterprise obligations to pay interest or stock dividends to private individuals or private institutions.*

This decree will need no enforcement, since enterprises are not going to insist on paying what they are no longer legally obligated to pay.

- *Second, we declare that legal authority over all businesses employing more than N full-time workers (where N is a relatively small number) now resides with those workers, one-person, one-vote.*

The workforce may keep the same managers that they now have, or replace them. The authority is now theirs—to determine what to produce, how to produce it, at what price to market it, how to distribute the profits among themselves, and so forth. Guidelines will be issued concerning the formation of worker councils (in those companies where such councils do not already exist), but the only restriction placed on the workforce is the obligation to keep intact the value of the capital assets of the business. These are now regarded as the collective property of the nation and are not to be looted or squandered.

- *Third, we announce that a flat rate tax will be levied on each firm's capital assets, all the revenue from which will go into the national investment fund.*

Firms may object to this new tax, but it will be pointed out that they are no longer paying dividends to their stockholders or interest on loans they have accumulated. This tax is the rent they pay for the use of assets now regarded, not as the private property of owners, but the social property of the nation. (If a capital assets tax has already been implemented under capitalism, as a part of the reform process, the mechanisms for calculating and collecting the tax will already be in place. The rate need merely be raised.)

- *Fourth, we nationalize all banks. These now-public banks will be charged with reviewing applications for new investment grants and with dispensing the funds generated by the capital assets tax according to the double criteria of profitability and employment creation.*

Nationalizing banks is not as "revolutionary" as one might think. The decidedly non-left *Far Eastern Economic Review* recently proposed doing just that to resolve Japan's banking crisis.[9] In our scenario, commercial banks would no longer be viable as private institutions anyway, since there is no longer any interest revenue coming in from their loans, so the government would have no choice but to take them over. These institutions, which now oversee the distribution of the investment fund, will still have a vital role to play under Economic Democracy, although they will no longer be profit-making institutions.

That's it—four simple reforms. The day after the revolution, virtually all businesses keep doing exactly what they did before, so the production and distribution of goods and services need not be disrupted. Workers still work, managers still manage, businesses still compete. Enterprises begin setting up new governing structures, the IRS puts into place a new tax code, banks begin the process of restructuring. The Federal Reserve may have to provide these banks with some liquidity to tide them over, but since it is authorized (even now) to create new money, it can readily do so.

Of course, the financial markets will crash—if they haven't already. Capitalists will try to cash in their stocks and bonds, but these will be worthless, since there will be no buyers. Huge amounts of paper wealth will evaporate—but the productive infrastructure of the nation will remain wholly intact. That's the lovely part. Producers keep producing; consumers keep consuming. Life goes on—after capitalism.

6.3.2 Once More, This Time with Feeling (for the Stockholders)

Too simple? Of course. The above is not meant to be a realistic scenario. Above all, it fails to take into account the fact that millions of ordinary citizens (not only capitalists) have resources tied up in the financial markets. People with savings accounts or holdings in stocks and bonds have been counting on their dividend and interest checks. (Nearly half of all American households have direct or indirect holdings in the stock market, mostly in pension plans.) Eliminating all dividend and interest income—which is what Radical Quick does—will not strike these fellow citizens as a welcome reform. Let us run through our story again, this time complicating it to take into account their legitimate concerns.

Let me first set the stage a little more fully than I did with Radical Quick. Let us suppose that a genuine counterproject to capitalism has developed, and that, gradually gaining in strength, it has been able to elect a leftist government that has put most of the reforms outlined earlier in this chapter on the table and has secured the passage of some of them. Suppose investors decide they've had enough and begin cashing in their stock holdings. A stock-market crash ensues. In reaction, the citizenry decide that they too have had enough—and give their leftist government an even stronger mandate to take full responsibility for an economy now tumbling into crisis.

Our new government declares a bank holiday, pending reorganization (as Roosevelt did following his election in 1932). All publicly traded corporations are declared to be worker-controlled. Note: This control extends only to corporations, not to small businesses or even to privately held capitalist firms. It is decided that it will be sufficient to redefine property rights only in those firms for which ownership has already been largely separated from management. (With the "commanding heights" of the economy now democratized, most other firms can be expected to come under increased pressure from their own workers, over time, to follow suit.)

All banks are nationalized, as in Radical Quick. Individual savings accounts are preserved, as are consumer loan obligations, including home mortgages. They remain in, or are transferred to, those banks now designated as savings and loan associations, which will continue to accept savings and make consumer loans, paying interest on the former, charging interest on the latter. (It might be the case that a prior reform has already separated savings and loan associations from other financial institutions.) Other banks are designated as commercial banks. These will facilitate short-run business transactions and will serve to distribute society's investment fund.

Funds for the commercial banks will now come from the capital assets tax. If such a tax is already in place as a result of prior reforms, it need only be raised sufficiently to compensate for that portion of the investment fund previously coming from private savings. If no tax is in place, the government can use the total value of a company's stock, as recorded on some specified date before the crash, as the value of the enterprise's capital assets, and set the tax rate so as to generate the desired quantity of funds.

At this point, the basic structure of Economic Democracy is in place. We have what we had with Radical Quick, except that worker self-management has been extended only to corporations, not to the rest of the private sector. One major issue still needs resolution—what to do with all those people who have relied on the income from their stocks and bonds to maintain or supplement their existing incomes, particularly retired people who have been depending on their private pension-fund investments.

In point of fact, most of these people will be desperate at this point, and looking to the government for help, because the stock market has just crashed, thereby wiping out their portfolios. A solution is relatively obvious. Our government will exchange all outstanding stock certificates and corporate bonds for long-term government annuities—guaranteeing a steady income to each holder until the value of his investment portfolio has been redeemed. The value of each portfolio will be set at the value of the person's stocks and bonds at a determined precrash date. In effect, we are nationalizing the corporate sector of the economy with compensation—generous compensation, since the stock market crash has rendered most stock certificates and corporate bonds almost valueless. Our socialist government will bail out those pension funds invested in the stock market—and all other stockholders as well, capitalists included. To recover a portion of these payments, a sharply graduated tax on annuity income will be instituted.

Is this a fair solution? Although stock ownership is widespread in the United States, it is massively maldistributed. Roughly half of all stocks are owned by only 1 percent of the population, whereas half of all households own none whatsoever. This means that half of all the annuity payments our socialist government makes will accrue to that 1 percent. Since these annuity payments must come from tax revenues, taxpayers are in effect maintaining its capitalist class in the style to which it has grown accustomed—much as the taxpayers in the United Kingdom and other monarchies maintain their kings and queens, despite the fact that they have been rendered functionless.

Let me make six points in support of this solution.

- The situation will not persist indefinitely. The government annuities that have been issued to stockholders are of finite duration, say thirty years. At the end of that period, payments stop. The capital "expropriated" has been fully repaid. Our capitalist kings and queens will not be maintained forever. In the meantime, they—and all other elements of society who had been counting on income from their financial holdings to supplement their wages, savings accounts, and social security incomes—will have had time to adjust to the new economy.

- The tax on annuity income will exempt those whose investments were in their pension funds. It will fall most heavily on the capitalist class—people with truly large holdings of stocks and bonds. This tax is not a punitive tax, however. In principle, it aims at allowing individuals to continue their existing lifestyles, while taxing away that portion of their income that would normally be reinvested. Recall that under capitalism, the very rich take in vastly more than they can possibly spend on personal goods and services; indeed, the health of the economy depends on their reinvesting most of their income. Since Economic Democracy does *not* depend on investment from private savings, a highly graduated tax on annuity income can be implemented that neither impedes the functioning of the economy nor compels the wealthy to cut back drastically on their consumption. The tax is designed so that poorer people who had invested in the financial markets to supplement their social security checks need pay no tax at all on their annuity income, whereas the wealthy, although paying a high tax, can still enjoy their estates, yachts, and other assorted luxuries. What the latter can no longer do is control the overall direction of the economy by their investment decisions. That power has been taken from them.

- To those who find it obscene that former capitalists should continue to maintain lifestyles far beyond the means of ordinary people (an understandable reaction), it should be pointed out that the livelihoods of many working people now depend on the consumption of the rich, and that it would be exceedingly disruptive to try to change this situation abruptly. If consumption by the rich were sharply reduced, the businesses that cater to this consumption would also suffer. People whose jobs depend on providing goods and services to the wealthy would find themselves unemployed. Our socialist government would find itself not only having to deal with the "reserve army of the unemployed" inherited from capitalism, but it would find this army suddenly grown larger. (As it is, most of Wall Street and employees of other financial institutions will find themselves out of work. It would needlessly complicate our government's task if it must also find jobs for the working people who now provide our capitalists with the goods and services they enjoy.)

- To the objection that we, as taxpayers, cannot afford to subsidize the rich, it should be answered that of course we can. We're doing it now. As was pointed out in chapter 1, the interest and stock dividends that now constitute the vast bulk of capitalists' income derive from the fact that workers are paid less than they otherwise would be. Since enterprises under Economic Democracy no longer pay these dividends or interest payments, the amount they would have paid can be taxed away without decreasing worker consumption at all. (The revenue generated by the capital assets tax will thus be divided into two parts: the bulk of it will constitute the economy's investment fund, and the rest will go to former holders of stocks and bonds—the great majority of whom are far from wealthy.)

- It is crucial to realize that the fundamental problem with capitalism is not on the supply side. Almost all enterprises are run at less than full capacity. The perennial problem with capitalism is lack of effective demand for all the goods it is capable of producing. The economy that Economic Democracy will inherit from capitalism can easily afford to maintain its ex-capitalists in the style to which they were accustomed. We need to be clear on this point: it is not the excessive consumption on the part of the capitalist class that generates our social and economic problems; it is what they do with what they *don't* consume. It is economic control that must be taken from them, not their expensive habits.

- Finally, we should remember that the capitalist qua capitalist is not an inherently immoral person, deserving of punishment. To be sure, many, perhaps most, will use their resources to block the coming into being of a genuinely democratic society. But most have made their fortunes by playing by rules that have been in effect for centuries. To be sure, these rules have been made, by and large, by the capitalist class—but not by the individuals whose holdings we propose to liquidate. Since competitive pressures have given them rather little room to maneuver in the economic sphere, they too may be regarded as trapped by the system— however gilded their cages may be. Economic Democracy has more leeway for generosity. (We might hope that this spirit of generosity will lessen the intensity of resistance on the part of at least some members of the capitalist class to the advent of a new order. Those who use violence or other illegal means to thwart the democratic process should be punished, but those capitalists who participate fairly in the process will not be forced to alter radically their style of living "after the revolution.")

6.4 A NEW COMMUNISM?

I have sketched a program for revolutionary structural reform that could be brought about peacefully, if conditions are right. One of these "conditions" is the coming to power of a leftist political party with a truly radical agenda. But how, given the enormous power of the capitalist class, could this ever happen?

If a leftist political party with a radical agenda is ever to come to power democratically—and I see no other plausible way for such a party to come to power, at least in an advanced capitalist society—the ground must be prepared. A sudden economic crisis will not suffice. Unless the counterproject is well developed, people will be tempted by simpler, uglier solutions, which will not, of course, be real solutions. Fortunately, the failure of racist, fascist, and militaristic experiments is well known, and this historical memory— which must be kept alive—provides an important counterweight to reactionary tendencies. But without a well-developed counterproject, this counterweight may prove insufficient. Although a moderate economic crisis might provide opportunities for meaningful reform, a severe crisis, too early, before the counterproject has become self-conscious, could give us fascism, not socialism.

As indicated in chapter 1, the counterproject must bring together, at least in collective spirit, the various movements now struggling, often in isolation from one another, for progressive social change: movements for gender and racial equality, for ecological sanity, for peace; struggles against poverty, against homophobia, against militarism, and against prisons and executions as solutions to our social problems.

It is clear that the labor movement will have to play a central role, since changing the nature and structure of the workplace is fundamental to the economic dimension of the counterproject. It is hard to imagine any of the economic reforms listed on our reform agenda being adopted without strong pressure from a revitalized labor movement.

Of course, economic issues are not solely the province of the labor movement, nor are issues of race, sex, ecology, peace, or prisons outside the purview of labor. None of these issues in fact can be treated in isolation from the others, although various movements will doubtless have distinctive emphases.

How are we to achieve unity in diversity, a dialectical unity that involves a genuine commonality of interests (and not just tactical alliances) but avoids the reductive subordination of one movement to another? Let us dream a little. Let us return to that short text I continue to find so provocative and inspiring, written 150 years ago by those two young men who had been drafted by their comrades to draw up a manifesto for their little, short-lived "Communist League." Let us dream of a New Communism.

> Communists do not comprise a separate political party opposed to other working class parties. They have no interests separate and apart from those of the proletariat as a whole. They do not set up any sectarian principles of their own, by which to shape and mold the proletarian movement.[10]

This, we observe, is something very different from the Leninist model that came to be dominant on the Left. There is no talk here of democratic centralism, of a tightly organized, tightly disciplined party with an unshakable confidence in its doctrinal correctness. Of course, "new communists" would be concerned not only with the "proletarian movement" but with the entire counterproject.

Communists, say Marx and Engels, must be both internationalist and nationalist.

> In the national struggles of the proletarians of different countries, [communists] point out and bring to the front the common interests of the entire proletariat, independently of all nationality. . . . [However,] the proletariat must first of all acquire political supremacy, must rise to be the leading class of the nation, must constitute itself as the nation. . . . The first step in the revolution by the working class is to . . . win the battle of democracy.[11]

Notice, although communism is envisaged as an international movement, Marx and Engels do not call for the abolition of nation-states, nor do they declaim on the futility of national struggles. On the contrary, they insist that the essential struggles must take place on precisely the terrain of the nation-state—and can be won only insofar as genuine democracy is truly established (which, as we have seen, is not yet the case).

As the *Manifesto* makes clear, Marx and Engels are "reformists." They not only endorse a reform agenda, but they see such reforms as essential means to radical transformation. At the same time, they remain clear-sighted about the insufficiency of "mere" reforms.

> The proletariat will use its political supremacy to wrest by degrees all capital from the bourgeoisie. . . . In the beginning, this cannot be effected except . . .

by means of measures which seem economically insufficient and untenable, but which, in the course of the movement, outstrip themselves, necessitate further inroads upon the old social order, and are unavoidable as a means of entirely revolutionizing the mode of production.[12]

To summarize briefly: The conception of a revolutionary movement that emanates from the pages of *The Communist Manifesto* is something different from the kinds of revolutionary movements that have in fact emerged in this century. Marx and Engels advocate an international association of committed activists who share a common global vision, who represent the most progressive elements of all progressive organizations and parties, who work primarily within the confines of their own nation-state, but who keep the international dimensions of the struggle in focus, and who recognize that many reforms are possible and desirable *before* global capitalism gives way to socialist reconstruction.

Might not some such concept of a revolutionary movement once again take root? If we assimilate sufficiently the lessons of our history, we will be on guard against excessive dogmatism, reductionism, and sectarianism. We will also assimilate the positive as well as negative lessons of the other monumentally important movements of our century: feminism, antiracism, environmentalism, pacifism, movements for human rights, and struggles everywhere against degrading and exploitative conditions. Perhaps this new revolutionary movement will see itself as something other than a "new communism." Perhaps it will want to eschew the word "revolution." The terms here are not important. What is important is that people regain that sense, which arises ever so often in human history, that we are faced with a collective task that will require the combined efforts of masses of people in all walks of life, and that will, if successful, change the world.

Nothing less will do.

NOTES

1. For an excellent critical analysis of the South Korea–Taiwan model that antedates and anticipates the crises of 1997–1998, see Walden Bello and Stephanie Rosenfeld, *Dragons in Distress: Asia's Miracle Economies in Crisis* (San Francisco: Institute for Food and Development, 1992).

2. As David Ellerman forcefully points out, "voucher privatization" was pushed for political reasons, when it would have made far more economic sense to allow workers to lease or buy their enterprises from the state. A natural evolution toward something like Economic Democracy was consciously blocked. "Lessons from Eastern Europe's Voucher Privatization," *Challenge: The Magazine of Economic Affairs* (July–August 2001): 14–37.

3. For these and other data on Chinese performance, see Peter Nolan, *China's Rise, Russia's Fall: Politics, Economics, and Planning in the Transition from Stalinism* (New

York: St. Martin's Press, 1995), 10–16; and Peter Nolan, *China and the Global Business Revolution* (New York: Palgrave, 2001), 912–16.

4. Karl Marx and Frederick Engels, *The Communist Manifesto* (London: Verso, 1998), 60.

5. For information on existing worker cooperatives in the United States, see *Resource Guide to Worker Co-ops and Sustainable Enterprises*, published by GEO (Grassroots Economic Organizing), which also publishes an informative newsletter. Consult www.geonewsletter.org for further information.

6. This tax was originally proposed by Nobel laureate James Tobin, building on a suggestion by Keynes. For a lucid explanation of the benefits of a Tobin tax in reasserting national control over financial policy and in generating significant government revenue, see Thomas Palley, "The Case for a Currency Transaction Tax," *Challenge: The Magazine of Economic Affairs* (May–June, 2001): 70–89.

7. See George Soros, *The Crisis of Global Capitalism: Open Society Endangered* (New York: Public Affairs, 1998).

8. For a recent, powerful statement of this case, see Robin Blackburn, "The New Collectivism: Pension Reform, Grey Capitalism, and Complex Socialism," *New Left Review*, no. 233 (January/February 1999): 3–65.

9. *Far Eastern Economic Review* (1 October 1998): 80.

10. Marx and Engels, *Manifesto*, 50.

11. Marx and Engels, *Manifesto*, 51, 58, 60.

12. Marx and Engels, *Manifesto*, 60.

Bibliography

Barber, Benjamin. "Beyond Jihad vs. McWorld." *The Nation* (21 January 2002): 11–18.

Bello, Walden, and Stephanie Rosenfeld. *Dragons in Distress: Asia's Miracle Economies in Crisis.* San Francisco: Institute for Food and Development, 1992.

Berlin, Isaiah. *Russian Thinkers.* New York: Penguin Books, 1978.

Berman, Katrina. "A Cooperative Model for Worker Management." In *The Performance of Labour-Managed Firms,* ed. Frank Stephens. New York: St. Martin's Press, 1982.

Blackburn, Robin. "The New Collectivism: Pension Reform, Grey Capitalism, and Complex Socialism." *New Left Review* (January–February 1999): 3–65.

Blinder, Alan. *Hard Heads, Soft Hearts: Tough-Minded Economics for a Just Society.* Reading, Mass.: Addison-Wesley, 1987.

———, ed. *Paying for Productivity: A Look at the Evidence.* Washington, D.C.: Brookings, 1990.

Bourdieu, Pierre. "A Reasoned Utopia and Economic Fatalism." *New Left Review* (January–February 1998): 125–30.

Bradley, Keith, and Alan Gelb. *Cooperation at Work: The Mondragon Experience.* London: Heinemann Educational Books, 1983.

Braverman, Harry. *Labor and Monopoly Capital: The Degradation of Work in the Twentieth Century.* New York: Monthly Review Press, 1974.

Brown, Lester, et al. *State of the World 1997.* New York: Norton, 1997.

———. *State of the World 1998.* New York: Norton, 1998.

———. *State of the World 2001.* New York: Norton, 2001.

Cheney, George. *Values at Work: Employee Participation Meets Market Pressure at Mondragon.* Ithaca, N.Y.: ILR/Cornell University Press, 1999.

Cherry, Robert, and Max Sawicky. "And Now for Something Completely Different: Progressive Tax Cuts That Republicans Can Support." *Challenge: The Magazine of Economic Affairs* (May–June 2001): 43–60.

Chomsky, Noam. *For Reasons of State.* New York: Random House, 1973.

————. *On Power and Ideology: The Managua Lectures*. Boston: South End Press, 1987.

Clark, John Bates. *The Distribution of Wealth*. New York: Kelley and Millman, 1956.

Cockburn, Alexander, and Jeffrey St. Clair. *Five Days That Shook the World*. London: Verso, 2000.

Cohen, Stephen. *Failed Crusade: America and the Tragedy of Post-Communist Russia*. New York: Norton, 2000.

Dahl, Robert. *Democracy and Its Critics*. New Haven, Conn.: Yale University Press, 1989.

Dahl, Robert, and Charles Lindblom. *Politics, Economics, and Welfare*. New York: Harper, 1953.

Dasgupta, Partha. *An Inquiry into Well-Being and Destitution*. Oxford: Clarendon Press, 1993.

Daly, Herman. *Beyond Growth*. Boston, Mass.: Beacon Press, 1996.

Ehrenreich, Barbara. *Nickel and Dimed: On (Not) Getting By in America*. New York: Metropolitan, 2001.

————. *Fear of Falling: The Inner Life of the Middle Class*. New York: Pantheon, 1989.

Ellerman, David. "Lessons from Eastern Europe's Voucher Privatization." *Challenge: The Magazine of Economic Affairs* (July–August 2001): 14–37.

Frank, Andre Gunder. *Dependent Accumulation and Underdevelopment*. New York: Monthly Review Press, 1979.

Franke, Richard, and Barbara Chasin. *Kerala: Radical Reform as Development in an Indian State*. San Francisco: Institute for Food and Development, 1989.

Friedman, Milton. *Capitalism and Freedom*. Chicago: University of Chicago Press, 1962.

Friedman, Robert. "And Darkness Covered the Land: A Report from Israel and Palestine." *The Nation* (24 December 2001): 13–20.

Fromm, Erich. *Marx's Concept of Man*. New York: Frederick Ungar, 1966.

Fukuyama, Francis. *The End of History and the Last Man*. New York: Free Press, 1992.

Galbraith, John Kenneth. *The New Industrial State*. Boston: Houghton Mifflin, 1967.

Golden, Lonnie, and Deborah Figart. "Doing Something about Long Hours." *Challenge: The Magazine of Economic Affairs* (November/December 2000): 15–37.

Gowan, Peter. "Western Economic Diplomacy and the New Eastern Europe." *New Left Review* (July–August 1990): 63–84.

Greider, William. *Secrets of the Temple: How the Federal Reserve Runs the Country*. New York: Simon and Schuster, 1987.

————. *One World Ready or Not: The Manic Logic of Global Capitalism*. New York: Simon and Schuster, 1997.

Hacker, Andrew. *Money: Who Has How Much and Why*. New York: Simon and Schuster, 1997.

Hawkins, Paul, Amory Lovins, and L. Hunter Lovins. *Natural Capitalism*. Boston: Little, Brown, 1999.

Hochschild, Arlie. *Time Bind: When Work Becomes Home and Home Becomes Work*. New York: Metropolitan Books, 1997.

Holmstrom, Nancy, and Richard Smith. "The Necessity of Gangster Capitalism: Primitive Accumulation in Russia and China." *Monthly Review* (February 2000): 1–15.

Howard, Michael. *Self-Management and the Crisis of Socialism: The Rose in the Fist of the Present*. Lanham, Md.: Rowman and Littlefield, 2000.

International Labour Organization. *World Employment Report 2001: Life at Work in the Information Economy*. Geneva: International Labour Office, 2000.

Issac, Jeffrey. "Marxism and Intellectuals." *New Left Review* (March–April 2000): 111–17.

Jackall, Robert, and Henry Levin, eds. *Worker Cooperatives in America*. Berkeley: University of California Press, 1984.

Johnson, Chalmers. *MITI and the Japanese Miracle: The Growth of Industrial Policy, 1925–1975*. Stanford, Calif.: Stanford University Press, 1982.

Jones, Derek, and Jan Svejnar, eds. *Participatory and Self-Managed Firms: Evaluating Economic Performance*. Lexington, Mass.: Lexington Books, 1982.

Kasmir, Sharryn. *The Myth of Mondragon: Cooperatives, Politics, and Working-Class Life in a Basque Town*. Albany, N.Y.: SUNY Press, 1996.

Keynes, John Maynard. *Essays in Persuasion*. New York: Norton, 1963.

——. *The General Theory of Employment, Interest, and Money*. New York: Harcourt Brace and World, 1936.

Krugman, Paul. *The Return of Depression Economics*. New York: Norton, 1999.

——. *The Age of Diminished Expectations: U. S. Economic Policies in the 1990s*. Cambridge, Mass.: MIT Press, 1990.

Lane, Robert. *The Loss of Happiness in Market Democracies*. New Haven, Conn.: Yale University Press, 2000.

Lawler, James. "Marx's Theory of Socialisms: Nihilistic and Dialectical." In *Debating Marx*, ed. Louis Pastouras. Lewiston, N.Y.: Edward Mellen Press, 1994.

Leisner, Thelma. *Economic Statistics 1900–1983*. New York: Facts on File Publications, 1985.

Lenin, V. I. *State and Revolution*. New York: International Publishers, 1932.

Lesnor, Carl. "War: The Health of the State." *Radical Philosophy Review* 2, no. 1 (1999): 41–49.

Lieber, James. *Friendly Takeover: How an Employee Buyout Saved a Steel Town*. New York: Viking, 1995.

Lindblom, Charles. *Politics and Market*. New York: Basic Books, 1977.

Lowenstein, Roger. *When Genius Failed: The Rise and Fall of Long-Term Capital Management*. New York: Random House, 2000.

Lydall, Harold. *Yugoslavia in Crisis*. Oxford: Clarendon Press, 1989.

MacLeod, Greg. *From Mondragon to America: Experiments in Community Economic Development*. Sidney, Nova Scotia: University College of Cape Breton Press, 1997.

Maddison, Angus. *Monitoring the World Economy, 1820–1992*. Washington, D.C.: OECD, 1995.

Mann, Michael. "Globalization and September 11." *New Left Review* (November/December 2001): 51–72.

Martin, Hans-Peter, and Harald Schumann. *The Global Trap*. London: Zed Books, 1997.

Marx, Karl. *Capital*. Vol. 1. New York: International Publishers, 1967.

Marx, Karl, and Frederick Engels. *The Communist Manifesto*. London: Verso, 1998.

McChesney, Robert. *Rich Media, Poor Democracy*. Champaign: University of Illinois Press, 1999.

McKibben, Bill. *Hope, Human and Wild*. Saint Paul, Minn.: Hungry Mind Press, 1995.

Mill, John Stuart. *Considerations on Representative Government.* Indianapolis, Ind.: Bobbs-Merrill, 1958.

Mills, Charles. *The Racial Contract.* Ithaca, N.Y.: Cornell University Press, 1997.

Morrison, Roy. *We Build the Road as We Travel.* Philadelphia: New Society Publishers, 1991.

Mosely, Bill. "The Lottery Scam." *Democratic Left* (Spring 1999).

Nolan, Peter. *China's Rise, Russia's Fall: Politics, Economics, and Planning in the Transition from Stalinism.* New York: St. Martin's Press, 1995.

———. *China and the Global Business Revolution.* New York: Palgrave, 2001.

Nozick, Robert. *Anarchy, State, and Utopia.* New York: Basic Books, 1974.

Ollman, Bertell, ed. *Market Socialism: The Debate among Socialists.* New York: Routledge, 1998.

Olsen, Mancur, and Hans Landsberg, eds. *The No-Growth Society.* New York: Norton, 1974.

Palley, Thomas. *Plenty of Nothing: The Downsizing of the American Dream and the Case for Structural Keynesianism.* Princeton, N.J.: Princeton University Press, 1998.

———. "The Case for a Currency Transaction Tax." *Challenge: The Magazine of Economic Affairs* (May–June 2001): 70–89.

Pastouras, Louis, ed. *Debating Marx.* Lewiston, N.Y.: Edward Mellen Press, 1994.

Pen, Jan. *Income Distribution: Facts, Theories, Policies.* New York: Praeger, 1971.

Rawls, John. *A Theory of Justice.* Cambridge, Mass.: Harvard University Press, 1971.

———. *The Law of Peoples.* Cambridge, Mass.: Harvard University Press, 1999.

Robinson, Joan, ed. *After Keynes.* New York: Barnes and Noble, 1973.

Rorty, Richard. "For a More Banal Politics." *Harper's* (May 1992): 16–21.

Samuelson, Paul. *Economics.* 11th ed. New York: McGraw-Hill, 1980.

Schor, Juliet. *The Overworked American: The Unexpected Decline of Leisure.* New York: Basic Books, 1992.

Schweickart, David. *Against Capitalism.* Cambridge: Cambridge University Press, 1993.

Sen, Amartya. *Resources, Values, and Development.* Cambridge, Mass.: Harvard University Press, 1984.

Soros, George. *The Crisis of Global Capitalism: Open Society Endangered.* New York: Public Affairs, 1998.

Stehle, Vince. "Righting Philanthropy." *The Nation* (30 June 1997): 14–19.

Stephens, Frank, ed. *The Performance of Labour-Managed Firms.* New York: St. Martin's Press, 1982.

Stiglitz, Joseph. "Quis Custodiet Ipsos Custodes?" ("Who Will Guard the Guardians?") *Challenge: The Magazine of Economic Affairs* (November/December 1999): 26–67.

Thomas, Henk, and Chris Logan. *Mondragon: An Economic Analysis.* London: George Allen & Unwin, 1982.

Thurow, Lester. *Head to Head: The Coming Economic Battle among Japan, Europe, and America.* New York: William Morrow, 1992.

United Nations Development Programme. *Human Development Report 1998.* Oxford: Oxford University Press, 1998.

United States Bureau of Labor Statistics and Bureau of the Census. *CPS Annual Demographic Survey: March 1999 Supplement.* Washington, D.C.: Government Printing Office, 1999.

United States Census Bureau. *Money Income in the United States: 1999*. Washington, D.C.: Government Printing Office, 2000.

———. *Fall 2000 Statistics of Income Bulletin*. Pub. 1136. Washington, D.C.: Government Printing Office, 2000.

United States Department of Commerce, *Statistical Abstract of the United States, 1999*. Washington, D.C.: Government Printing Office, 2000.

United States Department of Health, Education, and Welfare. *Work in America*. Cambridge, Mass.: MIT Press, 1973.

Van Parijs, Philippe. *Real Freedom for All: What (if Anything) Can Justify Capitalism?* (Oxford: Clarendon Press, 1995).

Weisman, Alan. *Gaviotas: A Village to Reinvent the World*. White River Junction, Vt.: Chelsea Green, 1998.

Whyte, William Foote, and Kathleen King White. *Making Mondragon: The Growth and Dynamics of the Worker Cooperative Complex*. Ithaca, N.Y.: Cornell University Press, 1988.

Zepezaurer, Mark, and Arthur Naiman. *Take the Rich Off Welfare*. Tucson, Ariz.: Odonian Press, 1996.

Index

About the Author

David Schweickart is a professor of philosophy at Loyola University Chicago. He holds doctorate degrees in both mathematics and philosophy. He is the author of *Capitalism or Worker Control: An Ethical and Economic Appraisal, Against Capitalism,* and numerous articles on social, political, and economic philosophy. His work has been translated into French, Spanish, Catalan, and Chinese.